U0633341

88有词

李森·编著

从词汇小白走向词汇大咖从串串有词开始

浙江工商大学出版社
ZHEJIANG GONGSHANG UNIVERSITY PRESS

图书在版编目(CIP)数据

串串有词 / 李森编著. — 杭州 : 浙江工商大学出版社, 2018.8

ISBN 978-7-5178-2882-2

Ⅰ. ①串… Ⅱ. ①李… Ⅲ. ①英语－词汇－记忆术 Ⅳ. ①H313

中国版本图书馆CIP数据核字(2018)第176266号

串串有词

李森 编著

特约策划	北京环球卓尔英才文化传播有限公司
责任编辑	张莉娅 李相玲
封面设计	王友蕾
责任印制	包建辉
出版发行	浙江工商大学出版社

（杭州市教工路198号 邮政编码 310012）

（E-mail:zjgsupress@163.com）

（网址:http://www.zjgsupress.com）

电话：0571-88904970，88831806（传真）

印　　刷	北京合众伟业印刷有限公司
开　　本	787mm×1092mm　1/16
印　　张	23
字　　数	511千
版 印 次	2018 年 8 月第 1 版　2018 年 8 月第 1 次印刷
书　　号	ISBN 978-7-5178-2882-2
定　　价	59.80元

F O R E W O R D

前　言

　　近些年来，留学低龄化的趋势愈加明显。在教英文词汇的这些年里，森哥遇到了很多低龄留学生，他们大多词汇基础薄弱，而又迫切需要提升词汇量，以应对出国留学考试。不少学生饱受词汇的折磨，记不住、忘得快是他们在词汇学习上遇到的最常见的问题。而当前市面上大多数的词汇书，除了按考试类型分类之外，其内容和格式与词典几乎无异，学生们除了死记硬背别无他法。森哥看到大家背单词如此之痛苦，决定要为同学们写一本既有趣又有文化，而且还能迅速有效地提升词汇量的词汇书。于是，就有了这本《串串有词》。

　　全书主要由词根词缀、追根溯源和锦囊妙计三大部分构成，紧扣出国留学考试核心词汇，同时兼具文化性和趣味性。

　　本书的主要内容有：

1 词根词缀

　　通过词根词缀记忆单词是学习英文单词最普遍、最科学的方法。本书包含了100多个最常见的词根，出国留学考试常用单词所涉及的词根都可以在本书中找到，因此本书可以说是学习词根词缀，提升英语词汇素养的实用书籍。本书的编排是把与词根相关的单词串到一起进行讲解，这样避免了学生为了学一个单词还要专门学习一个词根和前缀的问题，只要学习了词根再结合已经积累的前缀后缀便可以成串地搞定与词根相关的单词。比如我们只需要记住pel=push，便可以利用前缀与词根的结合，记住repel, expel, dispel, impel, propel, compel及其相关延伸的单词

impulse, impulsive, repulsive, propulsive, compulsory和repeal这一串词，这样的记忆方法极大地减少了学生们的记忆负担。把单词串起来记，是词根词缀能够给我们带来的最大好处。

词根词缀相当于汉语中的偏旁部首，上面所谈到的词根词缀是非常明显的偏旁部首，而还有一部分单词虽然没有明显的词根词缀，但是在词形和词义上都存在着联系。这部分单词的联系，特别容易被我们忽略，森哥对这一部分单词也进行了整理。

我们知道在汉语中，以"氵"为偏旁的汉字都跟水有关系。那么我们来看一组英语单词，drain（排水），drown（溺水），drizzle（毛毛细雨），drench（浸透），由此可知，以"dr"开头的这一串词大都跟水流有关系。诸如此类的单词，我们将其串起来记忆，对我们背单词也会起到事半功倍的效果。

2 追根溯源

追根溯源就是探索单词的来源，其中希腊神话是英语单词的重要来源。比如希腊神话中Prometheus（普罗米修斯）具备先知先觉的能力，所以pro-作为前缀就有了"before"的意思，而他的弟弟 Epimetheus（埃庇米修斯）比较愚笨，做事情总是后知后觉，所以epi-作为前缀表示"after; among"的意思。希腊神话为英语单词增色不少，每一个单词都有精彩的神话故事可以激发学生们学习单词的兴趣，因此本书尽可能收集全了与单词相关的神话故事。

在词源方面，单词除了来自希腊神话之外，还有一部分单词本身就有着自己的历史来源，比如，aghast（惊呆的，吓呆的）这个词对很多学生来说是很难的，但是如果森哥告诉你这个单词其实就是来自于ghost（鬼），那么这个单词就好记了，见到ghost（鬼）当然是aghast（吓呆了的）。这样很难的单词我们利用追根溯源就可以迎刃而解了。追根溯源是本书的一大亮点，这种处理让本书覆盖单词量大，趣味性强，并且紧扣留学考试核心词汇。

3 锦囊妙计

词根词缀法和追根溯源法都是有据可查的单词记忆方法，但是还有一部分单词既无词根词缀可用，又无词源可查，这时候我们就只能利用一些有趣的"偏方"了。这类"偏方"并没有什么词汇学的依据，但是可以帮助我们快速有效地记单词。森哥认为当前最常见的和最成体系的记忆方法主要包括谐音法、联想法、拆分法和串联法。

谐音法：靠读音记单词，比如pest（害虫），谐音：拍死它，是害虫（pest）当然要拍死它！

拆分法：famine（饥荒），fa（发）mi（米）ne（呢），什么时候发米呢？当然是饥荒（famine）的时候。

联想法：主要是通过联想比较容易的单词或是常见的事物来记住复杂的单词，比如exotic（外来的；异国的），我们可以联想EXO（一个韩国明星组合），韩国明星组合当然是外来的（exotic）。

串联记忆法：通过编口诀的方式把一组形近的单词串联到一起记忆，顺口又好记。例如-oast系列，我们在海边（coast），吃着烧烤（roast），喝着酒，干着杯（toast），吹着牛（boast），很惬意！

在每一个单元的最后，森哥都给大家提供了锦囊妙计，希望大家能够在欢笑声中把单词记住，为枯燥的单词背诵增添一抹亮彩。

森哥希望有一天学生们能够捧着森哥写的书，看着森哥录制的视频，听着森哥的声音，轻轻松松地把单词搞定。为此森哥又为每一个词根词缀、每一个单词都录制了视频，视频与书籍完全同步，建议大家把书和视频结合起来学习。从此，妈妈再也不用担心你们记不住单词了！

《串串有词》是森哥在词汇上的一次探索，相比同类词汇书，虽有出众之处，但仍有缺陷，欢迎亲爱的读者和同行们多多提出宝贵的意见和建议。

在词汇学习的漫漫长路上，我愿成为一盏路灯，虽然光芒微弱，但也尽力守候！

词汇学习路漫漫，森哥一路相伴！

2018年5月

C O N T E N T S

目录

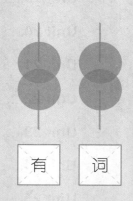

一个单词的构成可用以下结构表示：

前缀+词根+后缀

★三者的位置不同，职能亦不同

★ **前缀**：决定单词的方向，在形容词里决定单词是否定还是肯定；在动词里决定动词词根的方向，例如朝里(in)还是朝外(ex = out)，朝前(pro = forward)还是朝后(re = back)。

★ **词根**：决定单词的根本含义，是一个单词的灵魂。

★ **后缀**：决定单词的词性。

以invisible为例

vis作为词根有"看"的意思，那么这个单词肯定跟"看"有关系，-ble是形容词后缀，visible的意思是"可见的"，in-在形容词前面表示否定，因此invisible的意思就是"不可见的，隐形的"。

◆ 词根 ◆

词根的构成是辅音+元音+辅音，比如bal，pel等。有一条关于词根的原则是中间的元音字母在五个元音(a,e, i,o,u)之间发生变化，词根的意思不变。以bal为例：

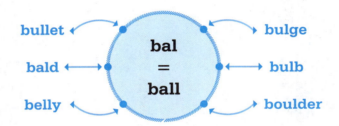

bald [bɔːld]	*adj.* 秃头的 (having no hair or very little hair on the head) He covered his bald head with a baseball cap. **bal** 跟球有关系，秃头当然也是圆形的。
bullet ['bʊlɪt]	*n.* 子弹 (a small piece of metal or another material that is shot out of a gun) He was killed by an assassin's bullet. **bul** 由a-u变化，bul仍然跟球有关系，而子弹为什么跟球有关系呢？这是因为一开始人们用来狩猎的子弹就是圆圆的小钢珠，后来子弹才发展成今天的各种形状。
bulb [bʌlb]	*n.* 电灯泡；球茎 (the glass part of an electric lamp; a root shaped like a ball that grows into a flower or plant) The stairwell was lit by a single bulb. 这也是一个由bal-bul的例子，电灯泡和球茎都是球状的。
bulge [bʌldʒ]	*v.* 膨胀；凸出 (to stick out in a rounded lump) His eyes seemed to bulge like those of a toad. 由bal-bul变化，像球一样鼓出来的意思。
bulky ['bʌlki]	*adj.* 庞大的；笨重的 (great in size or volume) He is a bulky man with balding hair.
belly ['beli]	*n.* 肚子；腹部 (the front part of the body between the chest and the hips) She laid her hands on her swollen belly. 由bal-bel变化，仍然具有球的意思。人的小腹像球凸面，而孕妇的belly完完全全就像一个球了。
boulder ['bəʊldə(r)]	*n.* 大圆石；巨石 (a very large stone or rounded piece of rock) The boulder sheltered them from the chilling wind. 由a向双元音ou变化，仍然是球的意思。

前缀

前缀主要决定了词根的方向，与词根结合产生新的单词含义，比如决定了单词是肯定词还是否定词，比如，a-, un-, in-, dis- 都是常见的否定前缀。另外，前缀决定了词根动作发出的方向，很多前缀有方向性特点，比如，re=back，pro=forward，ex=out，intro=inward，sub=under, super=over 等。词根pel=push，与re-结合，形成repel，便有了push back（推回去）的本意，引申为"击退；抵制"的意思；与ex-结合，形成expel，便有了push out（推出去）的本意，引申为"开除；驱逐"的意思。本书重点总结了最常用的前缀供同学们学习，前缀是用词根词缀记单词的基础，一定要牢记！

a- = no　　　　　　表示"否定"

typical *adj.* 典型的　　　　　　atypical *adj.* 不典型的

ab- = away; against; no　　　　　　表示"离开；反对；否定"

normal *adj.* 正常的　　　　　　abnormal *adj.* 反常的

ac-, ad-, af-, ag-, at-, as- = to　　　　　　表示"去干；加强"

1 to

custom *n.* 习惯　　　　　　accustom *v.* 使习惯

join *v.* 连接；毗邻　　　　　　adjoin *v.* 连接

2 表示加强

grand *adj.* 宏大的　　　　　　aggrandize *v.* 增强

grave *adj.* 沉重的　　　　　　aggravate *v.* 加重

ante- = before　　　　　　表示"之前"

date *n.* 日期　　　　　　antedate *v.* 先于；早于

auto- = self　　　　　　表示"自己；自动"

mobile *adj.* 移动的　　　　　　automobile *n.* 汽车

bene- = good
表示"好的"

bene**fit** *n.* 益处

bene**volent** *adj.* 慈善的

co-, con- = together
表示"共同；一起"

1 together

operation *n.* 操作   **co**operation *n.* 合作

centre *n.* 中心   **con**centric *adj.* 同一中心的

2 表加强

solid *adj.* 固体的   **con**solidate *v.* 巩固

contra- = against
表示"相反"

contrary *adj.* 相反的

controversy *n.* 争议

counter- = against
表示"相反"

clockwise *adj.* 顺时针方向的   **counter**clockwise *adj.* 逆时针的

current *n.* 水流   **counter**current *n.* 逆流

de- = down；away
表示"离向下；离开"

1 down

value *n.* 价值   **de**value *v.* 贬值

press *v.* 压   **de**press *v.* 压低

2 away

camp *n.* 营地   **de**camp *v.* 撤营

rail *n.* 铁轨   **de**rail *v.* 脱轨

dis- = no；away
表示"否定；离开"

1 no

agree *v.* 同意   **dis**agree *v.* 不同意

honest *adj.* 诚实的   **dis**honest *adj.* 不诚实的

2 away

distract *v.* 使分心

dispel *v.* 驱散

e- = out

表示"使……；出来"

1 表示"使……"

value *n.* 价值   evaluate *v.* 评价

long *adj.* 长的   elongate *v.* 使延长

2 out

erupt *v.* 喷发

eject *v.* 喷出

ex- = out

表示"使……；出来"

1 表示"使……"

exaggerate *v.* 夸大

2 out

export *n.* 出口

expel *v.* 驱逐

fore- = before

表示"之前"

tell *v.* 告诉   foretell *v.* 预言

head *n.* 头   forehead *n.* 前额

il- = no

表示"否定"

legal *adj.* 合法的   illegal *adj.* 非法的

logical *adj.* 符合逻辑的   illogical *adj.* 不合逻辑的

im- = no；into

表示"否定；进入"

1 no

possible *adj.* 可能的   impossible *adj.* 不可能的

polite *adj.* 礼貌的   impolite *adj.* 不礼貌的

2 into

imprison **v.** 投入监狱

import **n.** 进口

in- = no；into
表示"否定；进入"

1 no

formal **adj.** 正式的   informal **adj.** 非正式的

correct **adj.** 正确的   incorrect **adj.** 不正确的

2 into

inject **v.** 注入；注射

infuse **v.** 灌输

inter- = between
表示"在……之间"

nation **n.** 国家   international **adj.** 国际的

continent **n.** 大洲   intercontinental **adj.** 洲际的

mal- = bad；wrong
表示"坏；错"

nutrition **n.** 营养   malnutrition **n.** 营养不良

function **n.** 功能   malfunction **n.** 功能失调

mis- = bad；no
表示"坏；否定"

use **v.** 使用   misuse **v.** 误用

fortune **n.** 幸运   misfortune **n.** 不幸

mono- = single
表示"单一的"

tone **n.** 音调   monotonous **adj.** 单调的

cycle **n.** 自行车   monocycle **n.** 独轮车

per- = through；thoroughly
表示"贯穿；全部；彻底"

1 through

perspective **adj.** 透视的

permeate **v.** 渗透；弥漫

2 thoroughly

persist *v.* 坚持

permanent *adj.* 永久的

post- = after
表示"后面的"

war *n.* 战争　　　　　postwar *adj.* 战后的

human *n.* 人类　　　　posthumous *adj.* 死后的

pre- = before；forward
表示"在前；向前"

prehistory *n.* 史前

preview *v.* 预习

pro- = before；forward
表示"在前；向前"

prolong *v.* 延长

promote *v.* 促进；提升

re- = back；again；against
表示"反向；再次；反对"

1 back

call *v.* 呼唤；召唤　　　recall *v.* 召回

2 again

build *v.* 建造　　　　　rebuild *v.* 重建

consider *v.* 考虑　　　reconsider *v.* 重新考虑

3 against

resist *v.* 反抗；抵抗

rebel *v.* 反叛

se- = apart
表示"分离"

separate *v.* 分开；隔开

seclude *v.* 使隔绝

sub- = under；after

1 under

subway *n.* 地铁

submarine *n.* 潜水艇

2 after

substitute *n.* 替补

subtitle *n.* 副标题

super- = over

表示"超过"

superman *n.* 超人

supermarket *n.* 超市

sym-，syn- = same

表示"共同；相同"

sympathy *n.* 同情

synchronize *v.* 使同时发生

trans- = cross；change

表示"超过；转移"

1 cross

personal *adj.* 个人的   transpersonal *adj.* 超越个人的

2 change

form *n.* 形式   transform *v.* 改造

un- = no

表示"否定"

comfortable *adj.* 舒服的   uncomfortable *adj.* 不舒服的

fortunate *adj.* 幸运的   unfortunate *adj.* 不幸的

后缀

英语中的后缀多而且杂，我们只挑一些最常见、规律性最明显的后缀做讲解。

名词后缀

❶ 表示"人"

-or	act**or**　演员	profess**or**　教授
-er	teach**er**　教师	wait**er**　男服务员
-ress（表示"女性"）	act**ress**　女演员	wait**ress**　女服务员
-ant	assist**ant**　助手	peas**ant**　农民
-ist	art**ist**　艺术家	dent**ist**　牙医

❷ 其他名词后缀

-ity	abil**ity**　能力	activ**ity**　活动
-ness	ill**ness**　疾病	kind**ness**　善良
-ment	instru**ment**　乐器	advertise**ment**　广告
-itude	att**itude**　态度	alt**itude**　海拔高度
-ary, -ory　表示"场所"	libr**ary**　图书馆	laborat**ory**　实验室

形容词后缀

-ble	comforta**ble**　舒服的	availa**ble**　可获得的
-ous	curi**ous**　好奇的	seri**ous**　荒诞的
-ly	friend**ly**　友好的	sudden**ly**　突然的
-ed	pleas**ed**　满意的	puzzl**ed**　困惑的
-ful	beauti**ful**　漂亮的	color**ful**　多彩的

动词后缀

-ize	memor**ize**　记住	recogn**ize**　认出
-fy	satis**fy**　使满意	ampli**fy**　扩大；增强
-en	length**en**　使变长	strength**en**　增强

副词后缀

-ly	careful**ly**　认真地	dead**ly**　致命地

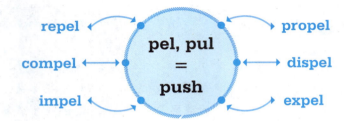

expel [ɪk'spel]	*v.* 驱逐 (to force somebody to leave a country) Trump wants to expel illegal immigrants already in the U.S. *v.* 开除 (to officially make somebody leave a school or an organization) She was expelled from school for bad behavior. *v.* 排出 (to force air or water out of a part of the body or from a container) Poisonous gas is expelled into the atmosphere.
propel [prə'pel]	*v.* 推进；推动 (to move, drive or push something forward or in a particular direction) The train is propelled by steam. *v.* 驱使 (to force somebody to move in a particular direction or to get into a particular situation) It was a shooting star that propelled me into astronomy in the first place .
propulsive [prə'pʌlsɪv]	*adj.* 有推进作用的 (having the force that drives something forward) Venture capital is the propulsive force of the high technology industry.
compel [kəm'pel]	*v.* 强迫；迫使 (to force somebody to do something) ① They compelled me to betray my country. ② Illness compelled him to stay in bed.
compulsory [kəm'pʌlsəri]	*adj.* 强制性的；强迫的 (that must be done because of a law or a rule) Many young men are trying to get away from compulsory military conscription.
compelling [kəm'pelɪŋ]	*adj.* 引人入胜的 (able to capture and hold your attention) The novel was so compelling that I couldn't put it down. *adj.* 非常强烈的；不可抗拒的 (so strong that you must do something about it) He felt a compelling need to tell someone about his idea.

adj. 令人信服的；有说服力的 (that makes you think it is true)

He made a compelling argument.

impel

[ɪmˈpel]

v. 激励；促使 (to cause someone to feel a strong need or desire to do something)

1 Hunger impelled the boy to steal.

2 His interest in the American Civil War impelled him to make repeated visits to Gettysburg.

impulsive

[ɪmˈpʌlsɪv]

adj. 冲动的；任性的 (acting suddenly without thinking carefully about what might happen because of what you are doing)

1 He needs to learn to control his impulsive behavior.

2 Young people now are often better known for impulsive spending than for saving money.

impulse

[ˈɪmpʌls]

n. 冲动 (a strong sudden desire to do something without thinking about the consequences)

He resisted an impulse to smile.

repel

[rɪˈpel]

v. 击退 (to cause somebody/something to move back by force or influence)

Their superior forces repelled the invasion.

v. 排斥；相斥 (if two things repel each other, they push each other away with an electrical force)

Magnets can both repel and attract one another.

repulsive

[rɪˈpʌlsɪv]

adj. 令人厌恶的；令人反感的 (causing a feeling of strong dislike;very unpleasant)

We must be clear. White supremacy is repulsive.

repeal

[rɪˈpiːl]

v. 撤销；废除 (to cancel officially)

He believes that death penalty will be repealed sooner or later.

dispel

[dɪˈspel]

v. 驱散 (to break up, drive away, or cause something to disappear)

The breeze dispelled the smog.

v. 消除（疑虑）(to make something, especially a feeling or belief, go away or disappear)

That fine performance dispelled any doubts about his abilities.

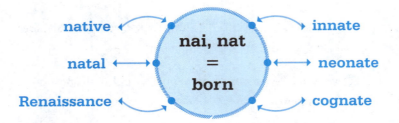

native ['neɪtɪv]	*adj.* 出生地的；本国的 (connected with the place where you were born and lived for the first years of your life) My native language is Spanish, but I also speak English. *adj.* （动植物）当地土生的；原产地的 (existing naturally in a place) These birds are native to Australia. *adj.* （能力或品质）天赋的；与生俱来的 (that you have naturally without having to learn it) She has a native ability to learn quickly.
natal ['neɪtl]	*adj.* 出生地的；出生时的 (relating to a place where or the time when somebody was born) The salmon are born in rivers, swim to the Atlantic and return to their natal river to spawn.
innate [ɪ'neɪt]	*adj.* 天生的；固有的 (determined by factors present in an individual from birth) She has an innate sense of rhythm.
neonate ['niːəʊneɪt]	*n.* 新生儿 (a baby from birth to four weeks) 0.2 percent of babies born at home died as neonates, compared with 0.09 percent of babies born in the hospital.
Renaissance [rɪ'neɪsns]	*n.* 文艺复兴 (the period of European history at the close of the Middle Ages and the rise of the modern world) The Renaissance was more than a "rebirth". It was also an age of new discoveries.
cognate ['kɒgneɪt]	*adj.* （词或语言）同源的，同语系的 (having the same origin as another word or language) Physics and astronomy are cognate sciences.

Form系列

form [fɔːm]	*n.* 形状；形式 (the shape and structure of something) They received a benefit in the form of a tax reduction. *v.* (使)形成 (to start to exist and develop;to make something start to exist and develop) They tried to form a study group on human rights.
reform [rɪˈfɔːm]	*v.* 改革 (to put or change something into an improved form or condition) The law needs to be reformed. *n.* 改革 (change that is made to a social system, an organization,especially in order to improve or correct it) The government took another step on the road to political reform.
deform [dɪˈfɔːm]	*v.* 改变……的外形；使成畸形 (to change or spoil the usual or natural shape of something) ① The trees had been completely deformed by the force of the wind. ② Heat deforms plastic.
uniform [ˈjuːnɪfɔːm]	*n.* 制服 (a special kind of clothing that is worn by all the members of a group) He was dressed in his uniform for parade. *adj.* 统一的 (having always the same form, manner, or degree) All departments have uniform training standards.
conform [kənˈfɔːm]	*v.* 符合 (to be similar, to be in line with) Your clothes must conform to the school regulations. *v.* 遵从 (to comply with) They persecute those who do not conform to their ideas.
transform [trænsˈfɔːm]	*v.* 改变；转换 (to change something completely and usually in a good way) The old factory has been transformed into an art gallery.
transformation [ˌtrænsfəˈmeɪʃn]	*n.* 转换；改变 (a complete or major change in someone's or something's appearance, form) The building underwent various transformations over the years.

Unit 01

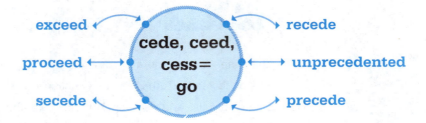

precede [prɪˈsiːd]	**v.** 在……之前发生或出现 (to come or happen before something in order) The president preceded the meeting with a brief welcoming speech.
precedent [ˈpresɪdənt]	**n.** 前例；先例 (an example that is used to justify similar occurrences at a later time) The trial could set an important precedent for dealing with large numbers of similar cases.
unprecedented [ʌnˈpresɪdentɪd]	**adj.** 前所未有的 (having no previous example) The team has enjoyed unprecedented success this year.
antecedent [ˌæntɪˈsiːdnt]	**n.** 先例 (something that came before something else and may have influenced or caused it) We shall first look briefly at the historical antecedents of this theory.
proceed [prəˈsiːd]	**v.** 行进；前进 (to move or travel in a particular direction) The troops proceeded north along the river. **v.** （尤指打断后）继续说 (to continue after a pause or interruption) After the interruption, she proceeded with her presentation.
procession [prəˈseʃn]	**n.** 队伍；行列 (a group of individuals moving along in an orderly often ceremonial way) ❶ There was a procession of children carrying candles. ❷ The cars moved in procession to the cemetery.
procedure [prəˈsiːdʒə(r)]	**n.** 程序；手续 (a series of steps followed in a regular definite order) We must follow proper court procedure.
exceed [ɪkˈsiːd]	**v.** 超过；超越 (to be greater than a particular numbers or amount) ❶ The cost must not exceed 10 dollars. ❷ His performance exceeded all expectations.
excessive [ɪkˈsesɪv]	**adj.** 过度的；极度的 (going beyond what is usual, normal or proper) Excessive drinking is harmful to the health.

access [ˈækses]	*n.* （使用或见到的）机会；权利 (the opportunity or right to use something or to see somebody/something) Only a few have access to the secret information. *n.* 入口；通道 (a way or means of approaching a place) We have Internet access at the library. *v.* 到达；进入；使用 (to reach, enter or use something) The new system makes it easier to access the money in your bank account.
accessible [əkˈsesəbl]	*adj.* 易到达的 (able to be reached) ① The resort is accessible by train. ② The centre is easily accessible to the general public. *adj.* 易得到的 (able to be used or obtained) The book is accessible in your school library.
necessary [ˈnesəsəri]	*adj.* 必要的；强制的 (so important that you must do it or have it) Food is necessary for life. *adj.* 必然的；无法避免的 (unable to be changed or avoided) The threat of a thunderstorm made it necessary to cancel the picnic.
recede [rɪˈsiːd]	*v.* 后退 (to move back or away) When the rain stopped, the floods receded. *v.* 减弱 (to become smaller or weaker) As time passed, his facial features receded from my mind.
recession [rɪˈseʃn]	*n.* 经济衰退；不景气 (a period of economic decline) The recession caused sales to drop off.
cede [siːd]	*v.* 放弃；割让 (to give up or surrender land, position, or authority) ① The General had promised to cede power by January. ② This island was ceded to Spain more than one hundred years ago.
secede [sɪˈsiːd]	*v.* 从……中脱离 (to separate from a nation or state and become independent) He suggested Americans should imagine what it would be like if the state Florida were to secede from the rest of the nation.
concede [kənˈsiːd]	*v.* 承认 (to acknowledge, often reluctantly, as being true) Although it seems clear that he has lost the election, he still refuses to concede. *v.* 让步 (to give something away, especially unwillingly) The company says that workers are not conceding enough in negotiations.

intercede	*v.* 斡旋；调解 (to speak to somebody in order to persuade them to have pity on somebody else or to help settle an argument)
[ˌɪntə'siːd]	Their argument probably would have become violent if I hadn't interceded.
supercede	*v.* 代替；取代 (take the place or move into the position of something)
[sjuː'pə'siːd]	Socialism will necessarily supercede capitalism.

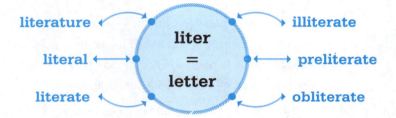

literature	*n.* 文学 (written works considered as having high quality and ideas of lasting and widespread interest)
['lɪtrətʃə(r)]	He's an expert in American literature.
literal	*adj.* 原义的；逐字的 (limited to the explicit meaning of a word or text)
['lɪtərəl]	They follow a literal interpretation of the Bible.
	adj. 缺乏想象力的 (lacking imagination)
	Her interpretation of the music was too literal.
literate	*adj.* 识字的 (able to read and write)
['lɪtərət]	About 65 percent of women were found to be literate, compared with 82 percent of men, according to the 2011 report.
illiterate	*adj.* 不识字的 (unable to read or write)
[ɪ'lɪtərət]	A large percentage of the population is illiterate.
	adj. （对某学科）了解不多的；外行的 (not knowing very much about a particular subject area)
	She is politically illiterate and has never voted in an election.
preliterate	*adj.* 没有文字的 (lacking a written language)
[priː'lɪtərɪt]	In preliterate societies oral literature was widely shared.
obliterate	*v.* 毁掉；清除 (to remove or destroy something completely so as to leave no trace)
[ə'blɪtəreɪt]	❶ The town was obliterated by the bombs.
	❷ He drank to obliterate the memory of what had occurred.

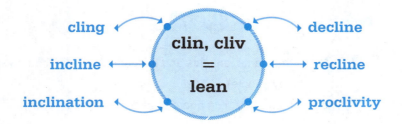

cling
[klɪŋ]

- **v.** 附着于；紧贴 (to hold fast or adhere to something)
  These wet socks are clinging to my feet.
- **v.** 牢牢抓住 (to hold onto something or someone very tightly)
  He appears determined to cling to power.

incline
[ɪnˈklaɪn]

- **v.** （使）倾斜 (to lean or slope in a particular direction;to make something lean or slope)
  The road inclines at an angle of about 12 degrees.
- **v.** （使）倾向于；有……趋势 (to tend to think or behave in a particular way; to make somebody do this)
  Those who fail incline to blame the world for their failure.

inclination
[ˌɪnklɪˈneɪʃn]

- **n.** 倾向；意愿 (a feeling that makes you want to do something)
  My first inclination was to say no, but I finally decided to do what she asked.

decline
[dɪˈklaɪn]

- **v.** 减少；下降；衰弱 (to become smaller, fewer or weaker)
  Her father's health has declined significantly in recent months.
- **v.** 拒绝 (to say that you will not or cannot do something)
  He changed his mind and declined the company's offer.
- **n.** 衰落 (a continuous decrease in the number,value,quality,etc.of something)
  The town fell into decline after the factory closed down.

recline
[rɪˈklaɪn]

- **v.** 斜倚；倚靠 (to sit back or lie down in a relaxed manner)
  He was reclining on the sofa, watching TV.

proclivity
[prəˈklɪvəti]

- **n.** （常指对坏事的）倾向 (a strong natural liking for something that is usually bad)
  He has a proclivity toward violence.

Nature系列

nature ['neɪtʃə(r)]	*n.* 自然 (all the plants, animals and things that exist in the universe that are not made by people) The most amazing thing about nature is its infinite variety.
nurture ['nɜːtʃə(r)]	*v.* 养育；培养 (to care for and protect somebody/something while they are growing and developing) Teachers should nurture their students' creativity.
nourish ['nʌrɪʃ]	*v.* 滋养 (to promote the growth of somebody/something) Vitamins are added to the shampoo to nourish the hair.
nutrition [nju'trɪʃn]	*n.* 营养；滋养 (the process by which living things receive the food necessary for them to grow and be healthy) The speaker discussed diet and nutrition with the class.
nutritional [njʊ'trɪʃənl]	*adj.* 营养的 (connected with the process by which living things receive the food necessary for them to grow and be healthy) Cooking vegetables reduces their nutritional value.

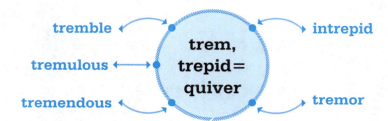

tremble ['trembl]	*v.* 发抖；颤动 (to shake slightly because you are afraid, nervous or excited) My voice trembled as I began to speak.
tremulous ['tremjələs]	*adj.* 颤抖的 (shaking slightly especially because of nervousness, weakness or illness) She opened the letter with tremulous hands. *adj.* 胆小的 (showing a lack of confidence or courage) The tremulous daughter never left her father's house.
tremendous [trə'mendəs]	*adj.* 巨大的；极大的 (very great) ① The engine's power is tremendous. ② Suddenly there was a tremendous explosion.

intrepid [ɪn'trepɪd]	*adj.* 无畏的；勇敢的 (feeling no fear; very bold or brave) The intrepid explorer probed parts of the rain forest never previously attempted.
tremor ['tremə(r)]	*n.* 震颤 (a shaking movement of the ground before or after an earthquake) Small tremors were still being felt several days after the earthquake. *n.* 波动 (a slight shaking movement) The news sent tremors through the stock market.

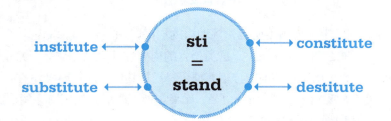

institute ['ɪnstɪtjuːt]	*v.* 建立；制定（体系、政策等）；实行 (to introduce a system, policy, etc. or start a process) They have instituted new policies to increase public safety. *n.* 协会；学院 (an organization created for a particular purpose such as research or education) They founded an institute for research into the causes of mental illness.
constitute ['kɒnstɪtjuːt]	*v.* 组成 (to be the elements or parts of something) Women constitute 70 percent of the student population at the college. *v.* 构成 (to form; to make up; to be) Nuclear waste constitutes a serious danger.
destitute ['destɪtjuːt]	*adj.* 贫困的 (poor enough to need help from others) Many families were left destitute by the horrible fire.
constitution [ˌkɒnstɪ'tjuːʃn]	*n.* 宪法 (the basic principles and laws of a nation, state or social group that determine the powers and duties of the government and guarantee certain rights to the people in it) The king was forced to adopt a new constitution which reduced his powers. *n.* 体格 (the physical character of the body as to strength or health) Only animals with strong constitutions are able to survive the island's harsh winters.

substitute

['sʌbstɪtjuːt]

> **v.** 代替；替换 (to take the place of somebody/something else; to use somebody/something instead of somebody/something else)
>
> **1** They were substituting violence for dialogue.
>
> **2** They substituted real candles with electric ones.
>
> **n.** 替补 (one that takes the place of another)
>
> Coming on as a substitute, he scored four crucial goals for his club.

追根溯源

在欧洲封建时期，土地为领主所有，领地内的居民归领主管辖。领主为了加强对领地居民的统治，经常会颁布公告（bannu）。这类公告的内容往往以禁令居多，禁止（ban）居民做某些事情，比如，禁止居民在领地内打猎、捕鱼，或是其他有损领地权益的活动。那么这些禁令颁布频繁，风格是陈腐平庸的（banal）。如果领地中的居民认真遵守领主颁布的禁令，那么一切安好。但是，如果居民违背了这些禁令，将会受到严重的惩罚，会被整个领地放弃（abandon），最终被领主驱逐（banish）。被驱逐的人无法在领地中正常生活，也不被其他人所接受，就只能落草为寇，沦为土匪（bandit）。

ban

[bæn]

> **v.** 禁止；下令禁止 (to prohibit especially by legal means)
>
> He was banned from driving for three years.

banal

[bə'nɑːl]

> **adj.** 陈腐的；平庸的 (very ordinary and containing nothing that is interesting or important)
>
> He made some banal remarks about the weather.

abandon

[ə'bændən]

> **v.** 放弃；抛弃 (to leave somebody/place completely and finally)
>
> The approaching fire forced hundreds of people to abandon their homes.

banish

['bænɪʃ]

> **v.** 放逐；驱逐 (to order somebody to leave a place, especially a country, as a punishment)
>
> The dictator banished anyone who opposed him.

bandit

['bændɪt]

> **n.** 土匪；强盗 (a robber, especially a member of a gang)
>
> Reports say he was killed in an attack by armed bandits.

abolish [ə'bɒlɪʃ]	**v.** 废除，废止 (法律、制度、习俗等) (to officially end a law, a system or an institution) ① They voted to abolish the death penalty. ② Slavery was abolished in the mid-19th century in America and in Russia. 谐音法 a—一，bolish-暴力史，一部暴力史，当然应该被废除 (abolish)。
amateur ['æmətə(r)]	**n.** 业余爱好者 (a person who takes part in sports or occupations for pleasure and not for pay) He is an amateur who dances because he feels like it. 谐音法 a-矮，mateur-模特，矮模特，当然只能是业余爱好者 (amateur)。
stern [stɜrn]	**adj.** 严厉的；严峻的 (very serious especially in an unfriendly way) Her father was stern and hard to please. 谐音法 stern-死瞪着，爸爸死瞪着你！对你很严肃 (stern)。
sweat [swet]	**v.** 流汗 (when you sweat, drops of liquid that appear on the surface of your skin, for example, when you are hot, ill/sick or afraid) He sweats a lot when he exercises. 联想法 只有流汗 (sweat) 才能浇灌出甜蜜的 (sweet) 果实。
rust [rʌst]	**n.** 铁锈 (a reddish coating formed on metal) The car was covered with rust. **v.** (使) 生锈 (to form rust) Your bicycle will rust if you leave it out in the rain. 联想法 大脑不能休，if you rest（休了), you will rust（锈）！

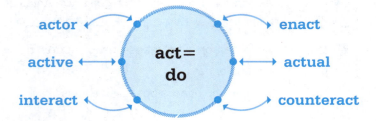

actor → enact

active ← → actual

interact ← act = do → counteract

actor ['æktə(r)]	*n.* 演员 (a person who acts in a play, film or broadcast, etc.) You have to be a very good actor to play that part.
actress ['æktrəs]	*n.* 女演员 (a female actor) She'll make a good actress, if she gets the right training.
active ['æktɪv]	*adj.* 积极的；活跃的 (in a state of action; moving, working or doing something) We stay active during the cold winter months by skiing and ice skating.
inactive [ɪn'æktɪv]	*adj.* 不活动的 (not active; dormant) It's easiest to catch snakes early in the morning, while they're still cold and inactive. *adj.* 懒散的 (not doing things that require physical movement and energy) Inactive people suffer higher rates of heart disease.
activate ['æktɪveɪt]	*v.* 使活动；启动 (to make something active or more active) ① The bomb was activated by remote control. ② Sunlight activates a chemical reaction in the plant's leaves.
react [ri'ækt]	*v.* 反应；做出反应 (to act or behave in response to something) ① The firefighters reacted quickly when they heard the alarm. ② When I told her what happened, she reacted with anger.
reaction [ri'ækʃn]	*n.* 反应 (behavior or attitude in response to something) There has been strong reaction against the government's policies.

interact	_v._ 相互作用 (to come together and have an effect on each other)
[ˌɪntərˈækt]	The chemicals interacted to produce smoke.
	_v._ 交流；沟通；合作 (to talk or do things with other people)
	Teachers have a limited amount of time to interact with each child.
counteract	_v._ 抵消；抵制 (to make something ineffective by applying an opposite force or amount)
[ˌkaʊntərˈækt]	
	1 The drug will counteract the poison.
	2 Many countries within the region are planning measures to counteract a missile attack.
enact	_v._ 通过（法律）(to pass a law)
[ɪˈnækt]	The bill would be submitted for discussion before being enacted as law.
proactive	_adj._ 积极主动的 (acting in advance to deal with an expected difficulty)
[ˌprəʊˈæktɪv]	The city is taking a proactive approach to fighting crime by hiring more police officers.
actual	_adj._ 真实的；实际的 (existing in fact or reality)
[ˈæktʃuəl]	She had written some notes, but she hadn't started the actual work.

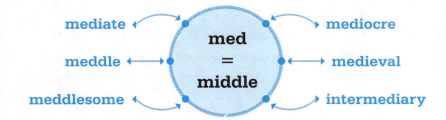

mediate	_v._ 调停；调解 (to try to end a disagreement between two or more people or groups by talking to them and tying to find things that everyone can agree on)
[ˈmiːdieɪt]	He is attempting to mediate a settlement between the company and the striking workers.
intermediary	_n._ 中间人；调解人 (a negotiator who acts as a link between parties)
[ˌɪntəˈmiːdiəri]	She wanted him to act as an intermediary in the dispute.
meddle	_v._ 干涉；插手 (to intrude into other people's affairs or business)
[ˈmedl]	Please stop meddling in your sister's marriage, even though you mean well.

meddlesome ['medlsəm]	*adj.* 好干预的；爱管闲事的 (enjoying getting involved in situation that do not concern them) He's accused of being meddlesome.
mediocre [ˌmiːdiˈəʊkə(r)]	*adj.* 普通的；平庸的 (of ordinary quality) The dinner was delicious, but the dessert was mediocre.
medieval [ˌmediˈiːvl]	*adj.* 中古的；中世纪的 (relating or belonging to the Middle Ages) The house is a textbook example of medieval domestic architecture.
medium ['miːdiəm]	*n.* 媒介物；介质 (the thing by which or through which something is done) Blood is the medium in which oxygen is carried to all parts of the body.

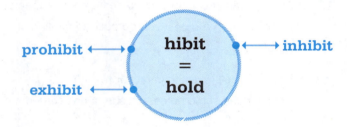

Unit 02

exhibit [ɪgˈzɪbɪt]	*v.* 陈列；展览 (to show or display outwardly especially by visible signs or actions) They will be exhibiting a collection of paintings. *v.* 表现；展现 (to show or reveal something) He first exhibited an interest in music when he was very young.
exhibition [ˌeksɪˈbɪʃn]	*n.* 陈列；展览 (a public showing as of works of art) There were several famous paintings at the exhibition.
prohibit [prəˈhɪbɪt]	*v.* 禁止；防止 (to prevent from doing something) We are prohibited from drinking alcohol during working hours.
prohibition [ˌprəʊɪˈbɪʃn]	*n.* 禁令 (a law or order that stops something from being used or done) The city's prohibition of smoking has taken effect in restaurants.
inhibit [ɪnˈhɪbɪt]	*v.* 抑制；阻止 (to hold back; restrain) It could inhibit the poor from getting the medical care they need.

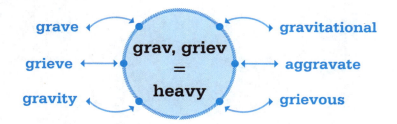

grave [greɪv]	*adj.* 严重的；重大的 (serious and solemn) He said that the situation in his country is very grave. *n.* 坟墓 (a grave is a place where a dead person is buried) She tore the rose apart and scattered the petals over the grave.
gravity ['grævəti]	*n.* 重力；万有引力 (the force that attracts objects in space towards each other,and that on the earth pulls them towards the centre of the planet, so that things fall to the ground when they are dropped) Increasing gravity is known to speed up the multiplication of cells. *n.* 重要性 (a very serious quality or condition) He doesn't think you realize the gravity of the situation.
gravitational [,grævɪ'teɪʃənl]	*adj.* 万有引力的 (relating to gravity) If a spacecraft travels faster than 11 km a second, it escapes the earth's gravitational pull.
aggravate ['ægrəveɪt]	*v.* 使严重；使恶化 (to make an illness or a bad or unpleasant situation severe) His bad temper aggravated the situation.
grieve [griːv]	*v.* 使伤心；使悲伤 (to make somebody feel very sad) He was deeply grieved by the sufferings of the common people.
grievous ['griːvəs]	*adj.* 极严重的；令人伤心的 (very serious and often causing great pain or suffering) Their loss would be a grievous blow to our engineering industries.

Unit 02

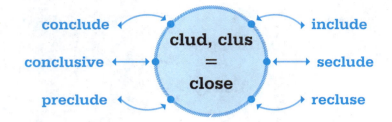

conclude ← → include
conclusive ← → seclude
clud, clus = close
preclude ← → recluse

include [ɪnˈkluːd]	*v.* 包括；包含 (to take in or have as part of a whole) The President is expected to include this idea in his education plan.
exclude [ɪkˈskluːd]	*v.* 排除；排斥 (to prevent somebody/something from entering a place or taking part in something) ❶ They excluded people under 20 from joining the club. ❷ We cannot exclude the possibility that he was lying.
exclusive [ɪkˈskluːsɪv]	*adj.* 排外的 (not very willing to allow new people to become members) An exclusive club does not readily accept newcomers. *adj.* 高档的；奢华的 (of a high quality and expensive and therefore not often bought or used by most people) She attended an exclusive private school. *adj.* 独家的；专有的 (only be used by one particular person or group;only given to one particular person or group) The story is exclusive to this newspaper.
conclude [kənˈkluːd]	*v.* 得出结论 (to decide or believe something as a result of what you have heard or seen) Many studies have concluded that smoking is dangerous. *v.* 结束；终止 (to bring something to an end) The chairman concluded his speech by wishing us all a happy holiday.
conclusive [kənˈkluːsɪv]	*adj.* 决定性的；确凿的 (showing that something is certainly true) Her attorneys claim there is no conclusive evidence that any murders took place.
conclusion [kənˈkluːʒn]	*n.* 结论 (a final decision or judgment) ❶ We came to the conclusion that it was too difficult to combine the two techniques. ❷ In conclusion, walking is a cheap, safe form of exercise.
preclude [prɪˈkluːd]	*v.* 阻止；排除 (to make something impossible, as by action taken in advance) Bad weather precluded any further attempts to reach the summit.

seclude [sɪˈkluːd]	*v.* 使隔开；使隔绝 (to keep somebody away from social contact with others) **1** He secluded himself in his room to study for the exam. **2** The patients will be secluded until they are no longer contagious.
recluse [rɪˈkluːs]	*n.* 隐居者 (a person who lives alone and likes to avoid other people) He was sick of cities and crowds, so he decided to go live by himself in the woods as a recluse.

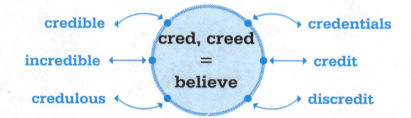

credible [ˈkredəbl]	*adj.* 可信的；可靠的 (reasonable to trust or believe) We've received credible information about the group's location.
incredible [ɪnˈkredəbl]	*adj.* 难以置信的 (difficult or impossible to believe) It's incredible to me that such a lazy person could be so successful. *adj.* 极好的；极大的 (extremely good, great, or large) The wildflowers will be incredible after this rain.
credulous [ˈkredjələs]	*adj.* 轻信的；易受骗的 (ready to believe things especially on slight or uncertain evidence) You must be credulous if she fooled you with that story.
credentials [krəˈdenʃlz]	*n.* 证明书；证件 (a letter or certificate giving evidence of the bearer's identity or competence) The new ambassador presented her credentials to the president.
credit [ˈkredɪt]	*n.* 信誉；信用 (the status of being trusted to pay back money to somebody who lends it to you) You need to have a strong credit history and a good job in order to get a mortgage. *n.* 荣誉；功劳 (a source of honor) All the credit must go to the play's talented director.

discredit	*v.* 使不可置信 (to refuse to accept something as true or accurate)
[dɪsˈkredɪt]	The prosecution discredited the witness by showing that she had lied in the past.
	v. 使丧失名誉 (to damage the reputation of someone; to disgrace)
	The candidates tried to discredit each other.
creed	*n.* 信条；教义 (statement of the basic beliefs of a religious faith)
[kri:d]	The centre is open to all, no matter what race or creed.

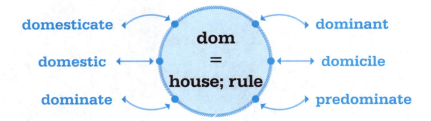

domestic	*adj.* 国内的 (of or inside a particular country; not foreign or international)
[dəˈmestɪk]	Today, almost 70 percent of our gross domestic product is dependent upon the purchasing power of consumers.
domesticate	*v.* 驯养 (to make a wild animal used to living with or working for humans)
[dəˈmestɪkeɪt]	Cattle, chickens and pigs were domesticated by people in different parts of the world between 8,000 and 11,000 years ago.
	adj. 家用的；家庭的 (used in the home; connected with the home or family)
	Woman are still the main victims of domestic violence.
domicile	*n.* 住处 (a dwelling place)
[ˈdɒmɪsaɪl]	You will need to report your change of domicile to your insurance company.
dominate	*v.* 支配；影响 (to have control of or power over somebody or something)
[ˈdɒmɪneɪt]	He denied that his country wants to dominate Europe.
	v. 占据优势 (to be much more powerful or successful than others in a game, competition)
	The stronger man dominates the weaker.
dominant	*adj.* 首要的；占支配地位的；占优势的 (more important, powerful or successful than other things)
[ˈdɒmɪnənt]	The company is now dominant in its market.

Unit 02

predominate	*v.*	占支配地位 (to be greater in number or amount than other types of people or things)
[prɪ'dɒmɪneɪt]		In this forest, pine trees predominate.
predominant	*adj.*	占优势的；主导的 (having more power or influence than others)
[prɪ'dɒmɪnənt]		Yellow is the predominant color this spring in the fashion world.

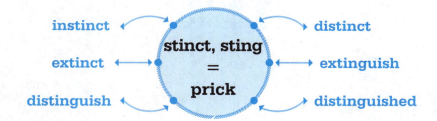

instinct · distinct

extinct · extinguish

distinguish · distinguished

stinct, sting = prick

instinct	*n.*	本能；天性 (a natural ability)
['ɪnstɪŋkt]		He has an instinct for making money.
instinctual	*adj.*	本能的 (derived from or prompted by a natural tendency)
[ɪn'stɪŋktʃuəl]		The relationship between a parent and a child is instinctual and stems from basic human nature.
extinct	*adj.*	灭绝的；绝种的 (no longer existing)
[ɪk'stɪŋkt]	①	Dinosaurs are extinct.
	②	The island's tallest volcano is long extinct.
extinction	*n.*	灭绝 (the state of being, becoming, or making extinct)
[ɪk'stɪŋkʃn]		30 percent of reptiles, birds, and fish are currently threatened with extinction.
extinguish	*v.*	熄灭 (火) (to make a fire stop burning or a light stop shining)
[ɪk'stɪŋgwɪʃ]		Firefighters tried to extinguish the flames.
	v.	使 (希望、爱情等) 不复存在 (to cause the end or death of something)
		News of the conflict extinguished our hopes for a peaceful resolution.
distinct	*adj.*	截然不同的；有区别的 (different in a way that you can see, hear, smell or feel)
[dɪ'stɪŋkt]		Each herb has its own distinct flavor.
	adj.	清楚的；明显的 (easily or clearly heard, seen or felt, etc.)
		The outline became less and less distinct as the light faded.

Unit 02

distinguish [dɪ'stɪŋgwɪʃ]	_v._ 区分；辨别 (to recognize the difference between two people or things) You're old enough to distinguish between fact and fantasy.
distinguished [dɪ'stɪŋgwɪʃt]	_adj._ 卓越的；著名的 (famous or outstanding) She is distinguished for her achievements in genetic research.

Arm系列

arm [ɑːm]	_n._ 武器 (a weapon, especially a firearm) They threatened to take up arms against the government if their demands were not met. _v._ 提供武器装备 (to supply or equip oneself with weaponry) The group of fighters was armed by a foreign government.
alarm [ə'lɑːm]	_n._ 警报 (a device that makes a loud sound as a warning or signal) He returned to the airport to find his car alarm going off. _n._ 惊恐 (a feeling of fear caused by a sudden sense of danger) His parents have expressed alarm about his safety. _v._ 使惊恐 (to make somebody anxious or afraid) The rapid spread of the disease has alarmed many people.
disarm [dɪs'ɑːm]	_v._ 解除武装 (to take a weapon or weapons away from somebody) The government has been unsuccessful at disarming the rebels.
armor ['ɑːmə(r)]	_n._ 盔甲 (defensive covering for the body) The officers are required to wear bulletproof body armor. _n._ （军舰，坦克等的）装甲，防弹钢板 (metal covers that protect ships and military vehicles such as tanks) The shots penetrated the tank's armor.

据希腊神话记载，天神乌拉诺斯（第一代主神）被他的儿子克洛诺斯（第二代主神）阉割，溅出的精血洒落在了大地女神，也是众神之母盖亚身上，于是盖亚生下了巨人族。这些巨人族被称为gigantes（癸干忒斯），他们身形雄伟、力大无穷，据说以两条蛇尾为足，大腿之上为人形，也被称为蛇足巨人。Giant（巨人）一词便来自巨人族，形容词是gigantic（巨大的）。

giant [ˈdʒaɪənt]	*n.* 巨人；巨兽；巨型植物 (an unusually large person, animal or plant)
	He has enormous charisma. He is a giant of a man.
	adj. 巨大的 (very large, much larger or more powerful than normal)
	A galaxy is a giant family of many millions of stars.
gigantic [dʒaɪˈɡæntɪk]	*adj.* 巨大的；庞大的 (extremely large)
	1 The earth may be thought of as a gigantic magnet.
	2 Gigantic waves crashed on the beach.

天神乌拉诺斯和众神之母盖亚结合生下了十二泰坦(Titan)。十二泰坦是希腊神话中曾统治世界的古老神族，他们身材巨大，力大无穷。titanic（巨大的）一词便来自泰坦，历史上著名的巨轮"泰坦尼克号"也由此得名。

后来第三代主神宙斯带领奥林匹斯诸神打败了十二泰坦。宙斯成为主神惹怒了盖亚。于是，盖亚鼓动巨人族（gigantes）向奥林匹斯发起进攻，巨人们手持燃烧的栎木大棒和巨大的石块，向奥林匹斯发起疯狂的进攻。奥林匹斯众神得到一个预言，必须有一个凡人参战才能击败巨人族。因此，宙斯通过雅典娜找到了民间伟大的英雄赫拉克勒斯（Hercules）前来参战。赫拉克勒斯力大无穷，射技精湛，帮助众神打败了巨人族。赫拉克勒斯惩恶扬善，敢于斗争，是希腊神话中最了不起的英雄，死后升入奥林匹斯圣山，成为大力神。在西方世界"赫拉克勒斯"一词已经成为了大力士和壮汉的同义词。herculean（力大无比的）一词便来于此。

titanic [taɪˈtænɪk]	*adj.* 十分巨大的 (very great in size, force or power)
	The world had witnessed a titanic struggle between two visions of the future.
herculean [ˌhɜːkjəˈliːən]	*adj.* 力大无比的 (of extraordinary power, extent, intensity or difficulty)
	His shoulders were herculean with long arms.
	adj. 费力的；需要决心的；艰巨的 (needing a lot of strength, determination or effort)
	He completed the translation of this monumental work with a herculean effort.

公元前292年，希腊的罗德岛人击败了马其顿人的入侵，把缴获的兵器熔化后制作了一尊高达100英尺的青铜太阳神巨像。巨像胯跨海港入口，船可从底下驶入港口，是古代七大奇观之一，被称为"Colossus of Rhodes"（罗德岛的巨型塑像）。"colossal"（巨大的）一词便来自于这尊巨像。

colossal [kə'lɒsl]	*adj.* 巨大的 (very large or great)
	① Even by modern standards, the 46,000 ton Titanic was a colossal ship.
	② The task they face is colossal.

《巨人传》是法国文学史上第一部长篇小说，作者是弗朗索瓦·拉伯雷(Francois Rabelais，约1493—1553)。书中的主人公叫高康大 (Gargantua)，他是巨人国王，食量惊人，出生的时候要喝17913头母牛的奶，穿的衣服要用几万尺布，长有十八层下巴，他把巴黎圣母院的大钟摘下来当马铃铛，他的一泡尿淹死了260416人。本书揭露了中世纪罗马教皇和教会的黑暗和腐朽，反映了文艺复兴时期人文主义者对个性解放的追求。"gargantuan"（巨大的；庞大的）一词就来自书的主人公Gargantua（高康大）。

gargantuan [gɑː'gæntʃuən]	*adj.* 巨大的；庞大的 (extremely large or great)
	A gargantuan corruption scandal has emerged in the past few years.

锦囊妙记

feeble ['fiːbl]	*adj.* 虚弱的；衰弱的 (lacking bodily strength; weak)
	The old lady has been rather feeble since her illness.
	谐音法 feeble-非薄，身体非常薄当然很feeble（虚弱）。
pest [pest]	*n.* 害虫 (an insect or other small animal that harms or destroys garden plants)
	The major pest was controlled and so the farmers stopped spraying insecticide.
	谐音法 pest-拍死它，是pest（害虫）当然要拍死它。
condemn [kən'dem]	*v.* 谴责 (to express strong disapproval of somebody/something)
	The school condemns cheating, and any student caught cheating will be expelled.
	拆分法 con-together（一起），demn-damn（该死的！），一起(con)骂某人该死的(damn)就是谴责！

schedule

['ʃedjuːl]

n. 日程安排 (a plan of things that will be done and the times when they will be done)

Students are planning their class schedules for next year.

v. 安排日程 (to arrange for something to happen at a particular time)

We scheduled a meeting for next week.

谐音法 sche-死车，dule-堵了，死车堵了，耽误了我的日程安排 (schedule)。

gist

[dʒɪst]

n. 要点；主旨 (the main point of a matter)

He spoke so fast that I only got the gist of the story.

谐音法 gist-记死它，对于要点和主旨当然要记死它！

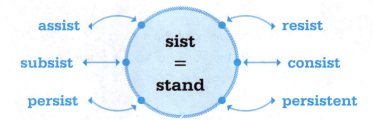

assist ←→ sist = stand ←→ resist
subsist ←→ consist
persist ←→ persistent

assist [ə'sɪst]	*v.* 协助；帮助 (to help somebody to do something) Robots will always assist humans, not replace them.
assistant [ə'sɪstənt]	*n.* 助手；助理 (a person who helps or supports someone, usually in their job) Her assistant was accused of theft and fraud by the police.
insist [ɪn'sɪst]	*v.* 坚持；强调 (to say something in a way that is very forceful and does not allow disagreement) 1 He insisted that his rights should be respected. 2 I insisted on driving him home.
consist [kən'sɪst]	*v.* 由……组成 (to be made up or composed) The atmosphere consists of more than 70 % of nitrogen. *v.* 在于 (to have something as an essential or main part) The beauty of the artist's style consists in its simplicity.
consistent [kən'sɪstənt]	*adj.* 一致的 (always behaving in the same way, or having the same opinions,standards,etc.) These new goals are not consistent with the existing policies. *adj.* 连续的；持续的 (happening in the same way and continuing for a period of time) He is a consistent supporter of the museum.
resist [rɪ'zɪst]	*v.* 抗拒；反对 (to refuse to accept something and try to stop it from happening) 1 It was hard to resist the temptation to open the box. 2 He tried to pin me down,but I resisted.

resistance [rɪˈzɪstəns]	*n.* 抵抗；阻力 (refusal to accept something new or different) In remote villages there is a resistance to change.
irresistible [ˌɪrɪˈzɪstəbl]	*adj.* 不可抗拒的 (impossible to resist) ① The force of the waves was irresistible. ② The music is irresistible.
persist [pəˈsɪst]	*v.* 坚持 (to keep on doing or saying something) You will succeed if you persist. *v.* 持续存在 (to continue to exist or occur) Rain persisted for days.
persistent [pəˈsɪstənt]	*adj.* 坚持不懈的 (refusing to give up or let go) She has been persistent in pursuing the job. *adj.* 持续存在的 (existing or continuing for a long time) Flooding has been a persistent problem in the area this year.
subsist [səbˈsɪst]	*v.* 维持生活 (to manage to stay alive, especially with limited food or money) They subsisted on bread and water. *v.* 生存；活着 (to continue living or being) The living things on the earth could not subsist on Mars.

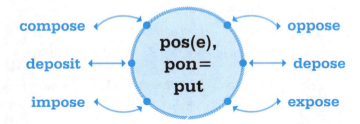

compose [kəmˈpəʊz]	*v.* 组成；构成 (to combine together to form a whole) This cloth is composed of silk and wool. *v.* 作曲；创作 (音乐) (to write music) Mozart began to compose when he was six years old.
composer [kəmˈpəʊzə(r)]	*n.* 作曲家 (a person who composes music) She prefers Mozart and Beethoven to modern composers.
component [kəmˈpəʊnənt]	*n.* 成分；零件 (one of the parts of something such as a system or mixture) Enriched uranium is a key component of nuclear weapons.

decompose
[ˌdiːkəmˈpəʊz]

v. 分解 (to separate something into components or basic elements)

1. Plastics take years to decompose.
2. Leaves decomposed on the forest floor.

expose
[ɪkˈspəʊz]

v. 使暴露 (to lay something open to danger, attack or harm)

Paintings should not be exposed to direct sunlight.

v. 揭露 (to tell the true facts about a person or a situation, and show them/it to be immoral, illegal, etc.)

After the scandal was exposed, he committed suicide.

oppose
[əˈpəʊz]

v. 反对 (to fight against, counter or resist strongly)

We're hoping we can get more senators to oppose the legislation.

opposite
[ˈɒpəzɪt]

adj. 相反的；截然不同的 (completely different)

The two scientists had the same information but reached opposite conclusions.

opponent
[əˈpəʊnənt]

n. 对手 (a person or thing that takes an opposite position in a contest, fight or controversy)

1. He knocked out his opponent in the third round.
2. She is a formidable opponent in the race for senator.

deposit
[dɪˈpɒzɪt]

v. 储蓄 (to put money in a bank account)

I deposited money in the bank.

v. 沉淀 (to let something fall or sink)

Layers of sediment were deposited on the ocean floor.

propose
[prəˈpəʊz]

v. 提议；建议 (to form or put forward a plan or intention)

The mayor proposed a plan for a new bridge.

v. 求婚 (to make an offer of marriage)

He proposed to her on bended knee.

proposal
[prəˈpəʊzl]

n. 提议；建议 (a plan that is proposed)

The committee is reviewing the proposal for the new restaurant.

dispose
[dɪˈspəʊz]

v. 处理；清除 (to get rid of something that you do not want or cannot keep)

They have no way to dispose of the hazardous waste they produce.

depose
[dɪˈpəʊz]

v. 罢免；免职 (to remove someone from a powerful position)

They have deposed the emperor.

postpone	*v.* 延期；延缓 (to put off to a later time)
[pə'spəʊn]	The baseball game was postponed until tomorrow because of rain.
impose	*v.* 强加 (to force someone to accept something)
[ɪm'pəʊz]	**1** They impose fines on airlines who bring in illegal immigrants.
	2 The government have imposed a new tax on cigarettes.

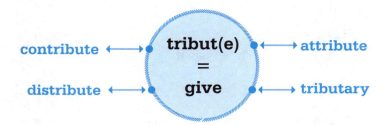

contribute ←→ **tribut(e)** ←→ attribute
=
distribute ←→ **give** ←→ tributary

tributary	*n.* 支流 (a stream feeding a larger stream or a lake)
['trɪbjətri]	The River Thames has many tributaries.
tribute	*n.* 致敬；颂词 (something that you say, give or do to show respect or affection for someone)
['trɪbjuːt]	Yellow ribbons were tied on trees as a tribute to the soldiers at war.
contribute	*v.* （为……）做贡献 (to give or supply something in common with others)
[kən'trɪbjuːt]	The volunteers contributed their time towards cleaning up the city.
	v. 导致；促成 (to help bring about a result)
	Design faults in the boat contributed to the tragedy.
	v. 投稿 (to submit articles to a publication)
	He contributed many poems to the magazine.
contribution	*n.* 贡献；捐赠 (the act of contributing)
[ˌkɒntrɪ'bjuːʃn]	As mayor, he made many positive contributions to the growth of the city.
attribute	*v.* 把……归于 (to say or believe that something is the result of a particular thing)
[ə'trɪbjuːt] *v.*	Women tend to attribute their success to external causes such as luck.
['ætrɪbjuːt] *n.*	*n.* 属性；特征 (a usually good quality or feature that someone or something has)
	Patience is a good attribute for a teacher.

distribute

[dɪ'strɪbjuːt]

v. 分发；分配 (to give things to a large number of people; to share something between a number of people)

1. He distributed sweets to all the children in the class.
2. The money was distributed among the poor.

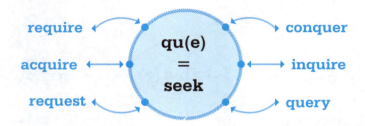

require

[rɪ'kwaɪə(r)]

v. 要求 (to make it necessary for someone to do something)

The law requires drivers to wear seat belts.

v. 需要 (to need something)

The work required infinite patience.

request

[rɪ'kwest]

n. 请求 (the act of asking for something)

After frequent requests, he eventually agreed to sing.

v. 请求；要求 (to ask for something)

Gentlemen are requested to wear a jacket and tie.

acquire

[ə'kwaɪə(r)]

v. 获得；取得 (to gain a new skill, ability usually by your own effort)

He is studying the way that language is acquired by children.

inquire

[ɪn'kwaɪə]

v. 询问；查询 (to ask somebody for some information)

I inquired about the schedule.

v. 调查 (to make an investigation)

The committee inquired into the matter.

query

['kwɪəri]

n. 问题；疑问 (a question; an inquiry)

The librarian responded to my query.

v. 询问 (to put as a question)

They conducted a survey in which several hundred people were queried about their dietary habits.

conquer

['kɒŋkə(r)]

v. 征服 (to take control of a country or city and its people by force)

The city was conquered by the ancient Romans.

v. 战胜 (to gain control of a problem or difficulty through great effort)

Scientists believe the disease can be conquered.

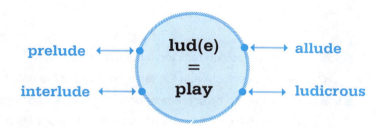

prelude ['preljuːd]	*n.* 序曲；前奏曲 (a short piece of music, especially an introduction to a longer piece) The musical had a brief prelude to get the audience in the proper mood.
interlude ['ɪntəluːd]	*n.* 插曲；幕间表演 (a usually short simple play or dramatic entertainment) We bought an ice-cream during the interlude. *n.* 间歇 (a period of time between events or activities) He has resumed his acting career after a two-year interlude.
ludicrous ['luːdɪkrəs]	*adj.* 可笑的；荒唐的 (funny because of being ridiculous) It was ludicrous to think that the plan could succeed.
allude [ə'luːd]	*v.* 暗指；影射 (to talk about or hint at somebody/something without mentioning directly) She only alluded to my past mistakes.
elude [i'luːd]	*v.* 躲避；避开 (to avoid or escape someone or something by being quick, skillful or clever) The killer was able to elude the police. *v.* 使⋯⋯迷惑 (to fail to be understood or remembered by someone) The cause of the disease continues to elude researchers.
elusive [i'luːsɪv]	*adj.* 难以找到的；琢磨不透的 (hard to find or capture) The giant squid is one of the ocean's most elusive inhabitants.

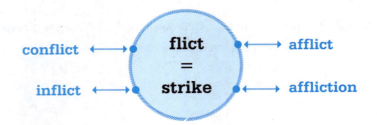

conflict ['kɒnflɪkt]	**v.** 矛盾；冲突 (to be contradictory or in opposition) His statement conflicts with the facts, as given in the police report. **n.** 矛盾；冲突 (strong disagreement between people or groups) The National Security Council has met to discuss ways of preventing a military conflict.
afflict [ə'flɪkt]	**v.** 使受痛苦；折磨 (to affect somebody/something in an unpleasant or harmful way) ❶ The disease afflicts an estimated two million people every year. ❷ Italy has been afflicted by political corruption for decades.
affliction [ə'flɪkʃn]	**n.** 苦恼；痛苦 (great suffering) She lost her sight and is now learning to live with her affliction.
inflict [ɪn'flɪkt]	**v.** 使遭受；给予打击 (to cause someone to experience something unpleasant or harmful) Rebels say they have inflicted heavy casualties on government forces.

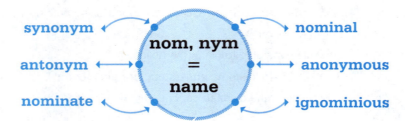

synonym ['sɪnənɪm]	**n.** 同义词 (a word that means the same thing as another word) In the eyes of many, it became a synonym for racism and anti-Semitism.
antonym ['æntənɪm]	**n.** 反义词 (a word that means the opposite of another word) The usual antonym of good is bad.

nominate ['nɒmɪneɪt]	*v.* 提名……为候选人；任命 (to propose somebody as a candidate for some honor) We expect the party to nominate him for president.
nominee [ˌnɒmɪ'niː]	*n.* 被提名者；候选人 (one who has been nominated to an office or for a candidacy) The presidential nominee was advised to choose a woman as a running mate.
nominal ['nɒmɪnl]	*adj.* 名义上的 (existing as something in name only) He was the nominal head of the government. *adj.* 微不足道的 (very small and much less than the normal cost or charge) The cells are provided at a nominal cost to research labs around the world.
anonymous [ə'nɒnɪməs]	*adj.* 无名的；匿名的 (having no known name or identity or known source) He made an anonymous phone call to the police.
ignominious [ˌɪgnə'mɪniəs]	*adj.* 耻辱的；不光彩的 (causing disgrace or shame) He made one mistake and his career came to an ignominious end.
pseudonym ['suːdənɪm]	*n.* 假名；化名 (a name that someone, often a writer, uses instead of their real name) Mark Twain is the pseudonym of the American writer Samuel L. Clemens.

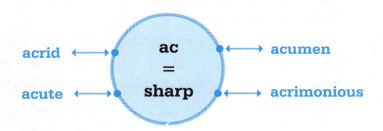

acute [ə'kjuːt]	*adj.* 严重的；剧烈的 (very serious or dangerous) The war has aggravated an acute economic crisis. *adj.* 敏锐的 (sensitive even to slight details or impressions) In the dark my sense of smell and hearing become so acute.
acrid ['ækrɪd]	*adj.* 辛辣的；刺鼻的 (having a noticeably sharp taste or smell) The room filled with the acrid smell of tobacco.

acumen ['ækjəmən]	*n.* 敏锐；聪明 (the ability to judge well) His sharp business acumen meant he quickly rose to the top.
acrimonious [ˌækrɪ'məʊniəs]	*adj.* （言辞）尖刻的，激烈的 (bitter and sharp in language or tone) There was an acrimonious debate between the two candidates.

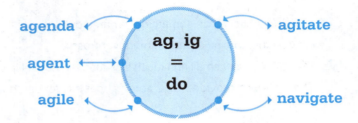

agent ['eɪdʒənt]	*n.* 代理人；中介 (a person who acts on behalf of another person, group) They worked with a travel agent to plan their vacation.
agenda [ə'dʒendə]	*n.* 议事日程 (a list of things to be done, especially at a meeting) The committee set the agenda for the next several years of research.
agile ['ædʒaɪl]	*adj.* 敏捷的；灵敏 (able to move quickly and easily) An acrobat has to be agile.
agitate ['ædʒɪteɪt]	*v.* （尤指为法律、社会状况的改变而）激烈争论，鼓动，煽动 (to argue strongly for something you want, especially for changes in a law, in social conditions, etc.) The women who worked in these mills had begun to agitate for better conditions. *v.* 使焦虑不安 (to make somebody feel angry, anxious or nervous) The thought of them getting her possessions when she dies agitates her.
navigate ['nævɪgeɪt]	*v.* (船只、飞机等)导航 (to direct, guide or move a ship, aircraft, etc. in a particular direction) They navigated by the sun and stars.

Social系列

social ['səʊʃl]	*adj.* 社会的 (connected with society and the way it is organized) We ought to organize more social events.

Unit 03

society [sə'saɪəti]	*n.* 社会 (people in general, living together in communities)
	We need to do more to help the poorer members of our society.
associate [ə'səʊʃieɪt]	*v.* 联想；联系 (to make a connection between people or things in your mind)
	He always associated the smell of tobacco with his father.
	n. 同事；伙伴 (a person who joins with others in some activity)
	They are the restaurant owner's business associates.
association [ə,səʊʃi'eɪʃn]	*n.* 团体；协会 (an organization of persons having a common interest)
	Research associations are often linked to a particular industry.
	n. 联系 (a connection or relationship between things or people)
	They denied having any association with terrorists.
dissociate [dɪ'səʊʃieɪt]	*v.* 使分离 (to separate from association or union with another)
	① It is getting harder for the president to dissociate himself from the scandal.
	② The director has tried to dissociate himself from his earlier films.

追根溯源

　　在古罗马时代，下至一般求职者，上至会计官、执行官乃至最高执政官等的候选人，都喜欢身穿白色宽外袍。白色象征洁白无瑕，表示谦卑真诚、忠实正直。拉丁语candidatus本意就是"身穿白袍的"，后延伸为candidate（候选人）。在拉丁语中，candere表示"发光"的意思。从中衍生出英语词根cand=shine；表"白色"之意。candid，candle，candor和incandescent等皆源于此。

candor ['kændə(r)]	*n.* 坦率；公正 (the quality of being honest and straightforward in attitude and speech)
	He covered a wide range of topics with unusual candor.
candid ['kændɪd]	*adj.* 率直的；坦白的 (open and sincere)
	He was candid about his dislike of our friends.
candidate ['kændɪdət]	*n.* 候选人 (a person who is trying to be elected)
	There were three candidates standing in the election.
incandescent [,ɪnkæn'desnt]	*adj.* 白炽光的；闪耀的 (white or glowing because of great heat)
	Because LEDs use up to 80 percent less energy than incandescent lights, the opportunity for savings is substantial.

incense ['ɪnsens]	*n.* 香 (material used to produce a fragrant odor when burned) In summer, they usually burn some coil incense to keep away the mosquitoes. *v.* 使愤怒；激怒 (to arouse the extreme anger) This proposal will incense conservation campaigners.
incendiary [ɪn'sendiəri]	*adj.* 引火的；燃烧的 (producing a fire) The fire was started by an incendiary bomb. *adj.* 煽动的 (causing strong feelings or violence) He recklessly made incendiary remarks during a period of heightened racial tensions.

锦囊妙记

plight [plaɪt]	*n.* 困境 (a bad condition or state) She was in a terrible plight, as she had lost all her money. 联想法 p-扑，light-光，扑灭灯光就进入了黑暗，陷入了困境（plight）。
blight [blaɪt]	*v.* 使凋萎；使颓丧 (to cause to suffer a blight) 1. The potatoes blighted. 2. His life was blighted by illness. 联想法 b-不，light-光，花儿如灯，使其不亮即是枯萎（blight）。
contest ['kɒntest] *n.* [kən'test] *v.*	*n.* 竞赛 (a struggle for victory) He won the contest for best photograph. *v.* 竞争 (to struggle or fight for or against something) He plans to contest a seat in Congress next year. 拆分法 con-together（一起），test-考试，一起参加考试就是竞争（contest）。
detest [dɪ'test]	*v.* 憎恶；嫌恶 (to dislike someone or something very strongly) I detest people who tell lies. 联想法 de-弟弟，test-考试，弟弟厌恶（detest）考试。
protest ['prəʊtest] *n.* [prə'test] *v.*	*n.* 抗议 (an expression or declaration of objection) The students launched a protest against the tuition increase. *v.* 抗议 (to express a strong objection to something) They were protesting against the death penalty. 拆分法 pro-前面，test-考试，走到前面抗议（protest）考试。

Unit 03

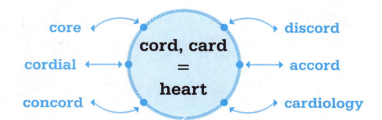

core → discord

cordial ↔ cord, card = heart ↔ accord

concord → cardiology

core [kɔː(r)]	*n.* （水果的）果心，核儿 (the hard central part of a fruit such as an apple, that contains the seeds) Peel the pears and remove the cores. *n.* 核心；要点 (the most important or central part of something) She has the ability to get straight to the core of a problem.
cordial ['kɔːdiəl]	*adj.* 热诚的；诚恳的 (warm and sincere) We received a cordial welcome at the university.
concord ['kɒŋkɔːd]	*n.* 和谐；协调 (agreement or harmony between people or nations) These states had lived in concord for centuries.
discord ['dɪskɔːd]	*n.* 不和谐；不一致 (lack of agreement among persons, groups or things) There are many discords in this family.
accord [əˈkɔːd]	*n.* 协议；条约 (a formal or official agreement) The two sides signed a peace accord last July. *v.* （与……）一致，符合 (to agree with or match something) Scientific evidence did not fully accord with the facts uncovered by the police.
according [əˈkɔːdɪŋ]	*adv.* 依照 (follwing, agreeing with or depending on something) According to the survey, independent private schools rate better than four other types of American educational institutions.
cardiac ['kɑːdiæk]	*adj.* 心脏的 (of or relating to the heart) The king was suffering from cardiac weakness.
cardiology [ˌkɑːdiˈɒlədʒi]	*n.* 心脏病学 (the study of the heart and its action and diseases) A doctor specializes in cardiology.

Unit 04

cardiologist [ˌkɑːdiˈɒlədʒɪst]	*n.* 心脏病专家 (a specialist in cardiology) In 1955 Eisenhower suffered a heart attack so severe that his primary cardiologist advised the president not to run for a second term.
cardinal ['kɑːdɪnl]	*n.* 红衣主教 (a priest of the highest rank in the Roman Catholic Church) The Pope appointed two new cardinals this year. *adj.* 基本的；最重要的 (basic or most important) My cardinal rule is to always be honest.

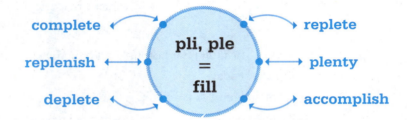

plenty ['plenti]	*n.* 充足；足够 (a full or more than adequate amount or supply) Most businesses face plenty of competition.
complete [kəm'pliːt]	*adj.* 完全的；完整的 (having all necessary parts; not lacking anything) I've collected the complete set.
deplete [dɪ'pliːt]	*v.* 耗尽；用尽 (to use up supplies, money or energy) Activities such as logging and mining deplete our natural resources.
replete [rɪ'pliːt]	*adj.* 充满的；充足的 (having much or plenty of something) The country's history is replete with stories of people who became successful by working hard.
replenish [rɪ'plenɪʃ]	*v.* 补充；重新装满 (to fill something that had previously been emptied) We need to replenish our supplies.
accomplish [ə'kʌmplɪʃ]	*v.* 完成；达到 (目的) (to succeed in doing something) The club accomplished its goal of raising money.
accomplished [ə'kʌmplɪʃt]	*adj.* 才华高的；技艺高超的 (having or showing the skill of an expert) She is one of the most accomplished authors of our time.

Unit 04

compliment ['kɒmplɪmənt]	**v.** 向……道贺；称赞 (to tell somebody that you like or admire something they have done, their appearance, etc.) We complimented her on her election victory. **n.** 恭维；称赞 (a remark that expresses praise or admiration of somebody) She blushed, but accepted the compliment with good grace.
complimentary [ˌkɒmplɪ'mentri]	**adj.** 赞美的 (expressing praise or admiration) We often get complimentary remarks regarding the quality of our service. **adj.** 免费赠送的 (given free as a courtesy or favor) He had complimentary tickets to take his wife to see the movie.
complement ['kɒmplɪment]	**n.** 补足；补充 (something that completes, makes up a whole, or brings to perfection) A good wine is a complement to a good meal. **v.** 补充；补足 (to serve as something necessary to make whole or better) The soup and salad complement each other well.
supplementary [ˌsʌplɪ'mentri]	**adj.** 增补的；追加的 (added to complete or make up a deficiency) The teacher's edition of the textbook comes with a lot of supplementary material.
implement ['ɪmplɪment]	**v.** 实施；执行 (to make something that has been officially decided start to happen or be used) Due to high costs, the program was never fully implemented. **n.** 工具；器械 (an object used to do work) The best implement for digging a garden is a spade.

Unit 04

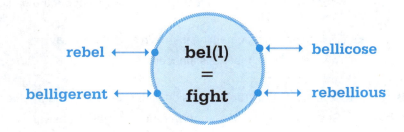

belligerent [bə'lɪdʒərənt]	**adj.** 好战的 (angry and aggressive) He is no less belligerent, no less dangerous than his father and grandfather.

bellicose	adj. 好战的；好争吵的 (having or showing a tendency to argue or fight)
	Bellicose hockey players always seem to spend more time fighting than playing.
['belɪkəʊs]	

rebel	n. 叛军 (a rebel is someone who fights authority)
	The government captured six armed rebels.
['rebl] n.	v. 反抗；反叛 (to oppose or take arms against a government or ruler)
[rɪ'bel] v.	When the government imposed more taxes, the people rebelled.

| **rebellious** | adj. 叛逆的；反对权威的 (refusing to obey rules or authority) |
| [rɪ'beljəs] | He grew older and more rebellious. |

Firm系列

firm	adj. 强有力的；坚决的 (strong and steady)
	He spoke to her in a soft but firm voice.
[fɜ:m]	adj. 坚定的；确定的 (not likely to change)
	They met two years ago and soon became firm friends.
	adj. 坚固的；结实的 (fairly hard; not easy to press into a different shape)
	Bake the cakes until they are firm to the touch.
	n. 公司 (a business unit or enterprise)
	The firm's employees were expecting large bonuses.

| **confirm** | v. 确认；证实 (to state or show that something is true or correct) |
| [kən'fɜ:m] | He confirmed that the area was now in rebel hands. |

| **confirmation** | n. 确认；认可 (the act of giving official approval to something or someone) |
| [ˌkɒnfə'meɪʃn] | Reporters awaited confirmation from the army about the battle. |

| **affirm** | v. 断言 (to say that something is true in a confident way) |
| [ə'fɜ:m] | The man affirms that he is innocent. |

| **affirmative** | adj. 肯定的；赞成的 (an expression as the word yes of agreement) |
| [ə'fɜ:mətɪv] | She gave an affirmative answer, not a negative answer. |

| **infirm** | adj. 体弱的；虚弱的 (weak in body or mind, especially from old age or disease) |
| [ɪn'fɜ:m] | The elderly and infirm have to be especially careful during the winter months. |

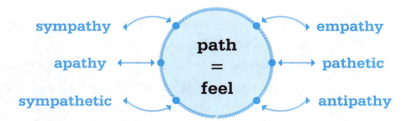

pathetic [pə'θetɪk]	*adj.* 令人同情的；可怜的 (causing feelings of sadness and sympathy) It was a pathetic sight, watching the people queue for food.
sympathy ['sɪmpəθi]	*n.* 同情；同情心 (a feeling of pity or sorrow for the distress of somebody) We expressed our sympathy for her loss.
sympathetic [ˌsɪmpə'θetɪk]	*adj.* 同情的；有同情心的 (having or showing feelings of sympathy) He received much help from sympathetic friends.
empathy ['empəθi]	*n.* 共鸣；同感 (the ability to share someone else's feeling) The nurse should try to develop empathy between herself and the patient.
apathy ['æpəθi]	*n.* 漠然；冷淡 (lack of feeling or emotion) People have shown surprising apathy toward these important social problems.
antipathy [æn'tɪpəθi]	*n.* 反感 (a feeling of intense dislike) I feel an antipathy against their behavior.

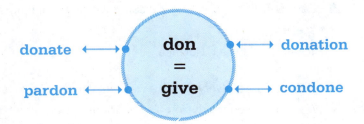

donate [dəʊ'neɪt]	*v.* 捐赠 (to give money, food, clothes, etc. to somebody/something) ① We donated our old clothes to charity. ② The computers were donated by local companies.
donation [dəʊ'neɪʃn]	*n.* 捐赠；赠送 (something given to help those in need) Employees make regular donations to charity.

pardon ['pɑːdn]	*v.* 赦免；特赦 (to officially allow somebody who has been found guilty of a crime to leave prison and/or avoid punishment) Hundreds of political prisoners were pardoned and released. *v.* 原谅 (to forgive somebody for something they have said or done) Pardon my ignorance, but what is a "duplex"?
condone [kən'dəʊn]	*v.* 容忍；纵容 (to accept behavior that is morally wrong or to treat it as if it were not serious) ① He could not condone lying. ② The government has been accused of condoning racism.

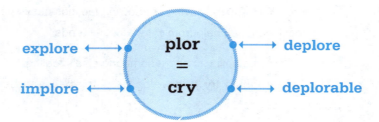

explore [ɪk'splɔː(r)]	*v.* 探索；勘查 (to travel over new territory for adventure or discovery) They were sent to explore unknown regions of Africa. *v.* 探究 (to investigate, study, or analyze something) Researchers are exploring how language is acquired by children.
deplore [dɪ'plɔː(r)]	*v.* 悲悼；哀叹 (to feel or express grief for somebody/something) They deplored the heavy loss of life in the earthquake. *v.* 谴责；强烈反对 (to strongly disapprove of something and criticize it, especially publicly) He says he deplores violence.
deplorable [dɪ'plɔːrəbl]	*adj.* 糟透的；可悲的 (very bad in a way that causes shock, fear or disgust) We condemned the deplorable conditions in which the family was living.
implore [ɪm'plɔː(r)]	*v.* 恳求；乞求 (to ask somebody to do something in an anxious way because you want or need it very much) ① Don't go. I implore you. ② Opposition leaders this week implored the president to break the deadlock.

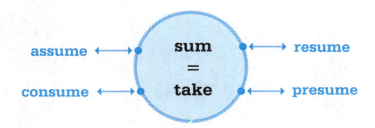

assume [əˈsjuːm]	*v.* 假定；认为 (to think that something is true or probably true without knowing that it is true)
	I assumed he was coming, so I was surprised when he didn't show up.
	v. 承担（责任）；取得（权利）(to take or begin to have power or responsibility)
	The king assumed the throne when he was very young.
	v. 假装；装出 (to pretend to have a particular feeling or quality)
	She assumed an air of confidence in spite of her nervousness.
assumption [əˈsʌmpʃn]	*n.* 假定；假设 (a belief or feeling that something is true or that something will happen, although there is no proof)
	Many scientific assumptions about Mars were wrong.
consume [kənˈsjuːm]	*v.* 消耗 (to use fuel, time, resources, etc.)
	The new lights consume less electricity.
	v. 吃；喝；饮 (to eat or drink something)
	Before he died he had consumed a large quantity of alcohol.
consumer [kənˈsjuːmə(r)]	*n.* 消费者；顾客 (a person who buys goods and services)
	Many consumers are still not comfortable making purchases on the Internet.
sumptuous [ˈsʌmptʃuəs]	*adj.* 豪华的；奢侈的 (very expensive or luxurious)
	The cruise ship claims to offer sumptuous meals.
resume [rɪˈzjuːm]	*v.* 重新开始 (to begin again something interrupted)
	After the war he resumed his study at the college.
presume [prɪˈzjuːm]	*v.* 假定；假设 (to believe that something is true without proof)
	When I found the room empty, I presumed that you had gone home.

Unit 04

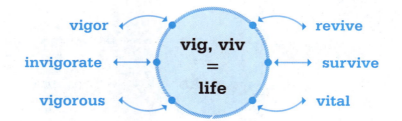

vigor
['vɪɡə(r)]

n. 精力；力量；活力 (energy, force or enthusiasm)

She was picked to lead the volunteer group because of her vigor and enthusiasm.

vigorous
['vɪɡərəs]

adj. 充满活力的；精力充沛的 (very active, determined or full of energy)

He was a vigorous, handsome young man.

adj. 有力的 (done with force and energy)

She gave a vigorous defense of her beliefs.

invigorate
[ɪn'vɪɡəreɪt]

v. 使生气勃勃；使精神焕发 (to give life and energy to somebody)

Take a deep breath in to invigorate you.

v. 振兴；刺激 (to cause something to become more active and lively)

The mayor planed to invigorate the downtown economy.

vigilant
['vɪdʒɪlənt]

adj. 警惕的；警觉的 (carefully noticing problems or signs of danger)

They were vigilant about protecting their children.

vivid
['vɪvɪd]

adj. 生动的 (producing a strong or clear impression on the senses)

The book includes many vivid illustrations.

adj. （光、颜色等）鲜艳的 (very bright)

The fabric was dyed a vivid red.

revive
[rɪ'vaɪv]

v. 使复苏；使恢复 (to return to consciousness or life)

They tried in vain to revive him.

v. 振兴 (to restore from a depressed, inactive or unused state)

Economists argued that freer markets would quickly revive the region's economy.

vital
['vaɪtl]

adj. 至关重要的 (necessary or essential in order for something to succeed or exist)

The port is vital to supply relief to millions of drought victims.

survive
[sə'vaɪv]

v. 幸存；活下来 (to remain alive or in existence)

① I don't see how any creature can survive under those conditions.

② The company survived the recession.

v. 比……活得长 (to live or exist longer than somebody or something)

She survived her husband by only a few years.

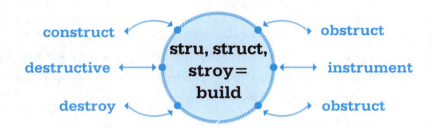

construct ← stru, struct, stroy = build → obstruct

destructive ↔ instrument

destroy ← → obstruct

construct [kən'strʌkt]	*v.* 修建；建造 (to make or form something by combining parts) ① They plan to construct a barn behind the house. ② The author constructs all the stories around one theme.
construction [kən'strʌkʃn]	*n.* 建筑；建造 (the process of constructing something) Construction of the new bridge will begin in the spring.
structure ['strʌktʃə(r)]	*v.* 构成；排列 (to arrange or organize something in a particular way) She structured the essay chronologically. *n.* 结构 (the manner of construction of something and the arrangement of its parts) Artists must study the structure of the human body.
reconstruct [ˌriːkən'strʌkt]	*v.* 重建 (to construct or form something again) The government must reconstruct the depressed economy.
destruction [dɪ'strʌkʃn]	*n.* 破坏；毁灭 (the act or process of killing, ruining or putting an end to something) War results in death and widespread destruction.
destroy [dɪ'strɔɪ]	*v.* 破坏；摧毁 (to cause something to end or no longer exist) ① The disease destroys the body's ability to fight off illness. ② The bomb blast destroyed the village.
destructive [dɪ'strʌktɪv]	*adj.* 破坏性的；毁灭性的 (causing a very large amount of damage) It was one of the most destructive storms in recent memory.
instruct [ɪn'strʌkt]	*v.* 讲授；指导 (to give knowledge to somebody) He instructs family members in nursing techniques.

Unit 04

	v. 指示；要求 (to give an order or command to somebody) She instructed us that we were to remain in our seats.
instruction [ɪnˈstrʌkʃn]	**n.** 指示；条令 (a statement that describes how to do something) The computer can handle one million instructions per second.
instrument [ˈɪnstrəmənt]	**n.** 器具 (a tool or device designed to do careful and exact work) An instrument was designed to measure the Earth's atmosphere. **n.** 乐器 (a device used to produce music) The piano was his favorite musical instrument.
instrumental [ˌɪnstrəˈmentl]	**adj.** 有帮助的；起作用的 (very important in helping or causing something to happen or be done) He was instrumental in bringing about an end to the conflict.
obstruct [əbˈstrʌkt]	**v.** 阻塞；堵塞 (to block or close up something by an obstacle) A piece of food obstructed his airway and caused him to stop breathing.
obstruction [əbˈstrʌkʃn]	**n.** 障碍物 (something that blocks a road, an entrance, etc.) They are removing trees and other obstructions from the path.

追根溯源

　　古希腊人和古罗马人在观看戏剧时，喜欢通过掌声（applaud）和喝彩声来表达喜爱和赞赏之情。当不喜欢演员的表演时，他们会通过嘘声、喝倒彩的方式表达对节目的不满。英语单词explode的本意就是"通过噪声把演员轰下台"，由ex（out，出去）+ plaudere（鼓掌；欢呼）构成。词义慢慢变为"突然而又大声地爆发，爆炸"。词根plaud=to clap由此而来。

applaud [əˈplɔːd]	**v.** 鼓掌欢迎；欢呼 (to express approval especially by clapping the hands) The audience stood and applauded her performance.
applause [əˈplɔːz]	**n.** 掌声；喝彩 (approval shown especially by clapping the hands) His speech was greeted with a storm of applause.
laudatory [ˈlɔːdətəri]	**adj.** 表示赞美的 (expressing praise or admiration) The play received mostly laudatory reviews.

explode [ɪkˈspləʊd]	*v.* 爆炸 (to burst or cause to burst with great violence as a result of internal pressure) They were clearing up when the second bomb exploded. *v.* （感情）爆发 (to give forth a sudden strong and noisy outburst of emotion) She looked like she was ready to explode with anger.
implode [ɪmˈpləʊd]	*v.* 内爆 (to burst inward) A blow can cause the vacuum tube to implode.

锦囊妙记

mourn [mɔːn]	*v.* 哀痛；哀悼 (to feel or express grief or sorrow) When he dies, people throughout the world will mourn. 谐音法 默哀
sorrow [ˈsɒrəʊ]	*n.* 痛苦 (a feeling of sadness caused especially by the loss of someone or something) I felt sorrow at the death of my friend. 联想法 给别人带来了sorrow（痛苦），感到很sorry。
bustle [ˈbʌsl]	*v.* 喧闹；忙乱 (to move or go in a busy or hurried way) She bustled around the kitchen getting ready for dinner guests. 联想法 每天挤bus，非常的bustle（忙乱）。
famine [ˈfæmɪn]	*n.* 饥荒；饥饿 (a very great shortage of food that affects many people over a wide area) The refugees are trapped by war, drought and famine. 拆分法 fa-发，mi-米，ne-呢！饥荒（famine）的时候才发米！
graze [greɪz]	*v.* 吃草 (to eat grass) The sheep usually graze in the grass land. *v.* 放牧 (to put cows, sheep, etc. in a field so that they can eat the grass there) The farmer grazed the cattle. 联想法 graze（放牧）就是吃grass（草）。
ranch [rɑːntʃ]	*n.* 大牧场 (a large farm for raising horses,cattle, or sheep) He lives on a cattle ranch in Australia. 拆分法 ran-跑，ch-吃，对于一头牛来说，又能ran（跑）又能ch（吃）的地方当然是ranch（牧场）。

Unit 05

victory [ˈvɪktəri]	*n.* 胜利 (the overcoming of an enemy) It was a decisive victory for the army.
evict [ɪˈvɪkt]	*v.* 依法驱逐 (to force someone to leave a place) His landlord has threatened to evict him if he doesn't pay the rent soon.
victim [ˈvɪktɪm]	*n.* 牺牲者；受害者 (a person who has been attacked, injured, robbed or killed by someone else) Food is being sent to the victims of the disaster.
convince [kənˈvɪns]	*v.* 使确信；使相信 (to make somebody believe that something is true) He convinced me that the story was true.
convincing [kənˈvɪnsɪŋ]	*adj.* 令人相信的 (causing someone to believe or agree something) There is no convincing evidence to support his theory.
invincible [ɪnˈvɪnsəbl]	*adj.* 不可战胜的，不能征服的 (impossible to defeat) He is an invincible wrestler who has never lost a match.
convict [kənˈvɪkt] *v.* [ˈkɒnvɪkt] *n.*	*v.* 证明……有罪 (to find or prove to be guilty) I have all the evidence necessary to convict this young criminal now. *n.* 罪犯 (a person convicted of and under sentence for a crime) The three escaped convicts were armed and dangerous.
vanquish [ˈvæŋkwɪʃ]	*v.* 征服；战胜 (to overcome somebody in battle; to subdue somebody completely) They were vanquished in battle.

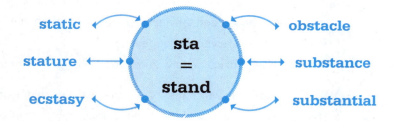

static ← → obstacle

stature ← → substance

sta = stand

ecstasy ← → substantial

static ['stætɪk]	*adj.* 静止的；不变化的 (showing little or no change, action or progress) The number of young people obtaining qualifications has remained static or decreased.
stationary ['steɪʃənri]	*adj.* 不动的；固定的 (not moving; standing still) The train was stationary for 90 minutes.
stature ['stætʃə(r)]	*n.* 身高；个子 (the natural height of a human) She was a little short in stature. *n.* 声望；名望 (the importance and respect that a person has because of their ability and achievements) This club has grown in stature over the last 20 years.
establish [ɪ'stæblɪʃ]	*v.* 建立；创建 (to begin or create something that is meant to last for a long time) ① They established the school in 1989. ② The company has established itself as a leader in the industry.
statue ['stætjuː]	*n.* 雕塑；雕像 (a figure usually of a person or animal that is made from stone or metal) A four-metre-high (13-foot) bronze statue stands in Che Guevara Square.
estate [ɪ'steɪt]	*n.* 房地产；不动产 (a large piece of land with a large house on it) His estate was valued at $150,000.
stable ['steɪbl]	*adj.* 稳定的 (not changing or fluctuating) Children need to be raised in a stable environment.
steady ['stedi]	*adj.* 稳定的；不变的 (showing little variation or fluctuation) ① Prices have remained steady over the last month. ② She used a tripod to keep the camera steady. *v.* 使稳定 (to keep something or someone from moving, shaking or falling) The doctor gave her medication to help steady her heart rate.

Unit 05

stagnant

['stægnənt]

adj. 不流动的；停滞的 (not flowing in a current or stream)

Mosquitoes have been thriving in stagnant water on building sites.

adj. 停滞不前的 (not advancing or developing)

He is seeking advice on how to revive the stagnant economy.

stalemate

['steɪlmeɪt]

n. 僵局 (a situation in which further action is blocked; a deadlock)

The new agreement could break the stalemate.

substance

['sʌbstəns]

n. 物质；材料 (a material of a particular kind)

This substance has now been cloned by molecular biologists.

n. 实质；基本内容 (the most basic or important part of something)

Syria will attend only if the negotiations deal with issues of substance.

substantiate

[səb'stænʃieɪt]

v. 证实；证明 (to prove the truth of something)

There is little scientific evidence to substantiate the claims.

substantial

[səb'stænʃl]

adj. 结实的；牢固的 (firmly constructed)

Substantial walls surround the castle.

adj. 大量的；重大的 (large in amount, value or importance)

① She purchased her tickets at a substantial discount.

② That is a very substantial improvement in the present situation.

insubstantial

[ˌɪnsəb'stænʃl]

adj. 无实体的；无实质的 (lacking substance or material nature)

Their thoughts seemed as insubstantial as smoke.

obstacle

['ɒbstəkl]

n. 障碍 (物) (something that makes it difficult to do something)

① Most competition cars will only roll over if they hit an obstacle.

② To succeed, you must learn to overcome obstacles.

constant

['kɒnstənt]

adj. 持续的；固定的 (staying the same, not changing)

① He suffers from constant headaches.

② The equipment should be stored at a constant temperature.

ecstasy

['ekstəsi]

n. 狂喜 (a state of very great happiness)

His performance sent the audience into ecstasies.

ecstatic

[ɪk'stætɪk]

adj. 狂喜的 (very happy or excited; feeling or showing ecstasy)

He was ecstatic when he heard that he was going to be a father.

instant

['ɪnstənt]

n. 瞬间；顷刻 (a very brief time; moment)

The pain disappeared in an instant.

Unit 05

	adj. 立即的 (happening immediately) The Internet provides instant access to an enormous amount of information.
instantaneous [ˌɪnstən'teɪnɪəs]	*adj.* 瞬间的 (happening very quickly) The thunder following the flash of lightning was nearly instantaneous.

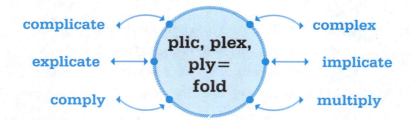

complicate ['kɒmplɪkeɪt]	*v.* 使复杂化 (to make something more difficult or less simple) You mustn't complicate the problem by raising new issues.
complicated ['kɒmplɪkeɪtɪd]	*adj.* 复杂的 (hard to understand, explain or deal with) The machine has a complicated design.
complex ['kɒmpleks]	*adj.* 复杂的；难懂的 (made of many different things or parts that are connected; difficult to understand) The situation is more complex than you realize.
perplex [pə'pleks]	*v.* 使迷惑；使混乱 (to confuse somebody very much) Questions about the meaning of life have always perplexed humankind.
explicate ['eksplɪkeɪt]	*v.* 解释；阐明 (to explain an idea or a work of literature in a lot of detail) The physicist did his best to explicate the wave theory of light for the audience of laymen.
explicit [ɪk'splɪsɪt]	*adj.* 明确的；清楚的 (fully and clearly expressed; leaving nothing implied) Criticism is hinted at, but never made explicit.
implicate ['ɪmplɪkeɪt]	*v.* 使……卷入；牵连 (to show to be connected or involved) His business partner was implicated in the theft.
implicit [ɪm'plɪsɪt]	*adj.* 不言明的；含蓄的 (suggested without being directly expressed) He wanted to make explicit in the film what was implicit in the play.

comply [kəm'plaɪ]	**v.** 遵从；依从 (to do what you have been asked or ordered to do) There will be penalties against individuals who fail to comply.
compliant [kəm'plaɪənt]	**adj.** 遵从的；依从的 (willing to do whatever you are asked or ordered to do) The student's shirt was not compliant with the school's dress code.
replica ['replɪkə]	**n.** 复制品 (an exact copy, especially of a work of art) The child was a replica of her mother.
duplicate ['djuːplɪkeɪt]	**v.** 复制；复印 (to make a copy of something) She duplicated the video to give to family and friends. **adj.** 完全一样的 (exactly the same as something else) I began receiving duplicate copies of the magazine every month.
multiply ['mʌltɪplaɪ]	**v.** 乘；(使) 相乘 (to add a number to itself a particular number of times) The teacher taught the children how to add, subtract, multiply and divide. **v.** 繁殖 (to increase in number by reproducing) The bacteria multiply rapidly in warm, moist conditions.

Mirror系列

mirror ['mɪrə(r)]	**n.** 镜子 (a polished or smooth surface as of glass that forms images by reflection) Breaking a mirror is supposed to bring seven years of bad luck.
mirage ['mɪrɑːʒ]	**n.** 海市蜃楼；幻景 (an illusion sometimes seen at sea, in the desert) In short, winter is a tomb, spring is a lie, and summer is a pernicious mirage. **n.** 幻想；妄想 (a hope or wish that you cannot make happen because it is not realistic) A peaceful solution proved to be a mirage.
miracle ['mɪrəkl]	**n.** 奇迹 (a very amazing or unusual event, thing or achievement) It's a miracle he wasn't killed in the plane crash.
miraculous [mɪ'rækjələs]	**adj.** 奇迹般的 (very wonderful or amazing like a miracle) He made a miraculous recovery after the accident.

admire

[əd'maɪə(r)]

v. 赞赏；称赞 (to think very highly of somebody)

You have to admire the way he handled the situation.

v. 欣赏 (to look at something and think that it is attractive and impressive)

We gazed out the window and admired the scenery.

admirable

['ædmərəbl]

adj. 令人钦佩的 (deserving great respect and approval)

He showed admirable courage.

Mark系列

mark

[mɑːk]

n. 斑点；污点 (a small area of dirt, a spot or a cut on a surface that spoils its appearance)

The dogs are always rubbing against the wall and making dirty marks.

v. 做记号；做标记 (to write or draw a symbol, line, etc. on something in order to give information about it)

I have marked the event on my calendar.

v. 留下痕迹；弄污 (to make a mark on something in a way that spoils or damages it)

Be careful not to mark the floor with your shoes.

remark

[rɪ'mɑːk]

n. 评论 (an expression of opinion or judgment)

I've heard many disparaging remarks about him.

v. 评论 (to express as an observation or comment)

She has made outspoken remarks on the issue.

remarkable

[rɪ'mɑːkəbl]

adj. 显著的；引人注目的 (unusual or surprising)

Competing in the Olympics is a remarkable achievement.

immaculate

[ɪ'mækjələt]

adj. 洁净的；无瑕疵的 (having no flaw or error)

① He managed to keep the white carpet immaculate.

② She had an immaculate record of service.

Unit 05

orbit

['ɔːbɪt]

n. 轨道 (the path of a celestial body or an artificial satellite)

The spaceship is in orbit round the moon.

v. 绕轨道而行 (to go round in space)

The spacecraft orbits the earth every 24 hours.

exorbitant

[ɪgˈzɔːbɪtənt]

adj. 极高的；高得离谱的 (going far beyond what is fair, reasonable or expected)

Exorbitant tuition imposes an immense strain on parent.

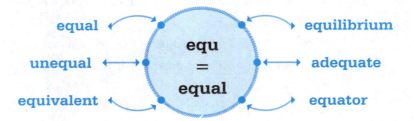

equal   equilibrium

equ = equal

unequal   adequate

equivalent   equator

equal

['iːkwəl]

adj. 相等的；平等的 (the same in number, amount, degree, rank or quality)

We divided the profits into three equal shares.

unequal

[ʌnˈiːkwəl]

adj. 不平等的；不公平的 (in which people are treated in different ways or have different advantages in a way that seems unfair)

This country still had a deeply oppressive, unequal and divisive political system.

equator

[ɪˈkweɪtə]

n. 赤道 (an imaginary line around the earth at an equal distance from the North and South Poles)

The equator is an imaginary line around the middle of the earth.

equivalent

[ɪˈkwɪvələnt]

adj. 相等的；相当的 (equal in force, amount or value)

Those less-known companies manufacture equivalent products at cheaper prices.

n. 对等物 (something like or equal to something else in number, value, or meaning)

Breathing such polluted air is the equivalent of smoking ten cigarettes.

Unit 05

equilibrium [ˌiːkwɪ'lɪbriəm]	*n.* 平衡 (a state of balance between opposing forces or actions) ① Supply and demand were in equilibrium. ② We must find an equilibrium between commercial development and conservation of our natural treasures.
adequate ['ædɪkwət]	*adj.* 足够的 (enough for some need or requirement) The school lunch should be adequate to meet the nutritional needs of growing children.
inadequate [ɪn'ædɪkwət]	*adj.* 不充足的 (not enough or not good enough) The food supplies are inadequate to meet the needs of the hungry.

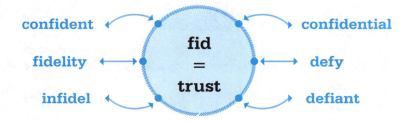

confident ['kɒnfɪdənt]	*adj.* 自信的 (having a feeling or belief that you can do something well or succeed at something) We are confident that conditions will improve soon.
confidence ['kɒnfɪdəns]	*n.* 自信 (a feeling or belief that you can do something well or succeed at something) The experience gave her the confidence to start her own business.
diffident ['dɪfɪdənt]	*adj.* 缺乏自信的；胆怯的 (lacking confidence; not feeling comfortable around people) For someone who makes a living performing for other people, the actress is remarkably diffident in real life.
confidential [ˌkɒnfɪ'denʃl]	*adj.* 机密的；秘密的 (meant to be kept secret and not told to or shared with other people) These documents are completely confidential. *adj.* （说话的方式）隐秘的 (showing that what you are saying is private or secret) She spoke in a confidential tone.

fidelity [fɪ'deləti]	*n.* 忠诚；忠实 (the quality or state of being faithful or loyal) They swore fidelity to the king.
infidel ['ɪnfɪdəl]	*n.* 异教徒 (one who is not a Christian or who opposes Christianity) Their leaders have declared publicly death to the infidels.
defy [dɪ'faɪ]	*v.* 不服从；公然反抗 (to challenge the power of somebody/something) She defied her parents and dropped out of school.
defiant [dɪ'faɪənt]	*adj.* 挑衅的；公然违抗的 (openly refusing to obey something or someone) He's taken a defiant stand on the issue.

Crak系列

crack [kræk]	*n.* 裂缝 (a very narrow space or opening between two things or two parts of something) The vase has a few fine cracks, but it is still usable. *v.* 断裂 (to break something so that there are lines in its surface but it is usually not separated into pieces) The mirror cracked when she dropped it.
crash [kræʃ]	*n.* 碰撞声 (a loud sound as of things smashing) She looked up when she heard the crash outside. *v.* 碰撞 (to break violently and noisily) She crashed the car into a tree, but no one was hurt.
crevice ['krevɪs]	*n.* (岩石) 裂缝 (a narrow opening or crack in a hard surface and especially in rock) Steam escaped from a long crevice in the volcano.
discrepancy [dɪs'krepənsi]	*n.* 差异；不符合；不一致 (a difference between two or more things that should be the same) There were discrepancies between their accounts of the accident.
decrepit [dɪ'krepɪt]	*adj.* 衰老的；破旧的 (old and in bad condition or poor health) The film was shot in a decrepit police station.

Unit 05

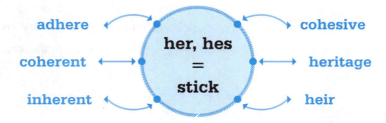

adhere [əd'hɪə(r)]	_v._ 黏附；附着 (to stick firmly to something)
	Wet clothes adhere to the skin.
	_v._ 坚持；遵守 (to behave according to a particular law, rule, set of instructions, etc.)
	We adhered to our original plan of swimming in spite of the bad weather.
coherent [kəʊ'hɪərənt]	_adj._ 有表达能力的；能表述清楚的 (able to talk and express yourself clearly)
	He was taken to a local hospital for treatment for dehydration but was not coherent enough to provide his name or other information at the time.
	adj. 条理分明的 (logical and well-organized)
	He proposed the most coherent plan to improve the schools.
cohesive [kəʊ'hiːsɪv]	_adj._ 有凝聚力的 (closely united)
	Their tribe is a small but cohesive group.
cohesion [kəʊ'hiːʒn]	_n._ 凝聚；内聚 (the act or state of keeping together)
	There was a lack of cohesion in the rebel army.
inherit [ɪn'herɪt]	_v._ 继承 (to get money, property, etc. by legal right from a person at his or her death)
	She inherited the family business from her father.
	_v._ 经遗传获得 (品质、身体特征等) (to have qualities, physical features, etc. that are similar to those of your parents, grandparents, etc.)
	She inherited her father's deep blue eyes.
heritage ['herɪtɪdʒ]	_n._ 遗产；继承物 (the traditions, achievements and beliefs that are part of the history of a group of people)
	① This farm is my heritage from my father, as it was for him from his father.
	② Manchester has a rich cultural, economic and sporting heritage.
heir [eə(r)]	_n._ 继承人 (a person who has the legal right to receive the property, money or title of someone who dies)
	She became the leader of her husband's organization and the heir to his estate, worth an estimated $10 million.

inherent [ɪnˈhɪərənt]	*adj.* 固有的；内在的 (belonging to the basic nature of someone or something) Individuality is a valued and inherent part of the British character.

追根溯源

　　卡俄斯（Chaos）是希腊神话中最早的神灵，代表宇宙形成之前模糊一团的景象。宇宙之初，只有卡俄斯，它是一个无边无际、一无所有的虚空。随后卡俄斯依靠无性繁殖从自身内部诞生了大地之神盖亚（Gaia）、地狱深渊神塔耳塔洛斯（Tartarus）、黑暗神俄瑞玻斯（Erebus）、黑夜女神倪克斯（Nyx）和爱神厄洛斯（Eros），世界由此开始。Chaos（混乱；混沌）一词用来表示当前一片混沌的状态。当时的宇宙充满了模糊的气体（gas）；卡俄斯代表了早期的宇宙（cosmos）。

chaos [ˈkeɪɒs]	*n.* 混乱；混沌 (complete confusion and disorder) The country had descended into economic chaos.
chaotic [keɪˈɒtɪk]	*adj.* 混沌的；一片混乱的 (completely confused or disordered) The traffic in the city is chaotic in the rush hour.
gas [gæs]	*n.* 气体 (a substance such as oxygen or hydrogen that is like air and has no fixed shape) The heated gas is piped through a coil surrounded by water.
cosmos [ˈkɒzmɒs]	*n.* 宇宙 (the universe especially when it is understood as an ordered system) Hundreds of scientists cycle through every year to study the deep history of the Earth and the great mysteries of the cosmos.
cosmopolitan [ˌkɒzməˈpɒlɪtən]	*adj.* 世界性的；全世界的 (belonging to all the world) London has always been a cosmopolitan city. *adj.* 见多识广的 (having or showing a wide experience of people and things from many different countries) The family are rich, and extremely sophisticated and cosmopolitan.

Unit 05

锦囊妙记

cautious ['kɔːʃəs]	*adj.* 小心的；谨慎的 (being careful about avoiding danger or mistakes) Any cautious tourist will guard her/his passport. 谐音法 cautious–靠蛇死，所以要小心谨慎(cautious)，不要靠近蛇!
humid ['hjuːmɪd]	*adj.* 潮湿的 (having a lot of moisture in the air) The air was so humid that our beach towels hanging on the line never really got dry. 拆分法 hu–湖，mid–中间，在湖(hu)中间(mid)，当然是潮湿的(humid)!
ambition [æmˈbɪʃn]	*n.* 雄心；抱负 (a desire to be successful, powerful, or famous) His ambition is to sail round the world. 谐音法 ambition–俺必胜! 很有雄心!
futile ['fjuːtaɪl]	*adj.* 无效的；无用的 (having no result or effect) Their efforts to win were futile. 谐音法 futile–"废头"，废头当然是无用的(futile)。
dread [dred]	*v.* 害怕；担心 (to fear something that will or might happen) She dreaded making speeches in front of large audiences. 联想法 省去r，dread 就变成了dead (死的)，每个人都害怕自己会死去。

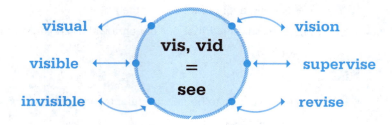

visual ← → vision
visible ← → supervise
invisible ← → revise

vis, vid
=
see

visual

['vɪʒuəl]

adj. 视觉的 (relating to the sense of sight)

She appreciates the visual arts such as painting and film.

visible

['vɪzəbl]

adj. 看得见的；明显的 (possible to see)

The house is visible through the tree.

invisible

[ɪn'vɪzəbl]

adj. 隐形的；看不见的 (impossible to see)

With the telescope we can see details of the planet's surface that are ordinarily invisible.

vision

['vɪʒn]

n. 视力；视觉 (the act or power of sensing with the eyes)

The disease causes blindness or serious loss of vision.

visionary

['vɪʒənri]

adj. 有远见的 (original and showing the ability to think about or plan the future with great imagination and intelligence)

She is known as a visionary leader.

adj. 空想的 (incapable of being realized or achieved)

I had a visionary schemes for getting rich.

n. 有眼力的人；有远见卓识的人 (a person who has the ability to think about or plan the future in a way that is intelligent or shows imagination)

Artists are often seen as visionaries, the first to arrive at truths that will someday be commonly held.

supervise

['suːpəvaɪz]

v. 监督；管理 (to manage and direct somebody or something)

The builder supervised the construction of the house.

supervisor

['suːpəvaɪzə(r)]

n. 上级；管理者 (a person who supervises someone or something)

The supervisor fired him after he showed up at work drunk.

revise [rɪˈvaɪz]	*v.* 修订；修改 (to make changes especially to correct or improve something) This dictionary has been completely revised.
evident [ˈevɪdənt]	*adj.* 明显的 (clear to the sight or mind) His footprints were clearly evident in the heavy dust.
evidence [ˈevɪdəns]	*n.* 证据 (a visible sign of something) Investigators could find no evidence linking him to the crime.
provident [ˈprɒvɪdənt]	*adj.* 有远见的 (having or showing foresight) Her provident measures kept us safe while the hurricane hit the city. *adj.* 节俭的 (careful about planning for the future and saving money for the future) It is possible to be provident without being miserly.
envision [ɪnˈvɪʒn]	*v.* 想象 (to picture something in your mind) She envisioned a better life for herself.

signal [ˈsɪgnəl]	*v.* 发信号；打手势 (to make a movement or sound to give somebody a message) He signaled us that it was time to begin the meeting. *n.* 信号 (something such as a sound, gesture or object that conveys notice) He likes her but he is sending the wrong signals with his constant teasing.
signify [ˈsɪgnɪfaɪ]	*v.* 表示；意味 (to be a sign of something) The recent decline of the stock market does not necessarily signify the start of a recession.
significant [sɪgˈnɪfɪkənt]	*adj.* 显著的；值得注意的 (large enough to be noticed or have an effect) A significant number of customers complained about the service.

	adj. 有重大意义的；显著的 (large or important enough to have an effect or to be noticed) This is the most significant outbreak of violence since October 2016, when nine policemen died in similar attacks on border posts.
insignificant [ˌɪnsɪɡˈnɪfɪkənt]	*adj.* 不重要的；无足轻重的 (small or unimportant) Looking up at the stars always makes me feel so small and insignificant.
signature [ˈsɪɡnətʃə(r)]	*n.* 签名 (a person's name written in that person's handwriting) We presented the document to the president for her signature.
resign [rɪˈzaɪn]	*v.* 辞职；放弃 (to give up one's office or position) The senator was forced to resign his position.
assign [əˈsaɪn]	*v.* 布置任务 (to give someone a particular job or duty) The teacher assigned us 50 math problems for homework. *v.* 选派 (to send someone to a particular group or place as part of a job) She was assigned to the embassy in India.
assignment [əˈsaɪnmənt]	*n.* 任务 (something as a job or task that is given out) The reporter's assignment is to interview the candidate.
designate [ˈdezɪɡneɪt]	*v.* 指定 (to appoint or choose somebody or something for a special purpose) Some of the rooms were designated as offices. *v.* 标明；指明 (to show something using a particular mark or sign) These lines designate the boundaries.

Cave系列

cave [keɪv]	*n.* 洞穴 (a large hole that was formed by natural processes in the side of a cliff or hill) Creatures such as bats and moths which shelter in caves.
cavity [ˈkævəti]	*n.* 洞 (a hole or space inside something) Some birds nest in tree cavities. *n.* 蛀牙 (a hole formed in a tooth by decay) There's a cavity in boy's tooth.

Unit 06

excavate ['ekskəveɪt]	*v.* 挖掘；发掘 (to dig out and remove something) They excavated an ancient city.
concave [kɒn'keɪv]	*adj.* 凹的 (having a shape like the inside of a bowl) Spoons are concave.

Gorge系列

gorge [gɔːdʒ]	*n.* 山峡；峡谷 (a deep narrow valley with steep sides) The south side of the gorge is now clothed in trees. *v.* 狼吞虎咽 (to eat something greedily) We gorged ourselves on chips and cookies.
gorgeous ['gɔːdʒəs]	*adj.* 极其漂亮的 (very beautiful or attractive) The cosmetics industry uses gorgeous women to sell its products. *adj.* 绚丽的；华丽的 (with very deep colors; impressive) Sunsets in Hawaii are just gorgeous.
gobble ['gɒbl]	*v.* 狼吞虎咽 (to swallow or eat something greedily) You'll be sick if you keep gobbling your meals like that.
guzzle ['gʌzl]	*v.* 狂饮 (to drink something greedily) My brother guzzled my soda before I could stop him.

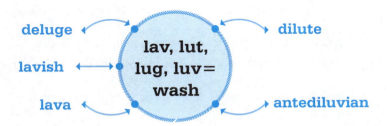

deluge — dilute

lavish — **lav, lut, lug, luv = wash** —

lava — antediluvian

deluge ['deljuːdʒ]	*n.* 洪水 (a large amount of rain that suddenly falls in an area) The deluge caused severe mudslides. *v.* 使涌来；使充满 (to send or give somebody/something a large number of things at the same time) things at the same time) The store was deluged with complaints.

lava

['lɑːvə]

n. 熔岩 (melted rock from a volcano)

The city was buried in volcanic lava.

antediluvian

[ˌæntɪdɪ'luːviən]

adj. 大洪水以前的 (relating to the period before the flood described in the Bible)

The archaeologists have found evidence in the Middle East of an antediluvian people previously unknown to history.

adj. 早已过时的 (very old-fashioned)

He has antediluvian notions about the role of women in the workplace.

dilute

[daɪ'luːt]

v. 稀释；冲淡 (to make a liquid thinner or less strong by adding water or another liquid)

You can dilute the medicine with water.

v. 削弱 (to lessen the strength of something)

The hiring of the new CEO diluted the power of the company's president.

lavish

['lævɪʃ]

adj. 过分慷慨的；非常浪费的 (giving or using a large amount of something)

Critics attack his lavish spending and flamboyant style.

Image系列

image

['ɪmɪdʒ]

n. 影像；图像 (a picture that is produced by a camera, artist, mirror, etc.)

The kids sat staring at the images on the TV screen.

n. 画面；形象 (a mental picture; the thought of how something looks or might look)

His poem evokes images of the sea and warm summer days.

imitate

['ɪmɪteɪt]

v. 模仿；效仿 (to follow as a pattern, model or example)

Her style has been imitated by many other writers.

imitation

[ˌɪmɪ'teɪʃn]

n. 模仿；仿效 (the act of copying someone or something)

① Children learn by imitation of adults.

② The restaurant was designed in imitation of a Japanese temple.

imitator

['ɪmɪteɪtər(r)]

n. 模仿者；仿效者 (someone who copies what someone else does, or copies the way they speak or behave)

He is an outstanding imitator and can impersonate all the well-known politicians.

emulate

['emjuleɪt]

v. 努力赶上；向……看齐 (to try to do something as well as somebody else because you admire them)

She grew up emulating her sports heroes.

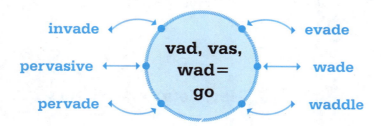

invade ← vad, vas, wad= go → evade

pervasive ← → wade

pervade ← → waddle

invade

[ɪnˈveɪd]

v. 入侵 (to enter a country, town, etc. using military force in order to take control of it)

The troops invaded at dawn.

n. (尤指造成损害或混乱地) 涌入；侵袭 (to enter a place in large numbers, especially in a way that causes damage or confusion)

Bacteria invaded and caused an infection.

invasion

[ɪnˈveɪʒn]

n. 入侵；侵略 (the incoming or spread of something usually hurtful)

① The people live under a constant threat of invasion.

② The enemy launched an invasion.

pervade

[pəˈveɪd]

v. 遍及；弥漫 (to spread through and be noticeable in every part of something)

① A feeling of great sadness pervades the film.

② Art and music pervade every aspect of their lives.

pervasive

[pəˈveɪsɪv]

adj. 弥漫的；渗透的 (existing in every part of something)

Televisions have pervasive influence on our culture.

evade

[ɪˈveɪd]

v. 逃避；躲避 (to avoid dealing with or facing something)

The governor has been accused of evading the issue.

evasive

[ɪˈveɪsɪv]

adj. 含糊其词的 (not willing to give clear answers to a question)

Direct questions would almost certainly result in evasive answers.

adj. 逃避的 (done to avoid harm, an accident, etc.)

They took evasive action to avoid capture.

wade [weɪd]	*v.* （从水、泥等）蹚，走过 (to walk through water or mud) I jumped off the boat and waded back to shore.
waddle ['wɒdl]	*v.* (鸭子似地) 蹒跚行走；摇摆地行走 (to walk with short steps, rocking slightly from side to side) A fat goose waddled across the yard.

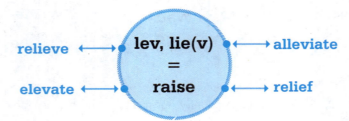

relieve [rɪ'liːv]	*v.* 解除；缓解 (to free from a burden) I took a pill to relieve my headache.
relief [rɪ'liːf]	*n.* 宽慰；缓解 (removal or lightening of something oppressive or distressing) I felt such a sense of relief after I finished my thesis. *n.* 救济；救援物资 (things that are given to help people who are victims of a war, earthquake, flood, etc.) Countries from around the world have been sending relief to the flood victims.
alleviate [ə'liːvieɪt]	*v.* 减轻；缓和 (痛苦) (to make less painful, difficult or severe) A good long rest alleviated her headache.
elevate ['elɪveɪt]	*v.* 提高；使升高 (to make the level of something increase) Emotional stress can elevate blood stress. *v.* 提拔 (to raise in rank or status) He elevated many of his friends to powerful positions within the government.
elevation [ˌelɪ'veɪʃn]	*n.* 海拔高度 (the height of a place) Atmospheric pressure varies with elevation and temperature.

Unit 06

Clear系列

clear [klɪə]	*adj.* 明显的；显然的 (obvious and leaving no doubt at all) There are clear differences between the two candidates.
clarify ['klærəfaɪ]	*v.* 澄清 (to make something clearer or easier to understand) The president was forced to clarify his position on the issue.
declare [dɪ'kleə(r)]	*v.* 宣布；声明 (to say or state something in an official or public way) The government has just declared a state of emergency. *v.* 申报 (to tell the government about money you have earned or received in order to pay taxes) Large purchases must be declared at customs.
declaration [ˌdeklə'reɪʃn]	*n.* 宣言；布告 (the act of making an official statement about something) The government has made a declaration of war on its enemies. *n.* 申报 (something that is stated or made known in an official or public way) You will need to make a declaration of your income.

Shri系列

shrimp [ʃrɪmp]	*n.* 虾 (a small shellfish that has a long body and legs and that is eaten as food) Experiments were made to adapt this variety of shrimp to fresh water.
shrink [ʃrɪŋk]	*v.* 收缩；蜷缩 (to become smaller in amount, size, or value) The town's population shrank during the war. *v.* 畏缩 (to refrain from doing something especially because of difficulty or unpleasantness) He did not shrink from telling the truth.
shrivel ['ʃrɪvl]	*v.* 枯萎 (to draw into wrinkles especially with a loss of moisture) The plant shrivels and dies.
cringe [krɪndʒ]	*v.* 畏缩 (to feel disgust or embarrassment and often to show this feeling by a movement of your face or body) Just the thought of eating broccoli makes me cringe.

wrinkle ['rɪŋkl]	**n.** 皱纹 (a small line or fold that appears on your skin as you grow older) His face was covered with wrinkles. **v.** 起皱 (to become marked with wrinkles) My shirt was wrinkled after being so long in the suitcase.

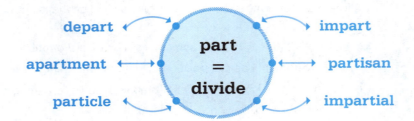

depart [dɪ'pɑːt]	**v.** 离开；出发 (to go away) The group is scheduled to depart tomorrow at 8:00 a.m.
apartment [ə'pɑːtmənt]	**n.** 公寓 (a building containing several individuals) We lived in an apartment for several years before buying a house.
department [dɪ'pɑːtmənt]	**n.** 部门 (one of the major parts of a company, organization, government or school) Your letter has been forwarded to our sales department.
particle ['pɑːtɪkl]	**n.** 微粒 (a very small piece of something) There is not a particle of evidence to support their claim.
participate [pɑː'tɪsɪpeɪt]	**v.** 参与 (to be involved with others in doing something) Most people joined the game, but a few chose not to participate.
impart [ɪm'pɑːt]	**v.** 传授；告知 (to pass information, knowledge, etc. to other people) I am about to impart knowledge to you that you will never forget.
counterpart ['kaʊntəpɑːt]	**n.** 职能 (或地位)相当的人 (someone or something that has the same job or purpose as another) The secretary of defense met with his counterparts in Asia to discuss the nuclear crisis.
partisan [ˌpɑːtɪ'zæn]	**adj.** 过分支持的；偏袒的 (showing too much support for one person,group or idea,especially without considering it carefully) Most newspapers are politically partisan.

impartial	*adj.* 不偏不倚的；公平的 (treating all people and groups equally)
[ɪm'pɑːʃl]	An impartial evaluation of the job applicant's qualifications does not consider age, gender or race.

Private系列

private	*adj.* 私有的；私人的 (belonging to or concerning an individual person, company or interest)
['praɪvət]	At work he was always very serious, but in his private life, he was actually very funny and relaxed.
privacy	*n.* 隐私 (the state of being away from public attention)
['prɪvəsi]	① Celebrities have a right to privacy.
	② The press invade people's privacy every day.
privilege	*n.* 特权 (a right or benefit that is given to some people and not to others)
['prɪvəlɪdʒ]	I had the privilege of meeting the president.
	v. 给……以特权 (to grant a privilege to somebody)
	The new tax laws unfairly privilege the rich.
deprive	*v.* 剥夺；夺去 (to prevent somebody from having or doing something, especially something important)
[dɪ'praɪv]	This law will deprive us of our most basic rights.

Front系列

frontier	*n.* 边界；边境 (a border between two countries)
['frʌntɪə(r)]	They were sent on an expedition to explore the western frontier.
forefront	*n.* 最前沿；最前线 (the most important part or position)
['fɔːfrʌnt]	The hospital is at the forefront of research in this area.
confront	*v.* 降临；使面临 (to face especially in challenge)
[kən'frʌnt]	She was confronted with severe money problems.
	v. 与……对峙；与……对抗 (to directly question the action or authority of someone)

Unit 06

1 They confronted the invaders at the shore.

2 We are learning how to confront death.

confrontation

[ˌkɒnfrʌnˈteɪʃn]

n. 对抗；冲突 (the clashing of forces or ideas)

There were several violent confrontations between rival gangs.

satisfy

[ˈsætɪsfaɪ]

v. 使满意；满足 (to cause somebody to be happy or pleased)

The movie's ending failed to satisfy audiences.

satiate

[ˈseɪʃieɪt]

v. 充分满足；使厌腻 (to give somebody so much of something that they do not feel they want any more)

A long drink of water at last satiated my thirst.

saturate

[ˈsætʃəreɪt]

v. 浸透 (to make something very wet)

He saturated the sponge with water.

v. 使充满；使饱和 (to fill something completely with something)

Their new products are saturating the market.

追根溯源

　　福尔图娜(Fortuna)是罗马神话中最古老的女神之一。作为时运女神，她司掌着人间的幸福和机遇。在西方神像中，福尔图娜常常一手拿着象征丰饶和富裕的羊角，一手拿着主宰人们时运的方向舵，站在旋转的飞轮之上。西方人认为，福尔图娜手中的方向舵和脚下的飞轮转到哪里，就把人们的时运带到哪里。但由于方向的变化不定，福尔图娜脚下飞轮也用以象征祸福无常，惩罚那些贪得无厌之人。fortunate（幸运的）就来自这位女神，因为她所代表的幸运有无常不定之意，fortuitous（偶然的）也来于此。

fortunate

[ˈfɔːtʃənət]

adj. 幸运的 (having good luck)

We should try to help others who are less fortunate than ourselves.

| **misfortune** | *n.* 不幸；厄运 (bad luck) |
| [ˌmɪsˈfɔːtʃuːn] | He blamed the party's misfortunes on poor leadership. |

| **unfortunate** | *adj.* 不幸的；倒霉的 (accompanied by or resulting in bad luck) |
| [ʌnˈfɔːtʃənət] | Every year we have charity days to raise money for unfortunate people. |

| **fortuitous** | *adj.* 偶然发生的 (happening by chance) |
| [fɔːˈtjuːɪtəs] | Their success is the result of a fortuitous combination of circumstances. |

锦囊妙记

schedule	*n.* 日程安排 (a list of times of departures and arrivals)
['ʃedjuːl]	Students are planning their class schedules for next year.
	拆分法 s（死）che（车）du（堵）le（了），耽误了日程（schedule）。

cargo	*n.* 货物 (the goods carried by a ship, airplane, or vehicle)
['kɑːgəʊ]	The ship was carrying a cargo of crude oil.
	拆分法 car（车）go（走）了，拉着cargo（货物）。

carpet	*n.* 地毯 (a heavy fabric cover for a floor)
['kɑːpɪt]	We bought a new carpet for the bedroom.
	拆分法 car（车）里有pet（宠物），要铺carpet（地毯）。

career	*n.* 职业生涯 (a job or profession that someone does for a long time)
[kəˈrɪə(r)]	During his long career in advertising he won numerous awards and honors.
	联想法 car（车）走过的轨迹就像人一生的职业生涯（career）。

carpenter	*n.* 木匠 (a worker who builds or repairs wooden things)
['kɑːpəntə(r)]	He left school at 15 and trained as an apprentice carpenter.
	拆分法 制作car（战车），用pen（笔）画图纸的er（人）就是carpenter（木匠）。

Unit 06

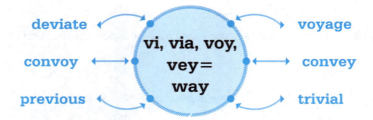

deviate ← → voyage

convoy ← **vi, via, voy, vey= way** → convey

previous ← → trivial

deviate ['diːvieɪt]	*v.* 脱离；越轨 (to turn aside from a course or way) ① He planned his schedule far in advance, and he didn't deviate from it. ② The recent pattern of weather deviates from the norm.
deviation [ˌdiːvi'eɪʃn]	*n.* 偏离 (an action, behavior or condition that is different from what is usual or expected) There have been slight deviations in the satellite's orbit.
obviate ['ɒbvieɪt]	*v.* 消除；排除 (to remove a problem or the need for something) The new treatment obviates many of the risks associated with surgery.
convoy ['kɒnvɔɪ]	*v.* 护送 (to travel with and protect someone or something) Police and FBI agents convoyed the President to the White House. *n.* 车队 (a group of vehicles or ships that are traveling together usually for protection) The President always travels in a convoy.
envoy ['envɔɪ]	*n.* 使节；外交官 (a representative sent by one government to another) The president sent the secretary of state as his personal envoy to gain the support of the country's allies.
convey [kən'veɪ]	*v.* 传达；传递 (to make something known to someone) We use words to convey our thoughts. *v.* 运送 (to carry somebody/something from one place to another) Travelers were conveyed to the airport by shuttle.
previous ['priːviəs]	*adj.* 先前的；以前的 (going before in time or order) She has a child from a previous marriage.

voyage ['vɔɪɪdʒ]	*n.* 旅行；航行 (a journey especially by water to a distant or unknown place) He aims to follow Columbus's voyage to the West Indies. *v.* 旅行；航行 (to take a long journey usually by ship or boat) The explorers voyaged to distant lands.
impervious [ɪm'pɜːviəs]	*adj.* 不可渗透的 (not letting something enter or pass through) The material for this coat is supposed to be impervious to rain. *adj.* 无动于衷的 (not bothered or affected by something) He's impervious to their criticism.
trivial ['trɪviəl]	*adj.* 琐碎的；无价值的 (of little worth or importance) Compared to her problems, our problems seem trivial.

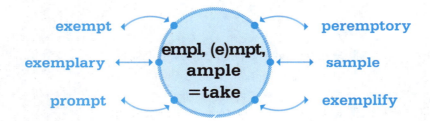

exemplary [ɪg'zempləri]	*adj.* 典型的；示范的 (serving as an example of something) His tact was exemplary, especially considering the circumstances.
exemplify [ɪg'zemplɪfaɪ]	*v.* 作为……的例证 (to be a very good example of something) The painting perfectly exemplifies the naturalistic style which was so popular at the time.
exempt [ɪg'zempt]	*v.* 使免除；豁免 (to release from a requirement that others must meet) His poor vision exempted him from military service. *adj.* 被免除的 (not required to do something that others are required to do) Men in college were exempt from military service.
sample ['sɑːmpl]	*n.* 样本 (used as an example of something) We based our analysis on a random sample of more than 200 males.
peremptory [pə'remptəri]	*adj.* 强硬的；强制的 (expecting to be obeyed immediately and without question or refusal) The governor's peremptory personal assistant began telling the crowd of reporters and photographers exactly where they had to stand.

prompt

[prɒmpt]

adj. 敏捷的；迅速的 (quick and ready to act)

The patient needed prompt attention.

v. 促使；导致 (to cause someone to do something)

Curiosity prompted her to ask a few questions.

v. 给提词 (to remind of something forgotten or poorly learned)

Sometimes it's necessary to prompt an actor.

announce

[ə'naʊns]

v. 宣布 (to make something known publicly)

The government announced a cut in taxes.

announcement

[ə'naʊnsmənt]

n. 通告；布告 (a public notice of something)

Many people were surprised by the government's announcement that there will be a cut in taxes.

pronounce

[prə'naʊns]

v. 宣布；宣称 (to declare officially or ceremoniously)

① He was pronounced dead upon arrival at the hospital.

② The judge pronounced sentence.

v. 发音 (to produce the components of spoken language)

He practiced pronouncing Spanish words.

renounce

[rɪ'naʊns]

v. 放弃；抛弃 (to give up, refuse, or resign usually by formal declaration)

The queen renounced the throne.

denounce

[dɪ'naʊns]

v. 谴责；痛斥 (to pronounce especially publicly to be blameworthy or evil)

The government called on the group to denounce the use of violence.

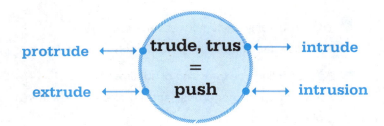

intrude [ɪnˈtruːd]	v. 侵入；侵犯 (to go or be somewhere where you are not wanted or are not supposed to be) ① The plane intruded into their airspace. ② Reporters constantly intruded into the couple's private life.
intrusion [ɪnˈtruːʒn]	n. 侵犯；侵扰 (the act of going or forcing in without being wanted) The phone call was an unwelcome intrusion.
protrude [prəˈtruːd]	v. 突出；伸出 (to stick out from a place or a surface) His lower jaw protrudes slightly.
extrude [ɪkˈstruːd]	v. 挤压出 (to force, press or push something out of something) The machine extrudes enough molten glass to fill the mold.
abstruse [əbˈstruːs]	adj. 难解的；深奥的 (difficult to understand) You're not the only one who finds Einstein's theory of relativity abstruse.

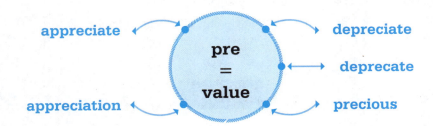

precious [ˈpreʃəs]	adj. 宝贵的；珍贵的 (of great value or high price) Diamonds and emeralds are precious stones.
appreciate [əˈpriːʃieɪt]	v. 欣赏 (to admire greatly and with understanding) In time you'll appreciate the beauty and subtlety of this language. v. 感激 (to be grateful for something that somebody has done) We appreciate your help.

	v. 增值 (to increase in number or value) My house has appreciated considerably over the last ten years.
appreciation [əˌpriːʃiˈeɪʃn]	*n.* 感谢 (a feeling or expression of admiration) You've been so generous, and I'd like to show my appreciation by cooking a meal for you.
depreciate [dɪˈpriːʃieɪt]	*v.* 贬值 (to cause something to have a lower price or value) These changes have greatly depreciated the value of the house.
deprecate [ˈdeprəkeɪt]	*v.* 不赞成；反对 (to criticize or express disapproval of someone or something) Movie critics tried to deprecate the comedy as the stupidest movie of the year.

Delete与Indelible

delete [dɪˈliːt]	*v.* 删除 (to take out something especially by erasing, crossing out or cutting) The e-mail was accidentally deleted.
indelible [ɪnˈdeləbl]	*adj.* 擦不掉的；永久的 (impossible to remove or forget) Winning the state basketball championship was our team's most indelible experience.
deleterious [ˌdeləˈtɪəriəs]	*adj.* 有害的；有毒的 (damaging or harmful) The drug has no deleterious effects on patients.

Evil系列

evil [ˈiːvl]	*adj.* 邪恶的 (morally bad) We are still being attacked by the forces of evil.
devil [ˈdevl]	*n.* 魔鬼 (an evil spirit) She is a tricky devil, so be careful.
devout [dɪˈvaʊt]	*adj.* 虔诚的 (deeply religious; devoted to a particular religion) She was a devout Christian.

Unit 07

vile [vaɪl]	*adj.* 极坏的；卑鄙的 (disgustingly or utterly bad) ① She has a vile temper. ② Her talk was full of vile curses.
villain ['vɪlən]	*n.* 恶棍 (a person who does bad things) She describes her first husband as a villain who treated her terribly. *n.* 反面人物 (a character in a story or play who opposes the hero) He plays the villain in most of his movies.
revile [rɪ'vaɪl]	*v.* 辱骂；痛斥 (to use abusive language) Many people reviled him for his callous behavior.
vilify ['vɪlɪfaɪ]	*v.* 中伤；诽谤 (to speak of harshly and often unfairly) The newspaper vilified him for his opinions.

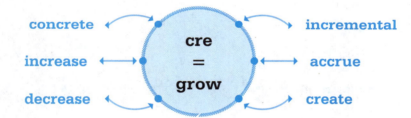

create [kri'eɪt]	*v.* 创造；产生 (to make or produce something) She enjoys creating new dishes by combining unusual ingredients.
increase [ɪn'kriːs] *v.* ['ɪnkriːs] *n.*	*v.* 增加 (to become progressively greater as in size, amount, number or intensity) The house increased in value. *n.* 增加 (the act or process of increasing) The construction will probably cause some increase in traffic delays.
decrease [dɪ'kriːs] *v.* ['diːkriːs] *n.*	*v.* 减少；减小 (to become smaller in size, amount or number) The driver decreased her speed as she approached the curve. *n.* 减少；减小 (the process of growing less) Studies report a recent decrease in traffic accidents.
incremental [ˌɪŋkrə'mentl]	*adj.* 增加的；递增的 (increasing in amount or value gradually and by a regular amount) We are seeking continuous, incremental improvements, not great breakthroughs.

crescent ['kresnt]	*n.* 新月形 (the shape of the visible part of the moon when it is less than half full) ① There is a flag with a white crescent on a red ground. ② A crescent moon peeped out from behind the clouds.
accrue [ə'kru:]	*v.* 逐渐增加 (to grow or build up slowly) I'll get back all the money I invested, plus any interest and dividends that have accrued.
concrete ['kɒŋkri:t]	*n.* 混凝土 (a hard strong building material made by mixing a cementing material) Eventually, the water will permeate through the surrounding concrete. *adj.* 具体的 (being specific and useful) We hope the meetings will produce concrete results.

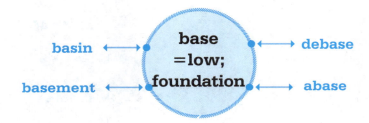

basement ['beɪsmənt]	*n.* 地下室 (the part of a building that is wholly or partly below ground level) We store our bicycles in the basement during the winter.
basin ['beɪsn]	*n.* 盆 (a wide shallow usually round dish or bowl for holding liquids) When he had finished washing he began to wipe the basin clean. *n.* 盆地 (a particular region of the world where the earth's surface is lower than in other places) The basin favors the development of farming and animal husbandry.
abase [ə'beɪs]	*v.* 表现卑微；屈从 (to act in a way that shows that you accept somebody's power over you) The president is not willing to abase himself before the nation.
debase [dɪ'beɪs]	*v.* 降低……的价值；败坏……的名誉 (to lower the value or reputation of someone or something) ① The governor debased himself by lying to the public. ② The holiday has been debased by commercialism.

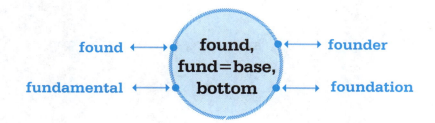

found
[faʊnd]

v. 建立；兴建（城镇或国家）(to be the first to start building and living in a town or country)
This town was founded in 1886.

founder
['faʊndə(r)]

n. 创始人；建立者 (a person who creates or establishes something)
Without the founder's drive and direction, the company gradually languished.

v. 沉没 (to sink below the surface of the water)
Three ships foundered in heavy seas.

v. 失败；倒塌 (to fail utterly; to collapse)
Her career foundered, and she moved from job to job for several years.

foundation
[faʊn'deɪʃn]

n. 地基；基础 (the support upon which something rests)
The inspector discovered a crack in the house's foundation.

n. 基金 (an organization which provides money for a special purpose such as research or charity)
They established a foundation to help orphaned children.

fundamental
[ˌfʌndə'mentl]

adj. 基本的；根本的 (forming or relating to the most important part of something)
1 The Constitution ensures our fundamental rights.
2 The revolution brought about a fundamental change in the country.

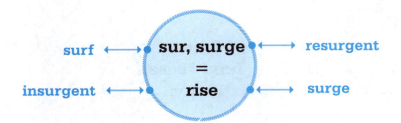

surf [sɜːf]	*v.* 冲浪 (to ride on ocean waves using a special board called a surfboard) ❶ I'm going to buy a surfboard and learn to surf. ❷ No one knows how many people currently surf the Net. *n.* 海浪 (the waves of the sea that splash on the shore) We could hear the roar of the surf.
surge [sɜːdʒ]	*v.* 波涛汹涌 (to rise and move in waves) The sea was surging. *v.* 急剧上升 (to suddenly increase to an unusually high level) Prices have surged recently. *v.* 蜂拥而来 (to move quickly and with force in a particular direction) Crowds were surging through the streets.
insurgent [ɪnˈsɜːdʒənt]	*n.* 起义者 (a person who revolts against an established government) Insurgents are trying to gain control of the country's transportation system.
resurgent [rɪˈsɜːdʒənt]	*adj.* 复活的；复兴的 (becoming popular, active, or successful again after a period of being less popular, active or successful) Today a resurgent, confident and globalizing China is rebuilding its naval strength.

Divide系列

divide [dɪˈvaɪd]	*v.* 分开；分散 (to separate something into two or more parts or pieces) She divided the pie into eight pieces. *v.* 出现分歧 (to be or make different in opinion or interest) The country was divided over the issue.
divisive [dɪˈvaɪsɪv]	*adj.* 引起分歧的 (causing a lot of disagreement between people and causing them to separate into different groups) Abortion has always been a divisive issue.

individual [ˌɪndɪˈvɪdʒuəl]	*adj.* 个体的；个性的 (existing as just one member or part of a larger group) The doctor carefully evaluates the individual needs of her patients. *n.* 个体 (a single human being as contrasted with a social group) They promote a philosophy that sacrifices the rights of the individual for the public welfare.
individualism [ˌɪndɪˈvɪdʒuəlɪzəm]	*n.* 个人主义 (the belief that the needs of each person are more important than the needs of the whole society or group) He was respected for his self-reliance and individualism.

Nerv系列

nerve [nɜːv]	*n.* 神经 (long thin fiber that transmit messages between your brain and other parts of your body) The optic nerve in the eye allows you to see. *n.* 勇气；胆量 (courage that allows you to do something that is dangerous or difficult) It takes a lot of nerve to start a new career.
nervous ['nɜːvəs]	*adj.* 紧张的 (showing feelings of being worried and afraid about what might happen) I get very nervous because I'm using a lot of expensive equipment.
enervate ['enəveɪt]	*v.* 使衰弱；使失去活力 (to make someone or something very weak or tired) The surgery really enervated me for weeks afterwards.

Error系列

erroneous [ɪˈrəʊniəs]	*adj.* 错误的 (containing error; mistaken; incorrect) The conclusions they have come to are completely erroneous.
aberrant [æˈberənt]	*adj.* 异常的；离经叛道的 (straying from the right or normal way) It reflects the aberrant personality of some American politicians hostile to China's development and becoming powerful.

英语单词awe来自原始日耳曼语，原本只含有"畏惧"之意。基督教传入英国后，《圣经》中多次使用awe一词来表示基督教徒对上帝的"既崇拜又害怕"的混合情感，awe才逐渐发展出"敬畏"的含义。

awe [ɔ:]	*n.* 敬畏 (a strong feeling of fear or respect and also wonder) She gazed in awe at the great stones. *v.* 使……敬畏 (to fill someone with awe) We were awed by the beauty of the mountains.
awful ['ɔ:fl]	*adj.* 糟糕的 (extremely bad or unpleasant) He has some awful disease. *adj.* 可怕的 (causing feelings of fear and wonder) Some of their offenses are so awful they would chill the blood.
awesome ['ɔ:səm]	*adj.* 令人惊叹的；很困难的；使人惊惧的 (very impressive or very difficult and perhaps rather frightening) We were impressed by the awesome sight of an erupting volcano.

阿多尼斯（Adonis）是植物神，也是王室美男子，他身高190cm以上，拥有如花一般俊美精致的五官，令世间所有人与物在他面前都黯然失色，连维纳斯都对其倾心不已。阿多尼斯是西方"美男子"的最早出处。**adore**（爱慕；崇拜）和**adorable**（讨人喜爱的）都来自这位美男子。

adore [ə'dɔ:(r)]	*v.* 爱慕；敬慕 (to be very fond of) ① People adore him for his noble character. ② We adore them for their generosity.
adorable [ə'dɔ:rəbl]	*adj.* 可爱的；讨人喜欢的 (very appealing or attractive) ① We have three adorable children. ② What an adorable old lady, so kind and sweet.

stroll [strəʊl]	*v.* 散步；溜达 (to walk slowly in usually a pleasant and relaxed way) They strolled along the street looking in the store windows. **联想法** 在street（大街）上stroll（散步）。

Unit 07

roam [rəʊm]	v. 漫游；漫步 (to go from place to place without purpose or direction) The chickens are able to roam around freely in the farmyard. 联想法 在road（马路）上，roam（漫步）。
meander [mi'ændə(r)]	v. 漫步；闲逛 (to wander aimlessly or casually without urgent destination) It's so restful to meander along Irish country roads. v. (河流或道路) 蜿蜒而行 (to curve a lot rather than being in a straight line) The path meanders through the garden. 拆分法 me（我）and（和）er（她）在meander（漫步）。
saunter ['sɔːntə(r)]	v. 闲逛；漫步 (to walk in a slow and relaxed manner) They sauntered slowly down the street. 联想法 s-s形路线，aunt-姑姑，姑姑走S形路线，在漫步（saunter）。

Unit 07

comprehend ← → comprise

enterprise ← → imprison

prehensile ← → apprehensive

prehen, pren, pris = seize

comprehend [ˌkɒmprɪ'hend]	*v.* 理解；领会 (to grasp the nature, significance or meaning of something) The infinite distances of space are too great for the human mind to comprehend.
comprehension [ˌkɒmprɪ'henʃn]	*n.* 理解力 (ability to understand) After reading the passage the teacher asked questions to test the children's comprehension.
comprehensive [ˌkɒmprɪ'hensɪv]	*adj.* 综合性的；全面的 (covering completely or broadly) The school curriculum is very comprehensive.
prehensile [prɪ'hensaɪl]	*adj.* 适于抓住的 (capable of grabbing or holding something by wrapping around it) ① The monkey has a prehensile tail. ② The elephant has a prehensile trunk.
apprehend [ˌæprɪ'hend]	*v.* 了解 (to understand or recognize something) Only now can I begin to apprehend the power of these forces. *v.* 逮捕 (to arrest someone for a crime) Within hours, police had apprehended the thief.
apprehensive [ˌæprɪ'hensɪv]	*adj.* 忧虑的 (viewing the future with anxiety or alarm) He was apprehensive about the surgery.
apprehension [ˌæprɪ'henʃn]	*n.* 不安；忧虑 (fear of or uncertainty about what may be coming) The thought of moving to a new city fills me with apprehension.

imprison [ɪmˈprɪzn]	*v.* 关押；监禁 (to confine in prison especially as punishment for a crime) He has threatened to imprison his political opponents.
reprisal [rɪˈpraɪzl]	*n.* 报复 (an act in return for harm done by another) ❶ There were fears that some of the Western hostages might be killed in reprisal. ❷ The allies threatened economic reprisals against the invading country.
comprise [kəmˈpraɪz]	*v.* 包含；由……构成 (to be made up of; to consist of) ❶ The play comprises three acts. ❷ Nine players comprise a baseball team.
enterprise [ˈentəpraɪz]	*n.* 进取心 (the ability or desire to do dangerous or difficult things or to solve problems in new ways) He was criticized for his lack of enterprise in dealing with the crisis. *n.* 企业 (a company or business) There are plenty of small industrial enterprises.
entrepreneur [ˌɒntrəprəˈnɜː(r)]	*n.* 企业家 (a person who starts a business and is willing to risk loss in order to make money) The entrepreneur takes business risks in the hope of making a profit.
apprentice [əˈprentɪs]	*n.* 学徒；徒弟 (a person who is learning a trade or art by experience under a skilled worker) He decided to be an apprentice to an electrician after he graduated. *v.* 使……做学徒 (to set at work as an apprentice) He apprenticed with a master carpenter for two years. 在古代西方的手工艺行业中，广泛采取学徒制（apprenticeship）的教育培训方式。学徒（apprentice）是手工艺行业中最低一级，要寄宿在行业中最高一级的师傅（master）家中充当学徒，一边为师傅干活，一边学习和实习。通常要学习3到6年后才能出师，升为熟练工（journeyman）。在大多数手工艺行业公会中，工匠的职称一般都划分为学徒（apprentice）、熟练工（journeyman）和师傅（master）这三个级别。

Custom系列

custom ['kʌstəm]	**n.** 习惯；习俗 (the usual way of doing things) It is the custom for the bride to wear a white dress on her wedding day. **n.** 海关 (the government department that collects taxes on goods bought and sold and on goods brought into the country, and that checks what is brought in) We went through customs at the airport without any difficulty. **Tip** custom意为"海关"时，必须用复数形式！
customary ['kʌstəməri]	**adj.** 习惯的 (usually done in a particular situation or at a particular place or time) It is customary to hold the door open for someone who is entering a building behind you.
accustom [ə'kʌstəm]	**v.** 使……习惯 (to make somebody familiar with something through use or experience) She could not accustom herself to a hot climate.
customer ['kʌstəmə(r)]	**n.** 顾客；客户 (someone who buys goods or services from a business) The customer used a credit card for the purchase.
costume ['kɒstjuːm]	**n.** 戏服；表演服 (the clothes worn by actors in a play or film/movie, or worn by somebody to make them look like something else) ① Even from a distance, the effect of his costume was stunning. ② I will probably go to a Halloween costume party.

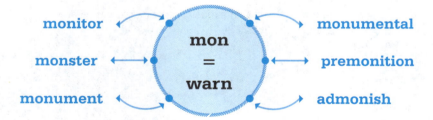

monitor ['mɒnɪtə(r)]	**v.** 监控 (to watch, keep track of or check something usually for a special purpose) Nurses monitored the patient's heart rate. **n.** 显示屏；监视器 (a video screen used for display) They watched the press conference on a video monitor in a back room.

monument

['mɒnjumənt]

n. 纪念碑 (a building, statue, etc. that honors a person or event)

They erected a monument in his honor.

monumental

[,mɒnju'mentl]

adj. 重要的；意义深远的；不朽的 (very important and having a great influence, especially as the result of years of work)

The discovery of antibiotics is a monumental contribution to the field of medicine.

adj. 巨大的 (very great or extreme)

Repairing the damage will be a monumental task.

admonish

[əd'mɒnɪʃ]

v. 劝告；（温和地）责备 (to criticize or warn somebody gently but seriously)

1 The principal admonished a student for talking.

2 The witness was admonished for failing to answer the question.

premonition

[,priːmə'nɪʃn]

n. 预感；预兆 (previous notice or warning)

She had a premonition that her cat would somehow get hurt that day.

premonitory

[prɪ'mɒnɪtəri]

adj. 预兆的 (giving warning)

Some patients develop premonitory signs and symptoms, such as nervousness and sweating.

monster

['mɒnstə(r)]

n. 怪物 (a strange or horrible imaginary creature)

The man must be a monster to treat his children so badly.

古罗马人相信各种奇异现象都是神灵所发出的信息。如果出现一些怪异、变态的生物 (monster)，则是神灵被激怒后发出的警告，预示着将有大灾大难发生。

monstrous

['mɒnstrəs]

adj. 巨大的；丑陋的；骇人的 (very large, ugly and frighting)

The monstrous creature approached.

adj. 丑恶的；骇人听闻的 (considered to be shocking and unacceptable because it is morally wrong or unfair)

She endured his monstrous behavior for years.

summon

['sʌmən]

v. 召唤 (to order somebody to come to you)

The queen summoned him back to the palace.

v. 鼓起；振作 (to make an effort to produce a particular quality in yourself, especially when you find it difficult)

She was trying to summon up the courage to leave him.

Crude系列

raw [rɔ:]	*adj.* 生的；未加工的 (in a natural state) We import raw materials and export mainly industrial products.
crude [kru:d]	*adj.* (油和其他自然物质) 天然的；自然的 (of oil and other natural substances in its natural state, before it has been treated with chemicals) A crude oil slick quickly spreads out over water. *adj.* 粗鲁的 (not having or showing good manners) He was critical of the people, disparaging of their crude manners.
crass [kræs]	*adj.* 愚笨的；粗鲁的 (stupid and does not show consideration for other people) A few people seemed shocked by her crass comments.
cruel [kru:əl]	*adj.* 残酷的 (wanting to cause others to suffer) These cruel devices are designed to stop prisoners bending their legs.
cruelty ['kru:əlti]	*n.* 残忍；残酷 (behavior that causes pain or suffering to others, especially deliberately) They protested against cruelty to animals.
rudimentary [ˌru:dɪ'mentri]	*adj.* 基本的；初步的 (basic and simple) This class requires a rudimentary knowledge of human anatomy. *adj.* 发育不完全的 (not very developed or advanced) Some insects have only rudimentary wings.
erudite ['erudaɪt]	*adj.* 博学的；有学问的 (having or showing knowledge that is learned by studying) Through hard work, he finally made himself into an erudite man.

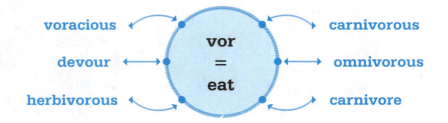

devour [dɪ'vaʊə(r)]	_v._ 狼吞虎咽地吃光 (to eat up greedily) She devoured half an apple pie. _v._ 吞噬；吞没 (to destroy somebody/something) Flames devoured the structure in minutes.
voracious [və'reɪʃəs]	_adj._ 贪吃的；贪婪的 (showing a tendency to eat very large amounts of food) He has a voracious appetite. _adj._ （对信息、知识）渴求的；求知欲强的 (wanting a lot of new information and knowledge) She's a voracious reader of all kinds of love stories.
herbivorous [hɜː'bɪvərəs]	_adj._ 食草的 (eating only plants) Mammoths were herbivorous mammals.
omnivorous [ɒm'nɪvərəs]	_adj._ 杂食性的 (eating both plants and animals) Black bears are classified as carnivores even though their omnivorous diet consists mainly of plant material.
carnivorous [kɑː'nɪvərəs]	_adj._ 食肉的 (eating only meat) Wolves are carnivorous animals.
carnivore ['kɑːnɪvɔː(r)]	_n._ 食肉动物 (any animal that eats meat) The lion is a carnivore.

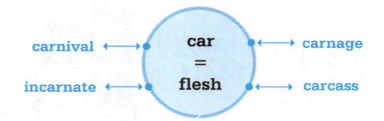

carnival ['kɑːnɪvl]	*n.* 狂欢节；嘉年华 (a public festival during which people play music and sometimes dance in the streets) The town is best known for its carnivals with masked balls and firework processions.
carcass ['kɑːkəs]	*n.* (人或动物的) 尸体 (the dead body) They divided the deer's carcass, the hunter took the hinder parts.
carnage ['kɑːnɪdʒ]	*n.* 大屠杀；残杀 (the killing of many people) Refugees crossed the border to escape the carnage in their homeland.
incarnate [ɪnˈkɑːnət]	*adj.* 化身的 (having a human body) Why should God become incarnate as a male. *v.* 使具体化 (to represent in a clear and obvious way) It is a community incarnates its founders' ideals.

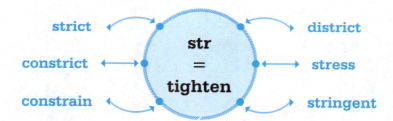

string [strɪŋ]	*n.* 绳子 (a cord usually used to bind, fasten or tie something) He tied the packages together with string.
strict [strɪkt]	*adj.* 严格的 (demanding that people obey rules or behave in a certain way) ① My parents were very strict. ② He insists on strict adherence to the rules.
restrict [rɪˈstrɪkt]	*v.* 限制；限定 (to confine within bounds) ① Villagers say the fence would restrict public access to the hills. ② They have accused the government of trying to restrict free speech.

constrict [kən'strɪkt]	*v.* 压缩；压紧 (to make something narrow or draw something together) These shoes are too small and they constrict my feet. *v.* 限制；束缚 (to prevent something or someone from developing freely) Men and women alike have been constricted by traditional sexual roles.
district ['dɪstrɪkt]	*n.* 地区 (an area established by a government for official business) Six police officers are in charge of the district.
strain [streɪn]	*n.* 压力；紧张 (something that causes great worry and concern or physical effort) Running the business was a strain on him. *v.* 拉伤 (to injure a body part or muscle by too much tension, use, or effort) I strained my back trying to lift the couch. *v.* 过度使用；使不堪承受 (to try to make something do more than it is able to do) Resources will be further strained by new demands for housing.
constrain [kən'streɪn]	*v.* 强迫 (to use pressure to force someone to do something) He was constrained to retire because of ill health. *v.* 束缚 (to restrict or limit somebody/something) She felt the rules constrained her creativity.
constraint [kən'streɪnt]	*n.* 束缚 (something that limits or restricts someone or something) Water shortages in the area will be the main constraint on development.
restrain [rɪ'streɪn]	*v.* 抑制；克制 (to keep from doing something) ① She was unable to restrain her desperate anger. ② He couldn't restrain his laughter.
restraint [rɪ'streɪnt]	*n.* 限制；克制 (control over your emotions or behavior) His angry response showed a lack of restraint.
strangle ['stræŋgl]	*v.* 扼死；勒死 (to kill a person or animal by squeezing the throat) He tried to strangle a border policeman and steal his gun. *v.* 抑制；压制 (to stop something from growing or developing) The country's economic plight is strangling its scientific institutions.
stress [stres]	*n.* 压力 (pressure put on something that can damage it or make it lose its shape) To reduce the amount of stress on your back, bend your knees when you lift something heavy.

Unit 08

	v. 强调 (to give special attention to something)
	They also stress the need for improved employment opportunities, better transport and health care.
distress [dɪ'stres]	*n.* 悲痛 (pain or suffering affecting the body, a bodily part or the mind)
	He suffered severe emotional distress as a result of the accident.
	v. 使忧虑；使悲伤 (to make somebody feel very worried or unhappy)
	Don't let the news distress you.
stringent ['strɪndʒənt]	*adj.* 严格的 (very strict or severe)
	There should be much more stringent laws against the dropping of rubbish in the streets.

Centre系列

centre ['sentə(r)]	*n.* 中心 (the middle point or part of something)
	The vaccine is being tested at several medical centres around the country.
concentrate ['kɒnsntreɪt]	*v.* 集中 (to focus thought or attention on something)
	Water companies should concentrate on reducing waste instead of building new reservoirs.
concentration [ˌkɒnsn'treɪʃn]	*n.* 专注 (the ability to give your attention or thought to a single object or activity)
	When you're tired it's easy to lose your concentration.
eccentric [ɪk'sentrɪk]	*adj.* 古怪的；异常的 (tending to act in strange or unusual ways)
	Geniuses are supposed to be eccentric and hopelessly impractical.

Force系列

forceful ['fɔːsfl]	*adj.* 强有力的 (having much strength)
	The government has threatened to use more forceful measures if necessary.

enforce [ɪnˈfɔːs]	*v.* 强行实施；强制执行 (to make sure that people do what is required by a law, rule, etc.) The duty of the police is to enforce the law.
reinforce [ˌriːɪnˈfɔːs]	*v.* 加固；使更结实 (to strengthen by adding more material for support) The wall needs to be reinforced. *v.* 给……加强力量 (或装备)；使更强大(to send more people or equipment in order to make an army, etc. stronger) The captain sent out another squad to reinforce the troops.

追根溯源

suit来自拉丁语"sequi"，字面意思是"跟随"，最早表示"随从"，后来表示这些随从所穿的统一制服，再后来表示成套的衣服，即常说的"套装西服"。单词suite其实是suit的变体，表示"一批随从；一套家具；套间"。另一方面，从"跟随"的词义出发，suit还发展出"追赶；请求"之意，从而进一步延伸出"对女性的追求"之意。在法律领域，suit表示"诉讼"，对应动词是sue（控告；请求）。同源单词还有动词pursue（追赶；继续；从事）和名词pursuit（追求；职业）。

Unit 08

suit [suːt]	*n.* 西装 (a set of clothing having matching top and bottom pieces) He wore his gray suit to the job interview. *v.* 适合；与……相称 (to be proper for somebody/something) She gave a serious speech that suited the occasion.
suitable [ˈsuːtəbl]	*adj.* 合适的 (being fit or right for a use or group) ❶ We upgraded the computer to make it suitable to our needs. ❷ The movie is suitable for children.
sue [suː]	*v.* 控告；起诉 (to seek justice or right by bringing legal action) He is suing the doctor who performed the unnecessary surgery.
pursue [pəˈsjuː]	*v.* 追赶 (to follow and try to catch or capture somebody/something) A dog pursued the fleeing cat. *v.* 追求 (to do something or try to achieve something over a period of time) She wants to pursue a legal career.
ensue [ɪnˈsjuː]	*v.* 接踵发生；继而产生 (to come after in time or as a result) The show ended, and a long standing ovation ensued.

锦囊妙记

babble ['bæbl]	*v.* 含糊不清地说 (to make meaningless sounds) The baby babbled in his crib. **联想法** 婴儿（baby）在含混不清地说（babble）。
drift [drɪft]	*v.* 漂移；漂流；飘 (to move slowly on water, wind) ① The climbing balloon drifted silently over the countryside. ② The boat slowly drifted out to sea. **谐音法** drift–追风的，随风飘动（drift）。
supercilious [ˌsuːpə'sɪliəs]	*adj.* 高傲的；傲慢的 (displaying arrogant pride, scorn or indifference) The shop assistant was very supercilious towards me when I asked for some help. **拆分法** super–超级，cili–silly（傻），认为别人都是超级（super）傻的（silly），这种人当然很高傲（supercilious）。
spurious ['spjʊəriəs]	*adj.* 虚假的；伪造的 (not genuine, sincere, or authentic) He was arrested in 1979 on spurious corruption charges. **拆分法** s–死，pure–纯洁，纯洁（pure）死（s）了，就变成虚假的（spurious）了。
irrigate ['ɪrɪɡeɪt]	*v.* 灌溉 (to supply as land with water by artificial means) He also wants to use the water to irrigate barren desert land. **联想法** i–一，rr 形似秧苗，一排排秧苗等待灌溉（irrigate）。

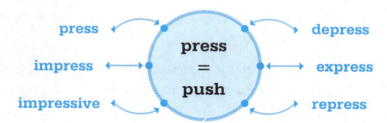

press [pres]	*v.* 压；按 (to push something closely and firmly against something) He pressed his back against the door. *v.* 压迫；迫使 (to exert pressure on somebody) Trade unions are pressing him to stand firm. *n.* 报刊杂志 (newspapers and magazines) Today the British press is full of articles on the subject.
pressing ['presɪŋ]	*adj.* 紧迫的；紧急的 (very important and needing immediate attention) It is one of the most pressing problems facing this country.
pressure ['preʃə(r)]	*n.* 心理压力 (difficulties and feelings of anxiety that are caused by the need to achieve or to behave in a particular way) She felt a constant pressure to earn more money.
impress [ɪm'pres]	*v.* 给……以深刻印象 (to affect somebody strongly or deeply, especially favorably) Her talent impressed me.
impressive [ɪm'presɪv]	*adj.* 给人印象深刻的 (deserving attention, admiration or respect) ① The film's special effects are particularly impressive. ② Her first performance was very impressive.
impression [ɪm'preʃn]	*n.* 印象；感觉 (the effect or influence that something or someone has on a person's thoughts or feelings) ① My first impression of him was that he was a kind and thoughtful young man. ② First impressions are important but can be misleading.

Unit 09

express [ɪkˈspres]	*v.* 表达；表示 (to represent in words) It was important for children to learn to express themselves clearly. *v.* 快递 (to send something by a quick method of delivery) They expressed the package to us.
expressive [ɪkˈspresɪv]	*adj.* 富于表现力的 (showing emotions and feelings clearly and openly) The teacher's expressive sigh showed that she had heard that excuse many times before.
expression [ɪkˈspreʃn]	*n.* 表达 (the act or process of making known especially in words) Laughter is one of the most infectious expressions of emotion. *n.* 表情 (the look on someone's face) Judging from her expression, I think the gift was a complete surprise.
depress [dɪˈpres]	*v.* 使抑郁；使沮丧 (to make someone feel sad) The rainy days always depress me. *v.* 降低；减少 (to lessen the activity or strength of something) Bad weather had depressed sales.
depression [dɪˈpreʃn]	*n.* 抑郁；沮丧 (a serious medical condition in which a person feels very sad, and unimportant and often is unable to live in a normal way) She has been undergoing treatment for severe depression. *n.* 萧条；低迷 (a period of low activity in business with much unemployment) After several years of an economic boom, it looks as though we may be heading toward a depression.
compress [kəmˈpres]	*v.* 压紧；压缩 (to press or squeeze something together) He never understood how to organize or compress large masses of material.
oppress [əˈpres]	*v.* 压迫；压制 (to treat a person or group of people in a cruel or unfair way) They condemned attempts by the government to oppress its citizens. *v.* 使心情沉重 (to make someone feel sad or worried for a long period of time) The atmosphere in the room oppressed her.
oppression [əˈpreʃn]	*n.* 压迫 (cruel or unjust use of power or authority) After five years of oppression, the peasants revolted.

Unit 09

oppressive [ə'presɪv]	*adj.* 沉重的；压迫的 (treating people in a cruel and unfair way and not giving them same freedom, rights, etc. as other people) The country is ruled by an oppressive regime. *adj.* 压抑的 (very unpleasant or uncomfortable) ① This region suffers from oppressive heat in the summer months. ② The situation was extremely tense; no one said a word, and the silence was oppressive.
suppress [sə'pres]	*v.* 镇压；压制 (to put down something by authority or force) Political dissent was brutally suppressed. *v.* 抑制 (to not allow yourself to feel, show, or be affected by an emotion) The girls could hardly suppress a smile.
repress [rɪ'pres]	*v.* 压抑；克制 (情感) (to not allow yourself to do or express something) ① On seeing his haircut, I had to repress a laugh. ② People who repress their emotions risk having nightmares.

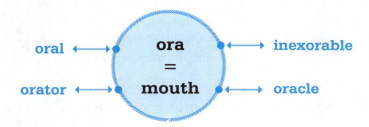

oral ['ɔːrəl]	*adj.* 口头的 (uttered by the mouth or in words) As part of her oral examination, she had to recite the names of all the presidents.
orator ['ɒrətə(r)]	*n.* 演说者；演说家 (a person who is very good at making speech) The orator gestured vigorously while speaking.
oracle ['ɒrəkl]	*n.* 神谕 (an answer given by a person through whom a god speaks) In times of difficulty, she pray for an oracle to guide her.
inexorable [ɪn'eksərəbl]	*adj.* 不可阻挡的；无法改变的 (not able to be stopped or changed) We cannot stop the inexorable passing of time.

Tect系列

protect [prəˈtekt]	*v.* 保护 (to cover or shield from exposure, injury or damage) He had no raincoat to protect himself from the rain.
detect [dɪˈtekt]	*v.* 查明；发现 (to discover the true character of something) 1 The test is used to detect the presence of alcohol in the blood. 2 This type of cancer is difficult to detect in its early stages.
detective [dɪˈtektɪv]	*n.* 侦探 (a person whose job is to find information about something or someone) She hired a detective to follow her husband.

Close系列

disclose [dɪsˈkləʊz]	*v.* 公开；揭露 (to make something known to the public) He refused to disclose the source of his information.
enclose [ɪnˈkləʊz]	*v.* 包围；围住 (to surround something) The rules state that samples must be enclosed in two watertight containers.
enclosure [ɪnˈkləʊʒə(r)]	*n.* 围场 (an area of land that is surrounded by a wall or fence and that is used for a particular purpose) During the day the horses are kept in an enclosure.
claustrophobia [ˌklɔːstrəˈfəʊbɪə]	*n.* 幽闭恐惧症 (abnormal dread of being in closed or narrow spaces) She doesn't go in elevators because of her claustrophobia.

Face系列

facial [ˈfeɪʃl]	*adj.* 面部的 (of or relating to the face) He didn't answer and his facial expression didn't change.
preface [ˈprefəs]	*n.* 序言；引语 (an introduction to a book or speech) The book's preface was written by the author.

deface

[dɪ'feɪs]

v. 损伤……的外观 (to ruin the surface of something especially with writing or pictures)

He was fined for defacing public property.

surface

['sɜ:fɪs]

n. 表面 (an outside part or layer of something)

① The bowl has a shiny surface.

② The surface of wood was rough.

superficial

[ˌsu:pə'fɪʃl]

adj. 表面的 (of or on the surface of something)

The storm only caused superficial damage to the building.

adj. 肤浅的；浅薄的 (not studying or looking at something thoroughly; seeing only what is obvious)

He has only superficial knowledge of the subject.

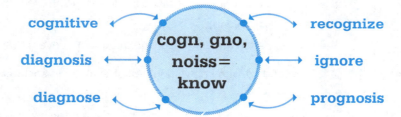

cognitive ← → cogn, gno, noiss= know → recognize
diagnosis ← → → ignore
diagnose ← → prognosis

cognition

[kɒg'nɪʃn]

n. 认识；认知 (mental process involved in knowing, learning and understanding things)

People have speculated about human cognition for 2000 years.

cognitive

['kɒgnətɪv]

adj. 认知的；认识的 (relating to the mental process involved in knowing, learning, and understanding things)

As children grow older, their cognitive processes become sharper.

recognize

['rekəgnaɪz]

v. 认出；识别 (to know and remember someone or something because of previous knowledge or experience)

I didn't recognize you at first with your new haircut.

v. 承认 (to accept and approve of something as having legal or official authority)

The U.S. government has now recognized the newly formed country.

v. 赞赏 (to take approving notice of something)

They recognized his bravery with a medal.

recognizable [ˈrekəgnaɪzəbl]	*adj.* 可识别的 (be easily recognized or identified) This tree is always recognizable by its extremely beautiful silvery bark.
ignore [ɪgˈnɔː(r)]	*v.* 忽视；不顾 (to pay no attention to something) Safety regulations are being ignored by company managers in the drive to profits.
ignorant [ˈɪgnərənt]	*adj.* 无知的；愚昧的 (lacking knowledge or information) She was ignorant about the dangers of the drug.
prognosis [prɒgˈnəʊsɪs]	*n.* 预测 (a judgment about what is going to happen in the future) The president had a hopeful prognosis about the company's future.
diagnose [ˈdaɪəgnəʊz]	*v.* 诊断；判断 (to recognize as a disease by signs and symptoms) The soldiers were diagnosed as having flu.
diagnosis [ˌdaɪəgˈnəʊsɪs]	*n.* 诊断 (the act of identifying a disease, illness or problem by examining someone or something) She is an expert in the diagnosis and treatment of eye diseases.
connoisseur [ˌkɒnəˈsɜː(r)]	*n.* 鉴赏家 (a person who knows a lot about something such as art, wine or food) He is the connoisseur who can discriminate between two equally fine wines.

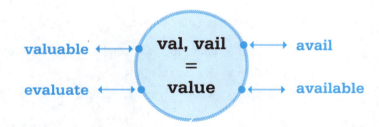

valuable ← → **val, vail** ← → avail
=
evaluate ← → **value** ← → available

valuable [ˈvæljuəbl]	*adj.* 很有用的；宝贵的 (very useful or important) He made many valuable contributions to the field of science.
evaluate [ɪˈvæljueɪt]	*v.* 评价 (to judge the value or condition of somebody or something in a careful and thoughtful way) Our research attempts to evaluate the effectiveness of the different drugs.

Unit 09

| **avail** | *n.* 效用；利益 (be useful or helpful to someone or something) |
| [ə'veɪl] | We tried to keep him alive but to no avail. |

available	*adj.* 可获得的；可用的 (present or ready for use)
[ə'veɪləbl]	① The family kept emergency supplies available.
	② Fresh fruit is available during the summer.

Root系列

root	*n.* 根 (the roots of a plant are the parts of it that grow under the ground)
[ruːt]	Pull weeds up by the roots so that they don't grow back.
	v. 扎根 (to grow roots or take root)
	Most plants will root in about six to eight weeks.

radical	*adj.* 根本的 (very basic and important)
['rædɪkl]	There are some radical differences between the two proposals.
	adj. 全新的；不同凡响的 (very new and different from what is traditional or ordinary)
	The computer has introduced radical innovations.
	n. 激进分子 (a person with radical opinions)
	He was a radical when he was a young,but now he is much more moderate.

| **eradicate** | *v.* 摧毁；完全根除 (to destroy or get rid of something completely, especially something bad) |
| [ɪ'rædɪkeɪt] | His ambition is to eradicate poverty in his community. |

Raze系列

| **eraser** | *n.* 橡皮擦 (a small piece of rubber or a similar substance,used for removing pencil marks from paper) |
| [ɪ'reɪzə(r)] | He rubbed out the last sentence on his paper with his eraser. |

| **erase** | *v.* 擦掉；抹去 (to cause to disappear by rubbing or scraping) |
| [ɪ'reɪz] | Several important files were accidentally erased. |

Unit 09

raze [reɪz]	*v.* 彻底摧毁，将……夷为平地 (to destroy something, such as a building completely) Dozens of villages have been razed.
abrasive [əˈbreɪsɪv]	*adj.* 摩擦的；粗糙的 (causing damage or wear by rubbing) An abrasive material is unsuitable for cleaning baths. *adj.* 生硬粗暴的；伤人感情的 (rude and unkind; acting in a way that may hurt other people's feelings) She was unrepentant about her abrasive remarks.
erode [ɪˈrəʊd]	*v.* 侵蚀；腐蚀 (to destroy or be destroyed by wearing away) Crashing waves have eroded the cliffs along the beach. *v.* 逐渐毁坏 (to gradually destroy something) Competition in the financial marketplace has eroded profits.
erosion [ɪˈrəʊʒn]	*n.* 腐蚀；侵蚀 (the process by which rock or soil is gradually destroyed by wind, rain or the sea) Centuries of erosion by wind have carved grooves in the rocks.

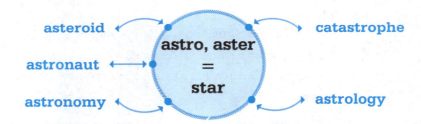

astronomy [əˈstrɒnəmi]	*n.* 天文学 (the branch of physics that studies celestial bodies and the universe as a whole) Astronomy is one of the oldest forms of science.
astronomer [əˈstrɒnəmə(r)]	*n.* 天文学家 (a person who is a specialist in astronomy) An astronomer can determine the brightness of each star.
astrology [əˈstrɒlədʒi]	*n.* 占星术 (the study of the supposed influences of the stars and planets on people's lives and behavior) This discovery seems to validate the claims of popular astrology.
astronaut [ˈæstrənɔːt]	*n.* 宇航员 (a person trained to travel in a spacecraft) The two American astronauts are scheduled to speak with President Donald Trump on Monday.

asterisk ['æstərɪsk]	*n.* 星号 (a star-shaped character used in printing) I've placed an asterisk next to the tasks I want you to do first.
asteroid ['æstərɔɪd]	*n.* 小行星 (any of numerous small celestial bodies composed of rock and metal that move around the sun mainly between the orbits of Mars and Jupiter) Planets and most asteroids revolve around the Sun in the same direction.
disaster [dɪ'zɑːstə(r)]	*n.* 灾难 (an event resulting in great loss and misfortune) The disaster killed nearly 9,000 people and damaged a million houses.
catastrophe [kə'tæstrəfi]	*n.* 大灾难 (a state of extreme ruin and misfortune) From all points of view, war would be a catastrophe.

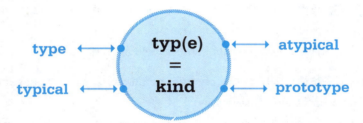

type [taɪp]	*n.* 类型 (a group of people or things that share particular features in common) There are various types of the disease.
typical ['tɪpɪkl]	*adj.* 典型的 (of the nature of or serving as a type or representative specimen) I am merely citing his reaction as typical of British industry.
atypical [ˌeɪ'tɪpɪkl]	*adj.* 非典型的 (departing from the normal) The economy of the province was atypical because it was particularly small.
prototype ['prəʊtətaɪp]	*n.* 原型；样本 (an original type, form or instance serving as a basis or standard) He has built a prototype of a machine called the wave rotor.

单词bar来自拉丁语barra，本意是"横梁；横木"。bar最开始指的是用来固定大门的长木棍，后来逐渐变成表示条棒做成的障碍物，进而有了"阻拦"之意。bar还可以表示酒吧中的吧台，用以隔开顾客和放酒水的货架，因此bar也有了酒吧的含义。与此同源的词还有barrier（障碍），barricade（路障），embargo（禁运）及barrage（连续的炮火）等。

bar [bɑː(r)]	*n.* 条；棒 (a rectangular solid piece or block of something)
	A crowd thrown stones and iron bars.
	n. 阻碍 (a thing that stops somebody from doing something)
	One of the fundamental bars to communication is the lack of a universally spoken, common language.
	v. 阻挡；拦住 (to block a road, path, etc.so that nobody can pass)
	Our path was barred by a chain.
barrier ['bæriə(r)]	*n.* 障碍 (something such as a fence or natural obstacle that prevents or blocks movement from one place to another)
	The mountain range forms a natural barrier between the two countries.
barricade [ˌbærɪ'keɪd]	*n.* 路障；障碍物 (an obstruction across a way or passage to check the advance of the enemy)
	The soldiers cut down some trees to make a barricade across the road.
embargo [ɪm'bɑːɡəʊ]	*n.* 禁运 (a legal prohibition on commerce)
	The UN has imposed an arms embargo against the country.
	v. 禁运 (to place an embargo on something)
	They embargoed oil shipments to the US.
barrage ['bærɑːʒ]	*n.* 连续的炮火；弹幕 (a heavy and continuous firing of weapons during a battle)
	The two fighters were driven off by a barrage of anti-aircraft fire.
	n. 一连串（批评或抱怨）(a large number of something, such as questions or comments, that are directed at somebody very quickly, one after the other,often in an aggressive way)
	He was faced with a barrage of angry questions from the press.

Unit 09

diligent ['dɪlɪdʒənt]	*adj.* 勤奋的 (showing steady and earnest care and hard work) The student who has been unceasingly diligent in pursuit of a degree in mathematics. 拆分法 dili（地里），gent-gentlemen，地里干活的gentlemen很diligent（勤奋）。
abundant [ə'bʌndənt]	*adj.* 丰富的；大量的 (existing or occurring in large amounts) Mosquitoes are extremely abundant in this dark wet place. 拆分法 a-一，bund-磅的，ant-蚂蚁，当然是abundant（大量的）。
indignant [ɪn'dɪgnənt]	*adj.* 愤怒的；愤慨的 (showing anger because of something that is unfair or wrong) I feel most indignant at the rude way I've been treated. 拆分法 in-里面，dign-挖，ant-蚂蚁，朝里面挖，挖到的不是财宝，而是蚂蚁，非常indignant（愤怒）。
indigent ['ɪndɪdʒənt]	*adj.* 贫穷的 (lacking money; very poor) The clinic provides free care for indigent patients. 拆分法 in-里，dig-挖，ent-表示"人"，在地里挖土的人是农民，很indigent（贫穷）。

Unit 09

Unit 10

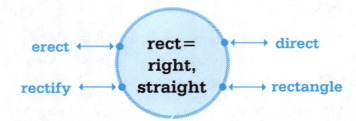

erect ←→ rect = right, straight ←→ direct

rectify ←→ rectangle

direct [dəˈrekt]	*v.* 指导；引导 (to cause someone or something to turn, move, or point in a particular way) He is responsible for directing the activities of the sales team. *adj.* 直接的；亲自的；亲身的 (happening or done without involving other people, actions, etc. in between) They are in direct contact with the hijackers.
director [dəˈrektə]	*n.* 导演 (a person who directs a play, movie, etc.) She's considered one of the best young directors in Hollywood. *n.* 主任 (the head of an organized group or administrative unit) The company will hire a new director of marketing.
rectangle [ˈrektæŋgl]	*n.* 矩形 (a flat geometric four-sided figure with right angles and with opposite sides parallel) The rectangle clearly shows each separate class in the distribution.
rectify [ˈrektɪfaɪ]	*v.* 改正；校正 (to correct something that is wrong) The hotel management promised to rectify the problem.
erect [ɪˈrekt]	*v.* 使直立；使竖起 (to set or place something so that it stands up) ❶ Demonstrators have erected barricades in the roads. ❷ They erected a statue in his memory. *adj.* 直立的；垂直的 (straight up and down) A lone tree remained erect after the terrible tornado had passed.

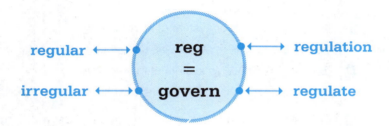

reg
=
govern

regular ←→ → regulation

irregular ←→ → regulate

regular ['reɡjələ(r)]	*adj.* 有规律的 (happening over and over again at the same time or in the same way)
	Most days she follows a regular routine.
	adj. 经常的 (happening or done very often)
	He's one of our regular customers.
irregular [ɪˈreɡjələ(r)]	*adj.* 不规律的 (not normal or usual; not following the usual rules about what should be done)
	She was taken to hospital, suffering from an irregular heartbeat.
regulate [ˈreɡjuleɪt]	*v.* 调节；调整 (to adjust the amount, degree or rate of something)
	The dam regulates the flow of water into the river.
	v. 管理；控制 (to make rules or laws that control something)
	Laws have been made to regulate working conditions.
regulation [ˌreɡjuˈleɪʃn]	*n.* 规则；规章 (an official rule or law that says how something should be done)
	Builders must comply with the regulations.

Region系列

region [ˈriːdʒən]	*n.* 地区；地域 (a large, usually continuous segment of a surface or space)
	He's the company sales manager for the entire Southwest region.
regional [ˈriːdʒənl]	*adj.* 地区的 (of or relating to a particular region)
	The book explores the connection between American ethnic and regional literature.
reign [reɪn]	*v.* 统治；治理 (to rule as a king, queen, emperor, etc.)
	The lion reigns as king of the jungle.
	v. (想法、情感或氛围) 盛行 (to be the most obvious feature of a place or moment)
	Enthusiasm reigned in the classroom.

regime [reɪ'ʒiːm]	*n.* 政权；政体 (a form or system of government) The military regime in power was unpopular and repressive. *n.* 管理制度；组织方法 (a system of management) Under the new regime, all workers must file a weekly report.
regiment ['redʒɪmənt]	*n.* 军团 (a military unit that is usually made of several large groups of soldiers) The regiment secured its position while awaiting the enemy attack. *v.* 严格地管制 (to control the behavior of people strictly) She criticized the way the school regiments its students by having strict rules.
sovereign ['sɒvrɪn]	*n.* 君主；最高统治者 (a person as a king or queen having the highest power and authority) After the current sovereign dies, the monarchy may be abolished. *adj.* 至高无上的 (having supreme rank or power) The government's sovereign duty is to protect the rights of its citizens.

glow [gləʊ]	*v.* 发光 (to shine with low light and heat but usually without flame) The coals glowed in the fireplace. *n.* 微弱而稳定的光 (a soft and steady light) We could see the glow of the lamp in the window. *n.* (脸上的) 红光 (pink color in your face from exercising, being excited) The fresh air had brought a healthy glow to her cheeks.
glisten ['glɪsn]	*v.* 闪耀；闪亮 (to shine with light reflected off a wet surface) 1 The calm sea glistened in the sunlight. 2 Her eyes glistened with tears.
glitter ['glɪtə(r)]	*v.* 闪烁；闪耀 (to sparkle brightly) Her eyes glittered with intelligence and amusement.

	n. 闪光 (light that shines in small, bright points)
	He was drawn to the glitter of the city's nightlife.
glimmer [ˈglɪmə(r)]	**v.** 发微光；隐约闪烁 (to shine faintly or unsteadily) The moon glimmered faintly through the mists. **n.** 微弱的闪光 (a faint unsteady light) In the east there is the slightest glimmer of light.
glare [gleə(r)]	**v.** 发出强光 (to shine with a harsh, bright light) **1** The sun glared down relentlessly. **2** The white snow glared in the morning sunlight. **n.** 刺眼的光 (a very bright, unpleasant light) I shielded my eyes from the glare of the sun. **n.** （长久的）怒视；瞪眼 (a long, angry look) She gave him a hostile glare.
gloss [glɒs]	**n.** 光彩；光泽 (brightness from a smooth surface) Her hair has a lovely gloss. **v.** 粉饰；掩饰 (to avoid talking about something unpleasant or embarrassing by not dealing with it in detail) Some governments are happy to gloss over continued human rights abuses.
glossy [ˈglɒsi]	**adj.** 有光泽的 (having a shiny, smooth surface) The leaves were dark and glossy.

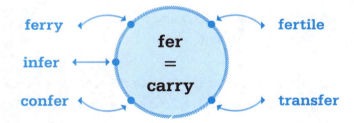

prefer [prɪˈfɜː(r)]	**v.** 更喜欢；偏爱 (to like one thing or person better than another or others) Some people like vanilla ice cream, but I prefer chocolate.
preference [ˈprefrəns]	**n.** 偏爱 (the selecting of someone or something over another or others) Car buyers have recently shown a growing preference for smaller vehicles.

confer [kən'fɜː(r)]	*v.* 商谈；商议 (to discuss something important in order to make a decision) The lawyer and judge conferred about the ruling. *v.* 授予；赋予 (to give something, such as a degree, award, title, right, etc. to someone or something) The university conferred degrees on two famous scientists.
conference ['kɒnfərəns]	*n.* 会议；讨论 (a formal meeting in which many people gather in order to talk about ideas or problems) The organization held its annual conference in New York this year.
infer [ɪn'fɜː(r)]	*v.* 推断；猜想 (to form an opinion from evidence) It's difficult to infer how these changes will affect ordinary citizens.
suffer ['sʌfə(r)]	*v.* 受痛苦 (to experience pain, illness or injury) ① He suffered a heart attack and died instantly. ② We suffered a great deal during the war.
transfer [træns'fɜː(r)]	*v.* 使转移 (to move from one place to another) ① The patient was transferred to a different hospital. ② The virus is transferred by mosquitoes.
fertile ['fɜːtaɪl]	*adj.* 肥沃的 (able to support the growth of many plants) This situation provides a fertile breeding ground for racists. *adj.* 能生育的 (able to reproduce and have babies) The operation cannot make her fertile again.
fertilizer ['fɜːtəlaɪzə(r)]	*n.* 肥料；化肥 (material added to soil to make it more fertile) We only use organic fertilizer in our gardens.
infertile [ɪn'fɜːtaɪl]	*adj.* 贫瘠的 (not suited for raising crops) The polluted waste is often dumped, making the surrounding land infertile. *adj.* 不能生育的 (not able to produce children, young animals, etc.) According to one survey, one woman in eight is infertile.
defer [dɪ'fɜː(r)]	*v.* 使推迟；使延期 (to put off to a future time) The test is deferred to next week. *v.* 服从 (to give in or yield to the opinion or wishes of another) Doctors are encouraged to defer to experts.
deferential [ˌdefə'renʃl]	*adj.* 恭敬的 (polite and respectful towards someone else) I am deferential and respectful in the presence of artists.

Unit 10

ferry	*n.*	渡船 (a boat that transports people or vehicles across a body of water)
['feri]		Ferries to both islands depart daily.
	v.	渡运 (to carry people or goods by boat over a body of water)
		The cars were ferried across the river.
interfere	*v.*	干预；干涉 (to get involved in and try to influence a situation that does not concern you, in a way that annoys other people)
[ˌɪntə'fɪə(r)]		The UN cannot interfere in the internal affairs of any country.

Suck系列

soak	*v.*	浸泡；浸透 (to put something in a liquid for a period of time)
[səʊk]	①	You should soak those dirty clothes before you wash them.
	②	The rain soaked us.
suck	*v.*	吮吸；吸入 (to draw something as liquid or air into the mouth)
[sʌk]	①	These plants suck moisture from the soil.
	②	He sucked chocolate milk through a straw.
absorb	*v.*	吸收 (液体、气体等) (to take in something, such as water in a natural or gradual way)
[əb'sɔːb]		The walls are made of a material that absorbs sound.
	v.	吸引……的注意 (to hold the complete attention of somebody)
		He was completely absorbed in his book.

Rod系列

rodent	*n.*	啮齿动物 (a usually small mammal as a squirrel, rat, mouse or beaver with sharp front teeth used in gnawing)
['rəʊdnt]		When there is a full moon, this nocturnal rodent is careful to stay in its burrow.
corrode	*v.*	使腐蚀 (to slowly break apart and destroy metal, an object, etc. through a chemical process)
[kə'rəʊd]		After a few weeks in the ocean, the boat began to corrode.
	v.	逐渐削弱 (to gradually destroy or weaken something)
		He warns that corruption is corroding Russia.

Unit 10

corrosion [kə'rəʊʒn]	*n.* 腐蚀；侵蚀 (the process or effect of destroying, weakening or wearing away little by little) All planes are being inspected for possible cracking and corrosion.

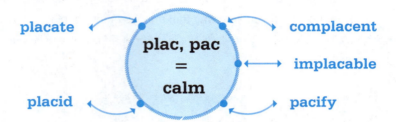

placate [plə'keɪt]	*v.* 安抚；抚慰 (to cause someone to feel less angry about something) The administration placated protesters by agreeing to consider their demands.
placid ['plæsɪd]	*adj.* 平和的 (not easily upset or excited) She was a placid child who rarely cried. *adj.* 平静的 (calm and peaceful) The placid waters stirred violently, and a loud noise broke the stillness.
complacent [kəm'pleɪsnt]	*adj.* 自满的；得意的 (too satisfied with yourself or with a situation, so that you do not feel that any change is necessary; showing or feeling complacency) The strong economy has made people complacent.
implacable [ɪm'plækəbl]	*adj.* 不能安抚的；不能缓和的 (impossible to please, satisfy or change) He has an implacable hatred for his political opponents.
pacify ['pæsɪfaɪ]	*v.* 安抚；抚慰 (to cause someone who is angry or upset to become calm or quiet) She resigned from her position to pacify her accusers. *v.* 平定；平息 (to cause or force a country, a violent group of people, etc. to become peaceful) Government forces have found it difficult to pacify the rebels.

Unit 10

Junior系列

junior [ˈdʒuːniə(r)]	*adj.* 职位低的 (having a low rank in an organization or a profession) She is a junior partner in the law firm.
juvenile [ˈdʒuːvənaɪl]	*adj.* 少年的 (connected with young people who are not yet adults) Juvenile crime is increasing at a terrifying rate. *adj.* 幼稚的；不成熟的 (silly or childish) He's a typical male, as he gets older he becomes more juvenile.
rejuvenate [rɪˈdʒuːvəneɪt]	*v.* 使变得年轻；使恢复活力 (to make somebody or something look or feel younger or more lively) ① The government pushed through schemes to rejuvenate the inner cities. ② The mountain air will rejuvenate you.

Sure系列

ensure [ɪnˈʃʊə(r)]	*v.* 确保 (to make sure that something happens or is definite) This victory will ensure his happiness.
insure [ɪnˈʃʊə(r)]	*v.* 为……保险 (to guarantee against loss or harm) For protection against unforeseen emergencies, you insure your house, your furnishings and your car.
insurance [ɪnˈʃʊərəns]	*n.* 保险 (an arrangement with a company in which you pay them regular amounts of money and they agree to pay the costs, for example, if you die or are ill/sick, or if you lose or damage something) We recommend that you take out travel insurance on all holidays.
assure [əˈʃʊə(r)]	*v.* 向……保证；使……确信 (to tell somebody that something is definitely true or is definitely going to happen, especially when they have doubts about it) I can assure you that you won't be disappointed.
reassure [ˌriːəˈʃʊə(r)]	*v.* 使安心；使消除疑虑 (to make someone feel less afraid, upset or doubtful) ① Experts reassured the public that the accident wouldn't happen again. ② I tried to reassure myself that the children were safe.

Unit 10

Stri系列

strive [straɪv]	*v.* 努力奋斗 (to try very hard to do or achieve something) ① They continue to strive toward their goals. ② We encourage all members to strive for the highest standards.
struggle ['strʌgl]	*v.* 艰难地行进 (to move with difficulty or with great effort) She struggled to lift the package by herself, but it was too heavy. *v.* 奋斗；努力；争取 (to try very hard to do something when it is difficult or when there are a lot of problems) He was living as a struggling artist in the city. *n.* 搏斗；奋斗 (a difficult or violent effort) It was a struggle getting out of bed this morning.
strife [straɪf]	*n.* 斗争；冲突 (very angry or violent disagreement between two or more people or groups) Bitter strife took place between the two political factions.
stretch [stretʃ]	*v.* 伸展；延伸 (to extend in length) She woke up and stretched her arms above her head.
strenuous ['strenjuəs]	*adj.* 费力的；艰苦的 (requiring or showing great energy and effort) ① Strenuous efforts had been made to improve conditions in the jail. ② Avoid strenuous exercise in the evening.

追根溯源

　　古罗马军队常常在旷野上扎营操练。英语中表示"军营，营地"等意的camp一词最初有"旷野"之义，来自拉丁语campus-field（旷野；场地）。出自此词源的还有campaign（战役），campus（校园），champion（冠军）和decamp（撤营；逃亡）。

camp [kæmp]	*n.* 营地 (a place where temporary shelters are erected) The hikers set up camp for the night. *v.* 宿营 (to make or occupy a camp) The travelers camped under a large tree.
decamp [dɪ'kæmp]	*v.* 逃亡；潜逃 (to go away from somewhere secretly or suddenly) He decamped to Europe soon after news of the scandal broke.

campus ['kæmpəs]	*n.* 校园；校区 (the grounds and buildings of a university, college or school) Freshmen at many universities are not allowed to live off campus.
campaign [kæm'peɪn]	*n.* 战役 (a series of planned movements carried out by armed forces) The allies are intensifying their air campaign. *n.* 运动 (a planned set of activities that people carry out over a period of time in order to achieve something such as social or political change) During his election campaign he promised to put the economy back on its feet.
champion ['tʃæmpiən]	*n.* 捍卫者 (one that does battle for another's rights or honor) He was once known as a champion of social reform. *v.* 捍卫；拥护 (to fight or speak publicly in support of a group of people or a belief) She is a lawyer who champions children's rights.

锦囊妙记

parsimony ['pɑːsɪməni]	*n.* 吝啬 (the quality of being very unwilling to spend money) Her parsimony was so extreme that she'd walk five miles to the store to save a few cents on gas. **谐音法** parsi-怕失，mony-money，一个总是怕失去金钱的人当然吝啬 (parsimony)！
greedy ['griːdi]	*adj.* 贪婪的；贪心的 (wanting more money, power, etc. than you really need) He was a ruthless and greedy businessman. **联想法** gree-green，贪婪的 (greedy)人两眼放绿光 (green)！
thrifty ['θrɪfti]	*adj.* 节俭的；节约的 (managing or using money in a careful or wise way) Except for smoking and drinking, he is a thrifty man. **联想法** thri-three，想到三块钱，每天只花三块钱，日子过得很节俭 (thrifty)。
avaricious [ˌævə'rɪʃəs]	*adj.* 贪婪的，贪得无厌的 (greedy for riches) He sacrificed his own career so that his avaricious brother could succeed. **拆分法** a-啊，va-哇，rice-大米！贪婪的 (avaricious)老鼠看到大米就会有这样的感叹！
avarice ['ævərɪs]	*n.* 贪婪 (strong desire for riches) He paid a month's rent in advance, just enough to satisfy the landlord's avarice.

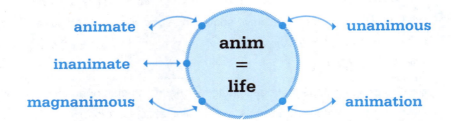

animate

['ænɪmeɪt]

v. 使有生气 (to make something more lively or full of energy)

The writer's humor animates the novel.

adj. 有生命的 (having life)

The lecture was about ancient worship of animate and inanimate objects.

inanimate

[ɪn'ænɪmət]

adj. 无生命的；无生气的 (not living; not capable of life)

A rock is an inanimate object.

animation

[ˌænɪ'meɪʃn]

n. 动画制作 (the process of making films/movies, videos and computer games in which drawings or models of people and animals seem to move)

The animation for the film took over two years to complete.

n. 活泼；热烈 (a lively or excited quality)

She spoke with animation about her trip.

unanimous

[juˈnænɪməs]

adj. 全体一致的 (agreed by everyone in a group)

The judges made a unanimous ruling.

magnanimous

[mægˈnænɪməs]

adj. 宽宏大量的 (having or showing a generous and kind nature)

He was magnanimous in defeat and praised his opponent's skill.

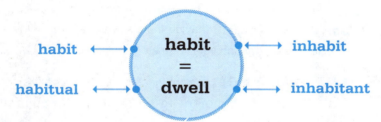

habit	*n.* 习惯 (something that a person does often in a regular and repeated way)
['hæbɪt]	It was his habit to take a nap after dinner every evening.
habitual	*adj.* 习惯的 (done regularly or repeatedly)
[hə'bɪtʃuəl]	Other countries retained their traditional and habitual ways of doing things.
inhabit	*v.* 居住 (to live in a place)
[ɪn'hæbɪt]	① Several hundred species of birds inhabit the island.
	② This part of the country is inhabited by native tribes.
inhabitant	*n.* 居民；住户；栖息动物 (a person or animal that lives in a particular place)
[ɪn'hæbɪtənt]	The inhabitants of the town don't like the tourists.

compete	*v.* 竞赛；竞争 (to strive for something as a prize or a reward for which another is also striving)
[kəm'piːt]	Thousands of applicants are competing for the same job.
competition	*n.* 竞争；比赛 (a contest in which all who take part strive for the same thing)
[ˌkɒmpə'tɪʃn]	Prices are lower when there is competition among the stores.
competitor	*n.* 竞争者；对手 (one that competes with another, as in sports or business)
[kəm'petɪtə(r)]	One of the oldest competitors in the race won the silver medal.

competent
['kɒmpɪtənt]

adj. 有能力的；能胜任的 (having the ability to perform well)

He was a loyal and very competent civil servant.

incompetent
[ɪn'kɒmpɪtənt]

adj. 无能力的；不胜任的 (lacking necessary ability or skills)

He is too incompetent to be trusted with such an important responsibility.

repeat
[rɪ'piːt]

v. 重复 (to do or to say something again)

He often has to ask people to repeat themselves because he's a little deaf.

repetitive
[rɪ'petətɪv]

adj. 重复乏味的；多次重复的 (happening again and again; repeated many times)

He left the job because the work was too repetitive.

appetite
['æpɪtaɪt]

n. 食欲 (a physical desire for food)

Exercise gives you a good appetite.

n. 欲望 (a desire or liking for something)

They had no appetite for further fighting.

petition
[pə'tɪʃn]

n. 请愿书 (a formal written request made to an official person or organized body)

We recently presented the government with a petition signed by 4,500 people.

v. 请求；请愿 (to make a formal request to somebody in authority, especially by sending them a petition)

The organization petitioned the government to investigate the issue.

perpetual
[pə'petʃuəl]

adj. 永久的；不断的 (continuing for a very long time without stopping)

The rest of the world struggles on with its perpetual problems, poverty and debt.

adj. 没完没了的 (frequently repeated in a way that is annoying)

I thought her perpetual complaints were going to prove too much for me.

perpetuate
[pə'petʃueɪt]

v. 使延续 (to cause something to last a long time)

Fears about an epidemic are being perpetuated by the media.

petulant
['petjulənt]

adj. 易怒的；任性的 (unreasonably angry and upset in a childish way)

A petulant man who is always blaming everyone else for his problems.

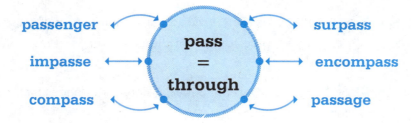

passenger | surpass
impasse | encompass
compass | passage

pass = through

passage ['pæsɪdʒ]	*n.* 通路；通道 (a long, narrow space that connects one place to another) We squeezed through a narrow passage between the rocks. *n.* 流逝 (the process of time passing) With the passage of time, the number of children suffering with the disease has decreased dramatically. *n.* 段落 (a brief part of a speech or written work) That is my favourite passage from the Bible.
passenger ['pæsɪndʒə(r)]	*n.* 乘客；旅客 (a person who is travelling in a car, bus, train, plane or ship and who is not driving it or working on it) There were two passengers in the car in addition to the driver.
impasse ['æmpɑːs]	*n.* 绝境；僵局 (a situation in which no progress seems possible) An arbitrator was called in to break the impasse.
compass ['kʌmpəs]	*n.* 罗盘；指南针 (a device that is used to find direction by means of a needle that always points north) **1** He always carries a compass when he walks in the woods. **2** His religion is the compass that guides him.
encompass [ɪn'kʌmpəs]	*v.* 围绕；包围 (to cover or surround an area) Mountains encompass the peaceful valley.
passport ['pɑːspɔːt]	*n.* 护照；通行证 (a government document needed to enter or leave a country) You should take your passport with you when changing money. *n.* 途径 (a thing that makes something possible or enables you to achieve something) Meeting that movie director could be your passport to a big acting career.
trespass ['trespəs]	*v.* 擅自进入 (to go on someone's land without permission) He told me I was trespassing on private land.

	v. 侵犯；侵害（权利等）(to do something that hurts or offends someone) They were acting to prevent the state from trespassing on family matters.
surpass [sə'pɑːs]	*v.* 超过；优于 (to become better, greater or stronger than somebody/ something) He was determined to surpass the achievements of his older brothers.

Tone系列

tone [təʊn]	*n.* 声调；语气 (the quality of a person's voice) He replied in a friendly tone.
monotonous [mə'nɒtənəs]	*adj.* 单调乏味的 (never chaning and therefore boring) Our trip across the ocean was monotonous.

All系列

alloy ['ælɔɪ]	*n.* 合金 (a metal made by melting and mixing two or more metals) Brass is an alloy of copper and zinc.
alliance [ə'laɪəns]	*n.* 结盟；同盟 (a union between people, groups or countries) We need to form a closer alliance between government and industry.
ally ['ælaɪ]	*n.* 同盟国 (a country that supports and helps another country in a war) Washington would not take such a step without its allies' approval. *v.* 与……结盟 (to give one's support to another group or country) ① He allied himself with a wealthy family by marriage. ② They've allied with their former enemies.
rally ['ræli]	*v.* 召集；集合 (to bring or come together for a common purpose) He rallied his own supporters for a fight. *n.* 集会 (a mass meeting intended to arouse group enthusiasm) Protesters staged an antiwar rally.

Unit 11

Life系列

enliven	*v.* 使活泼；使生动 (to make something more interesting, lively or enjoyable)
[ɪnˈlaɪvn]	① He enlivened his speech with a few jokes.
	② A few touches of color will enliven the room.

proliferate	*v.* 激增；剧增 (to increase in number or amount quickly)
[prəˈlɪfəreɪt]	① Rumors about the incident proliferated on the Internet.
	② Rabbits proliferate when they have plenty of food.

prolific	*adj.* （作家，画家）多产的 (producing many works, etc.)
[prəˈlɪfɪk]	She is a prolific writer of novels and short stories.
	adj. 高产的；多育的 (producing young or fruit in large numbers)
	Closer planting will give you a more prolific crop.

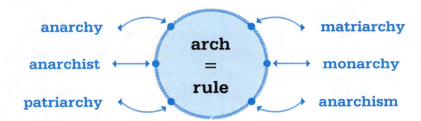

| **patriarchy** | *n.* 父权制；家长制 (a social system in which the father is the head of the family) |
| [ˈpeɪtriɑːki] | For 20 years, the country was ruled as a patriarchy. |

| **matriarchy** | *n.* 母权制 (a social system in which the mother is the head of the family) |
| [ˈmeɪtriɑːki] | Women owned the country and women governed it; suddenly the matriarchy existed. |

anarchy	*n.* 无政府状态；混乱 (a situation in a country, an organization, etc.in which there is no government, order or control)
[ˈænəki]	① The overthrow of the military regime was followed by a period of anarchy.
	② When the teacher was absent, there was anarchy in the classroom.

| **anarchist** | *n.* 无政府主义者 (a person who believes that government and laws are not necessary) |
| [ˈænəkɪst] | He was apparently quite converted from his anarchist views. |

Unit 11

anarchism ['ænəkɪzəm]	**n.** 无政府主义 (a belief that government and laws are not necessary) He was inclined to anarchism; he hated system and organization and uniformity.
monarchy ['mɒnəki]	**n.** 君主专制 (a country that is ruled by a monarch such as a king or queen) The country was a monarchy until 1973.

Fla系列

flap [flæp]	**v.** 飘动；摆动 (to move something up and down or back and forth) **1** The flag flapped in the breeze. **2** The bird's wings were flapping.
flip [flɪp]	**v.** (用手指) 轻弹，抛 (to throw something somewhere using your thumb and/or fingers) I pulled a coin from my pocket and flipped it. **v.** 翻动 (to cause something to turn and especially to turn over) She was sitting in the waiting room, flipping the pages of a magazine.
flippant ['flɪpənt]	**adj.** 轻浮的；无礼的 (lacking proper respect or seriousness) He made a flippant response to a serious question.
flicker ['flɪkə(r)]	**v.** 闪烁；摇曳 (to burn or glow in an unsteady way) The lights flickered and went out. **v.** 掠过，闪过 (to appear or pass briefly or quickly) A smile flickered across her face.
flutter ['flʌtə(r)]	**v.** (鸟或昆虫) 拍 (翅)；振 (翅) (to fly lightly with quick beats of the wings) We watched the butterflies fluttering in the garden. **n.** 颤振；挥动 (an act of moving or flapping quickly) With a flutter of wings, the birds settled into the nest. **n.** 紧张；激动不安 (a state of excitement or confusion) The contestants were all in a flutter.

Unit 11

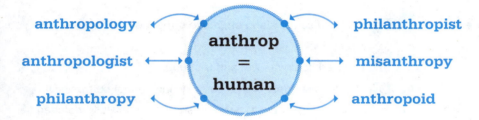

anthropology [ˌænθrəˈpɒlədʒi]	*n.* 人类学 (the study of the human race, especially of its origins, development, customs and beliefs) Social anthropology examines family relationships in detail.
anthropologist [ˌænθrəˈpɒlədʒɪst]	*n.* 人类学家 (a social scientist who specializes in anthropology) An eminent anthropologist, Fred Gelman investigated the remnants of ancient structures.
philanthropy [fɪˈlænθrəpi]	*n.* 博爱；慈善活动 (love of humankind in general) He shows his philanthropy by helping people who have been in prison.
philanthropist [fɪˈlænθrəpɪst]	*n.* 慈善家 (a person who practices philanthropy) The university was founded by a millionaire philanthropist.
misanthropy [mɪˈsænθrəpi]	*n.* 厌恶人类 (a general dislike of people) An abandoned child, his natural state is isolation, his faith a kind of misanthropy.
anthropoid [ˈænθrəpɔɪd]	*n.* 类人猿 (any type of ape that is similar to a human) About 38 million years ago, some anthropoids migrated to Africa.

Slip系列

slip [slɪp]	*v.* 滑；滑倒 (to slide a short distance by accident so that you fall or nearly fall) He had slipped on an icy pavement. *v.* 滑落 (to slide into or out of a place or away from a support) The book slipped out of my hand. *v.* 不知不觉地过去 (to pass or let pass or escape without being noted) Time slipped by.

slippery

['slɪpəri]

adj. 滑的 (difficult to stand on, move on, or hold because of being smooth, wet and icy)

The tiled floor was wet and slippery.

adj. 狡猾的 (dishonest in a clever way and cannot be trusted)

He is a slippery customer, and should be carefully watched.

slide

[slaɪd]

v. (使) 滑行，滑动 (to move smoothly along a surface)

Cars were slipping and sliding all over the roads during the snowstorm.

elapse

[ɪ'læps]

v. (时间) 消逝 (to slip past)

Nearly a year elapsed before his return.

relapse

[rɪ'læps]

n. 旧病复发 (the fact of becoming ill/sick again after making an improvement)

The treatment is usually given to women with a high risk of relapse after surgery.

v. 退回原状；(好转后) 再倒退 (to go back into a previous condition or into a worse state after making an improvement)

If you don't continue your treatment, you could relapse.

collapse

[kə'læps]

v. 崩溃；瓦解 (to break apart and fall down suddenly)

1 The roof collapsed under a heavy load of snow.

2 He warned that such measures could cause the economy to collapse.

n. 倒塌；垮掉 (the action of a building suddenly falling)

The building is in danger of collapse.

slipper

['slɪpə(r)]

n. 拖鞋 (loose, soft shoes that you wear at home)

I rescued the remains of my slipper from the dog.

sloppy

['slɒpi]

adj. 懒散的；草率的 (showing a lack of care, attention or effort)

A sloppy child always seems to have spilled something on his clothes.

Por系列

pore

[pɔː(r)]

n. (皮肤上的) 毛孔；(植物的) 气孔 (a very small holes on the surface of your skin; one of the similar small holes in the surface of a plant or a rock)

A plant's lungs are the microscopic pores in its leaves.

porous ['pɔːrəs]	*adj.* 多孔的；能渗透的 (having small holes that allow air or liquid to pass through) The water slowly drained away, down through the porous soil.
pierce [pɪəs]	*v.* 刺穿；戳穿 (to make a hole in or through something) The needle pierced into her skin.
permeate ['pɜːmieɪt]	*v.* 渗透；弥漫 (to pass or spread through something) ❶ The rain permeated through the soil. ❷ The smell of smoke permeated the room.
permeable ['pɜːmiəbl]	*adj.* 可渗透的；具渗透性的 (allowing liquids or gases to pass through) A number of products have been developed which are permeable to air and water.

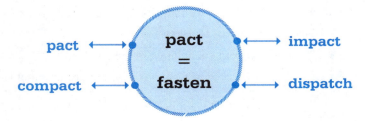

pact [pækt]	*n.* 条约 (a formal agreement between two countries, people or groups especially to help each other or to stop fighting) We supported a peace pact between the two countries.
compact [kəm'pækt]	*v.* 压紧 (to press something together firmly) The snow had compacted into a hard icy layer. *adj.* 紧凑的；体积小的 (using or filling only a small amount of space) The cabin was compact but perfectly adequate. *adj.* 矮小而健壮的 (small and strong) He is compact and muscular.
impact ['ɪmpækt] *n.* [ɪm'pækt] *v.*	*n.* 碰撞；冲击 (the force of impression of one thing on another) A running track should be capable of absorbing the impact of a runner's foot landing on it. *n.* 影响 (a significant or major effect) We need to be concerned about the environmental impacts of all this construction.

	v. 对……产生影响 (to have a strong and often bad effect on something or someone) No one is sure how these changes will impact our relations with other countries.
dispatch [dɪ'spætʃ]	*v.* 派遣 (to send someone or something quickly to a particular place for a particular purpose) Rescue workers were immediately dispatched to the area.

Cumul系列

accumulate [ə'kjuːmjəleɪt]	*v.* 堆积；累积 (to gather or pile up something especially little by little) As evidence began to accumulate, experts felt obliged to investigate.
cumulative ['kjuːmjələtɪv]	*adj.* 累积的；渐增的 (increasing or becoming better or worse over time through a series of additions) ❶ The benefits from eating fish are cumulative. ❷ The effect of human activity on the world environment is cumulative.
cumulus ['kjuːmjələs]	*n.* 积云 (a type of thick cloud that is rounded on top and has a flat base) The day will start off sunny with afternoon cumulus clouds developing.
encumber [ɪn'kʌmbə(r)]	*v.* 阻碍；拖累 (to make it difficult for somebody to do something or for something to happen) ❶ These rules will only encumber the people we're trying to help. ❷ Lack of funding has encumbered the project.
cumbersome ['kʌmbəsəm]	*adj.* 笨重的 (hard to handle or manage because of size or weight) Although the machine looks cumbersome, it is actually easy to use.

追根溯源

　　camera（照相机）的外形很像一个小房子，因此词根camer表示"房间"（room）的意思，chamber（大房间）与此同源。由camer向comra变形得到comrade（同志；战友）一词，comrade本意是指住在一个屋檐下的亲密伙伴，后来引申出今天的"同志；战友"之意。

Unit 11

camera [ˈkæmərə]	*n.* 照相机 (a piece of equipment that is used for taking photographs) The company commanded 90% of the market for photographic film and 85% of the market for cameras.
chamber [ˈtʃeɪmbə(r)]	*n.* 大房间 (a large room, especially one that is used for formal meetings) We are going to make sure we are in the council chamber every time he speaks. *n.* 议会；议院 (a group of people who form part of a government) The U.S. legislature is separated into two chambers: the Senate and the House of Representatives.
comrade [ˈkɒmreɪd]	*n.* 同志；战友 (a close friend you have worked with, been in the military with, etc.) He enjoys spending time with his old army comrades.

Calculus系列

　　在两千多年前，古罗马商人用拉丁文称为calculus的小圆石来计算损益。古罗马时代的人们也是以小圆石（calculus）作为算珠。今天我们所使用的calculate（计算）一词正源于此。recalcitrant（倔强的）也是来自小圆石，指的是一个人像石头一样非常固执、倔强。

calculate [ˈkælkjuleɪt]	*v.* 计算 (to determine by mathematical processes) We need to calculate our chances of success before we invest more money in the business.
recalcitrant [rɪˈkælsɪtrənt]	*adj.* 倔强对抗的 (stubbornly refusing to obey rules or orders) The danger is that recalcitrant local authorities will reject their responsibilities.

锦囊妙记

baffle [ˈbæfl]	*v.* 使困惑；把……难住 (to confuse someone completely) I was baffled by many of the scientific terms used in the article. **谐音法** baffle-拜佛，人生感到baffle（困惑），要去拜拜佛！
pompous [ˈpɒmpəs]	*adj.* 浮华的；自命不凡的 (excessively elevated or ornate) She found it difficult to talk about her achievements without sounding pompous. **谐音法** pomp-泡沫，ous-多，泡沫很多当然非常浮华(pompous)！

mystery ['mɪstri]	*n.* 神秘；奥秘；秘密 (something that has not been or cannot be explained) Her disappearance remains a mystery. 拆分法 my-my, stery-story. 我的故事是秘密(mystery)！
violate ['vaɪəleɪt]	*v.* 违反；违背 (to do something that is not allowed by a law, rule) ❶ They went to prison because they violated the law. ❷ They violated the ceasefire agreement. 拆分法 vio-我，late-晚了，我上学迟到 (late)了，违背了 (violate)学校的规则。
enhance [ɪn'hɑːns]	*vt.* 增强；提高 (to increase or further improve the value, quality or attractiveness of somebody/something) The company is looking to enhance its earnings potential. 谐音法 en-使得，hance-汉子，使得汉子，就要不断增强，提高(enhance)！

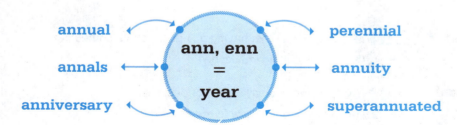

annual [ˈænjuəl]	*adj.* 年度的 (happening or done once every year) The economy grew at a 2.1% annual rate in the fourth quarter of last year.
annals [ˈænlz]	*n.* 编年史；历史记载 (an official record of events or activities year by year; historical records) He has become a legend in the annals of military history.
annuity [əˈnjuːəti]	*n.* 年金；养老金 (a fixed amount of money paid to somebody each year, usually for the rest of their life) Part of her retirement income will come from an annuity.
anniversary [ˌænɪˈvɜːsəri]	*n.* 周年纪念 (a date remembered or celebrated every year because of something special that happened on it in an earlier year) This year marks the 50th anniversary, with a large number of celebrations planned.
perennial [pəˈreniəl]	*adj.* 终年的；长久的 (present at all seasons of the year) Flooding is a perennial problem for people living by the river.
superannuated [ˌsuːpərˈænjueɪtɪd]	*adj.* 落伍的；废弃的 (old and therefore no longer very effective or useful) Roughly 6% of energy pumped out for public consumption is wasted thanks to America's superannuated electricity grid.

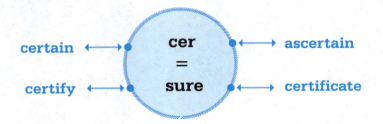

certain ←→ cer = sure ←→ ascertain

certify ←→ cer = sure ←→ certificate

certain ['sɜːtn]	*adj.* 必然的；肯定的 (not having any doubt about something) Our plan is certain to succeed.
uncertain [ʌn'sɜːtn]	*adj.* 不确定的 (not exactly known or decided) I'm uncertain about how to respond.
certify ['sɜːtɪfaɪ]	*v.* 证明 (to say officially that something is true, correct, or genuine) The document has been certified by the court.
certificate [sə'tɪfɪkət]	*n.* 证明书；文凭 (a document that is official proof that something has happened) He earned his teaching certificate last year.
ascertain [ˌæsə'teɪn]	*v.* 查明；弄清 (to find out the true or correct information about something) Police tried to ascertain the cause of the accident.
assert [ə'sɜːt]	*v.* 声称；断言 (to state something in a strong and definite way) He asserted that there were spies in the government. *v.* 坚持要求 (to demand that other people accept or respect something) She asserted her independence from her parents by getting her own apartment.
assertive [ə'sɜːtɪv]	*adj.* 坚定自信的；坚决主张的 (expressing opinions or desires strongly and with confidence, so that people take notice) If you want people to listen to your opinions, you'll need to learn to be more assertive.

Unit 12

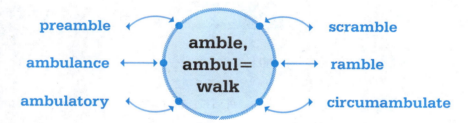

preamble ← → scramble
ambulance ← → ramble
ambulatory ← → circumambulate

amble,
ambul=
walk

preamble [priˈæmbl]	_n._ 序言 (an introductory statement) He ended the debate by reciting the preamble to the US Constitution, but messed up a word.
perambulate [pəˈræmbjʊleɪt]	_v._ 漫步；闲逛 (to travel over or through especially on foot) She perambulated around the outside of the house, investigating, looking to see if windows and shutters were secure and in order.
ambulatory [ˈæmbjələtəri]	_adj._ 可移动的；流动的 (that is not fixed in one place and can move around easily) The same procedure with the same doctor costs thousands more in a hospital than at an ambulatory surgical centre.
ambulance [ˈæmbjələns]	_n._ 救护车 (a vehicle that takes people to and from hospitals) Witnesses described ambulances racing toward the airfield, where a huge fire was blazing.
ramble [ˈræmbl]	_v._ 漫游；漫步 (to move about aimlessly or without any destination) They rambled about and shouted in joy like kids everywhere.
circumambulate [ˌsɜːkəmˈæmbjʊleɪt]	_v._ 绕行；巡行 (to walk around something) In the evening, hundreds of pilgrims circumambulate the stupa or meditate quietly in its shadows.
somnambulate [sɒmˈnæmbjʊleɪt]	_v._ 梦游 (to walk in one's sleep) I'm a somnambulist, only I somnambulate faster than most people.
scramble [ˈskræmbl]	_v._ (迅速地)爬 (to move or climb over something quickly especially while also using your hands) We scrambled over the boulders and kept climbing up the mountain.

Unit 12

bland

[blænd]

adj. 淡而无味的 (lacking strong flavor)

The vegetable soup was rather bland.

adj. 沉稳的；无动于衷的；讲话枯燥的 (showing no strong emotions or excitement not saying anything very interesting)

The diplomat's bland statement did nothing to calm the situation.

blank

[blæŋk]

adj. 空白的；空的 (having empty spaces to be filled in with information)

She turned to a blank page in her notebook.

n. (记忆中的) 空白；遗忘 (a state of not being able to remember anything)

Everything after the accident is a blank.

bleach

[bliːtʃ]

v. 漂白；晒白；使褪色 (to become white or pale by a chemical process or by the effect of light from the sun; to make something white or pale in this way)

These products don't bleach the hair.

bleak

[bliːk]

adj. 没有希望的；前景暗淡的 (not hopeful or encouraging)

The future looks bleak.

adj. 荒凉的；凄清的 (of a place exposed, empty or with no pleasant features)

The island is pretty bleak.

blind

[blaɪnd]

adj. 失明的 (unable to see)

Our old blind cat kept walking into walls and furniture.

v. 使……失明 (to make somebody blind)

She was blinded as a child in a terrible fire.

blunder

['blʌndə(r)]

v. 跌跌撞撞地走 (to move in an awkward or confused way)

We blundered along through the woods until we finally found the trail.

v. 犯愚蠢的错误 (to make a stupid or careless mistake)

The government blundered by not acting sooner.

n. 大错；疏忽 (a bad mistake made because of stupidity or carelessness)

The accident was the result of a series of blunders.

Unit 12

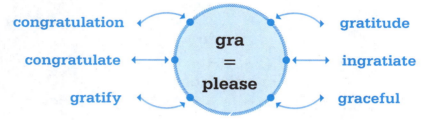

gratify ['grætɪfaɪ]	*v.* 使高兴 (to make someone happy or satisfied) The loud applause gratified her. *v.* 使满足 (to satisfy a wish, need, etc.) He only wants to gratify his wishes.
gratitude ['grætɪtjuːd]	*n.* 感激；感谢 (a feeling of thankfulness and appreciation) Let me express my sincere gratitude for all your help.
grateful ['greɪtfl]	*adj.* 感激的；感谢的 (feeling or showing thanks) I'm grateful for your help.
congratulate [kən'grætʃuleɪt]	*v.* 祝贺；向……道贺 (to tell someone that you are happy because of his or her success or good luck) I'd like to congratulate you on your success.
congratulation [kən,grætʃu'leɪʃn]	*n.* 祝贺；恭喜 (expressing pleasure at another person's success or good fortune) Let me offer you my congratulations for being elected.
ingratiate [ɪn'greɪʃieɪt]	*v.* 讨好；谄媚 (to do things in order to make somebody like you, especially somebody who will be useful to you) ❶ She quickly sought to ingratiate herself with the new administration. ❷ He ingratiates himself with teachers by being helpful.
gratuitous [grə'tjuːɪtəs]	*adj.* 无正当理由的；无谓的 (done without any good reason or purpose and often having harmful effects) The film was criticized for its gratuitous violence.
graceful ['greɪsfl]	*adj.* 优美的；优雅的 (moving in a smooth and attractive way) She has become a very graceful dancer. *adj.* 得体的 (polite or kind) There was no graceful way to say no to their offer.

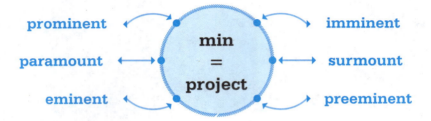

mountainous ['maʊntənəs]	adj. 多山的 (having many mountains) Nowadays tractors are used even in remote mountainous regions.
paramount ['pærəmaʊnt]	adj. 至为重要的；首要的 (more important than anything else) Maintaining the secrecy of the agreement is of paramount importance.
mount [maʊnt]	v. 登上；骑上 (to go or climb up something) The cowboy mounted his horse and then quickly dismounted. v. 增加；上升 (to increase in amount) The pressure mounted as the crisis continued.
surmount [sə'maʊnt]	v. 战胜；克服 (to deal with a problem or a difficult situation successfully) 1 I realized I had to surmount the language barrier. 2 The Olympic swimmer surmounted endless obstacles to achieve her goals.
prominent ['prɒmɪnənt]	adj. 杰出的；突出的 (standing out or projecting beyond a surface or line) His stomach had grown more prominent with every passing year.
eminent ['emɪnənt]	adj. 知名的；杰出的 (successful, well-known and respected) We are expecting the arrival of an eminent scientist.
eminence ['emɪnəns]	n. 显赫；卓越 (a condition of being well-known and successful) The brilliant scientist had earned eminence in her field.
preeminent [prɪ'emɪnənt]	adj. 卓越的；杰出的 (more important, skillful, or successful than others) The poem is a preeminent example of his work.
imminent ['ɪmɪnənt]	adj. (通常指不愉快的事) 即将发生的 (happening very soon) The black clouds show that a storm is imminent.

Unit 12

State

state [steɪt]	*v.* 规定；公布 (to fix or announce the details of something, especially on a written document) The rules clearly state that you can only draw one card.
statute ['stætʃuːt]	*n.* 法令；法规 (a law enacted by the legislative branch of a government) The new statute covers the care for, bringing up and protection of children.
statement ['steɪtmənt]	*n.* 声明 (something that you say or write in a formal or official way) His office issued an official statement concerning his departure.
understate [ˌʌndə'steɪt]	*v.* 对……轻描淡写 (to say that something is smaller, less important than it really is) She's trying to understate the issue.
overstate [ˌəʊvə'steɪt]	*v.* 夸大 (某事) (to say that something is larger or greater than it really is) It would be overstating the case to say that it was a matter of life or death.

Measure系列

measure ['meʒə(r)]	*v.* 测量；度量 (to find out the size, extent or amount of something) ❶ You should measure the cloth before cutting. ❷ The room measures 15 feet wide by 30 feet long. *n.* 措施；手段 (particular actions in order to achieve a particular result) The government warned that police would take tougher measures to contain the trouble.
dimension [daɪ'menʃn]	*n.* 尺寸 (the length, width, height or depth of something) She carefully measured each dimension of the room. *n.* 方面 (an aspect, or way of looking at or thinking about something) The social dimensions of the problem must also be taken into account.
immense [ɪ'mens]	*adj.* 极大的；巨大的 (very great in size or amount) He inherited an immense fortune.

Moist系列

mist [mɪst]	*n.* 薄雾；水汽 (water in the form of very small drops floating in the air or falling as rain) ① We could barely see the shore through the mist. ② The hills were veiled in a fine mist. *v.* 使……模糊 (to become covered with very small drops of water) The temperature in the car was misting the window.
misty ['mɪsti]	*adj.* 多雾的 (full of very tiny drops of water) The air was cold and misty.
moist [mɔɪst]	*adj.* 潮湿的；微湿的 (slightly wet) The plant grows best in direct sunlight and with rich, moist soil.
moisture ['mɔɪstʃə(r)]	*n.* 水分；潮湿 (a small amount of a liquid) ① These flowers grow best with moisture and shade. ② The leaves absorb moisture from the air.
moss [mɒs]	*n.* 苔藓 (a type of green plant that has very small leaves and no flowers and that grows on wet ground) Moss covered the fallen logs.
muzzy ['mʌzi]	*adj.* 模糊的；不清晰的 (confused or unclear in the mind especially after drinking alcohol) He stopped drinking when his head started getting muzzy.

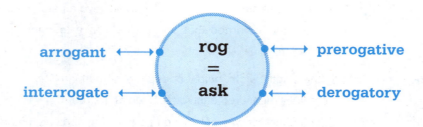

interrogate [ɪn'terəgeɪt]	*v.* 询问；审问 (to ask someone questions in a thorough and often forceful way) The police took a long time to interrogate the offenders fully.
interrogation [ɪn,terə'geɪʃn]	*n.* 讯问；审问 (the act of interrogating someone) Under interrogation, he refused to say anything at first.

arrogant [ˈærəgənt]	*adj.* 傲慢的；自大的 (behaving in a proud, unpleasant way, show little thought for other people) The arrogant young lawyer elbowed his way to the head of the line of customers, declaring that he was too busy to wait like everybody else.
prerogative [prɪˈrɒgətɪv]	*n.* 特权 (a special right or privilege that some people have) Constitutional changes are exclusively the prerogative of the parliament.
derogatory [dɪˈrɒgətri]	*adj.* 贬低的；贬义的 (expressing a low opinion of someone or something) Fans made a steady stream of derogatory remarks about the players on the visiting team.
abrogate [ˈæbrəgeɪt]	*v.* 废除 (法律等) (to abolish a law, an agreement, etc. by authoritative, official, or formal action) The U.S. Congress can abrogate old treaties that are unfair to Native Americans.
rogue [rəʊg]	*n.* 流氓；无赖 (a man who is dishonest or immoral) I wouldn't buy a car from a rogue like him.

追根溯源

idiom 一词的词源可以追溯至希腊语，表示各种特性或特色，尤指语言特色和文体特色。英语借用了这个词，用以表示"习语"或"习惯用语"。英语中的另外两个词 idiot（白痴）和 idiosyncrasy（癖好；特征），亦来源于此。

idiom [ˈɪdiəm]	*n.* 习语；成语 (the language peculiar to a people or to a district, community, or class) Mastering the use of idioms can be hard for a learner.
idiot [ˈɪdiət]	*n.* 傻瓜；笨蛋 (a very stupid or foolish person) What an idiot I was to leave my cell phone in the taxi!
idiosyncrasy [ˌɪdiəˈsɪŋkrəsi]	*n.* (某人特有的) 气质；癖好 (an unusual way of behaving or thinking that is characteristic of a person) Her habit of using 'like' in every sentence was just one of her idiosyncrasies.

| idol
['aɪdl] | *n.* 偶像；崇拜物 (a person or thing that is loved and admired very much)
A great cheer went up from the crowd as they caught sight of their idol. |

锦囊妙记

insolent ['ɪnsələnt]	*adj.* 傲慢的；无礼的 (rude or impolite; having or showing a lack of respect for other people) Insolent behavior will not be tolerated. **拆分法** in-内心，so-很，lent-冷的，内心很冷的人，肯定很傲慢，无礼（insolent）。
indolent ['ɪndələnt]	*adj.* 懒惰的；懒散的 (not liking to work or be active) He is an indolent boy who had to be forced to help out with the chores. **拆分法** in-不，do-做，什么都不做的人当然是懒惰的（indolent）。
idle ['aɪdl]	*adj.* 无事可做的；闲散的 (not working, active, or being used) Over ten per cent of the workforce is now idle. **谐音法** i-爱，dle-斗，爱斗的人当然很闲散（idle）。
moral ['mɒrəl]	*adj.* 道德的 (relating to what is right and wrong in human behavior) Animals are not moral creatures and are not responsible for their actions. **谐音法** moral-猫肉，有道德的（moral）人是不吃猫肉的，因为猫咪很可爱！
Deft [deft]	*adj.* 熟练的；敏捷的 The photographer is known for her deft use of lighting. **谐音法** deft-大夫，大夫做手术都是熟练，敏捷的（deft）。

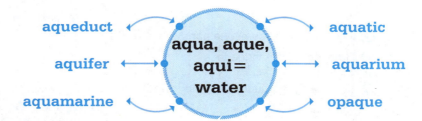

aqueduct ⟷ aquatic

aqua, aque, aqui = water

aquifer ⟷ aquarium

aquamarine ⟷ opaque

aquifer [ˈækwɪfə(r)]	*n.* 蓄水层 (a layer of rock or soil that can absorb and hold water) These key countries import or export crops irrigated from the world's most stressed aquifer systems.
aqueduct [ˈækwɪdʌkt]	*n.* 沟渠；导水管 (a pipe or channel designed to transport water from a remote source) A nationwide system of aqueducts was built to carry water to the arid parts of this country.
aquatic [əˈkwætɪk]	*adj.* 水生的；水上的 (living or growing in water) Seaweed also provides a key habitat for marine creatures, and the first link in the aquatic food chain.
opaque [əʊˈpeɪk]	*adj.* 难懂的；不透明的 (difficult to understand; not transmitting light) The opaque legal system often provides little or no explanation for why someone is detained or punished.
aquamarine [ˌækwəməˈriːn]	*n.* 海蓝宝石 (a transparent gem that is greenish-blue) Beads made of aquamarine can bring luck in love.
aquarium [əˈkweəriəm]	*n.* 水族馆 (a tank or pool or bowl filled with water for keeping live fish and underwater animals) The first time I saw seals was in an aquarium.

Unit 13

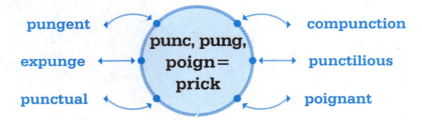

punch [pʌntʃ]	**v.** 用拳猛击 (to hit someone hard with one's fist) He punched me in the face.
pounce [paʊns]	**v.** 突袭；猛扑 (to suddenly jump toward and seize something with or as if with claws) He pounced on the photographer, beat him up and smashed his camera.
pungent ['pʌndʒənt]	**adj.** 辛辣的；刺激性的 (having a strong, sharp taste or smell) The more herbs you use, the more pungent the sauce will be. **adj.** 尖刻的 (having a strong effect on the mind because of being clever and direct) He enjoyed the play's shrewd and pungent social analysis.
expunge [ɪk'spʌndʒ]	**v.** 删除；清除 (to remove something completely) Time and the weather have expunged any evidence that a thriving community once existed here.
punctual ['pʌŋktʃuəl]	**adj.** 准时的；正点的 (arriving or doing something at the expected or planned time) I have to go now because I must be punctual for class.
punctilious [pʌŋk'tɪliəs]	**adj.** 循规蹈矩的 (very careful about behaving properly and doing things in a correct and accurate way) She's very punctilious about grammar.
punctuation [ˌpʌŋktʃu'eɪʃn]	**n.** 标点符号 (the act of adding punctuation marks to writing) He was known for his poor grammar and punctuation.
compunction [kəm'pʌŋkʃn]	**n.** 内疚；后悔 (anxiety arising from awareness of guilt) He feels no compunction about his crimes.
poignant ['pɔɪnjənt]	**adj.** 令人沉痛的；悲惨的；酸楚的 (having a strong effect on your feelings, especially in a way that makes you feel sad) The photograph was a poignant reminder of her childhood.

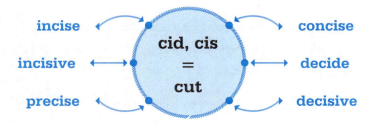

incise ← → concise

incisive ← → decide

cid, cis = cut

precise ← → decisive

---

decide

[dɪˈsaɪd]

v. 决定；决心 (to make a final choice or judgment about something)

❶ She is having difficulty deciding about the offer.

❷ Few hundred votes could decide the election.

---

decisive

[dɪˈsaɪsɪv]

adj. 坚定的 (firmly determined)

You must be decisive and persistent to succeed in this competitive field.

adj. 决定性的 (determining what the result of something will be)

The poverty of his childhood played a decisive role in his adult life.

---

suicide

[ˈsuːɪsaɪd]

n. 自杀 (the act of killing yourself because you do not want to continue living)

Authorities have officially ruled the death a suicide.

---

homicide

[ˈhɒmɪsaɪd]

n. 凶杀；杀人 (a killing of one human being by another)

The number of homicides increased last year.

---

insecticide

[ɪnˈsektɪsaɪd]

n. 杀虫剂 (a substance used for killing insects)

The world's most widely used insecticides would be banned from all fields across Europe.

---

patricide

[ˈpætrɪsaɪd]

n. 弑父 (when a father is killed by his child, it's called patricide)

Patricide is the worst crime a Roman can commit.

---

precise

[prɪˈsaɪs]

adj. 明确的；精确的 (clear and accurate)

The dating of very old materials has become more precise with new instruments.

---

precision

[prɪˈsɪʒn]

n. 精确；精密 (the quality or state of being precise)

I admire the precision of her work.

---

incise

[ɪnˈsaɪz]

v. 雕；刻 (to cut or carve into a surface)

The clay is incised to create a design.

incisive [ɪn'saɪsɪv]	*adj.* 尖锐的；深刻的 (very clear and direct; sharp) What viewers will actually find in both films is an incisive commentary on the current state of our country.
excise ['eksaɪz]	*v.* 切除；删去 (to remove by cutting; to cancel) One way filmmakers avoid alienating the audience is by excising any offending material.
concise [kən'saɪs]	*adj.* 简明的；简洁的 (consisting of few words that are carefully chosen) The explanation in this dictionary is concise and to the point.

Breast系列

breast [brest]	*n.* 乳房 (two soft parts on a woman's chest that produce milk when she has a baby) Cancer of the breast in young women is uncommon. *n.* 胸脯 (the front part of the body between the neck and the stomach) The president beat his breast and called that deal a mistake.
breed [briːd]	*v.* 饲养；哺育 (to produce young animals, birds, etc.) She believes that we are breeding a generation of children who know nothing about the history of their country. *v.* 滋生；导致 (to be the cause of something) Poverty breeds despair.
brood [bruːd]	*n.* 一家的孩子；一窝幼雏 (a group of young birds or children) ① She flew to the defence of her brood. ② Mrs. Smith took her brood to church every Sunday. *v.* 沉思 (to think a lot about something in an unhappy way) He brooded over his mistake.
embryo ['embrɪəʊ]	*n.* 胚胎 (a human or animal in the early stages of development before it is born) The mother provides the embryo with nourishment and a place to grow. *n.* 初期 (very early stages of development, but is expected to grow stronger) These developments were foreseen in embryo more than a decade age.

bracket ['brækɪt]	*n.* 括号 (one of a pair of marks)
	The prices in brackets are special rates for the under 18s.
	n. 支架 (pieces of metal, wood or plastic that are fastened to a wall in order to support something such as a shelf)
	The shelf is held up with two brackets.
embrace [ɪmˈbreɪs]	*v.* 拥抱 (to hold someone in your arms as a way of expressing love or friendship)
	At first people were sort of crying for joy and embracing each other.
	n. 拥抱 (the act of holding someone in your arms)
	He held her in a warm embrace.
	v. 欣然接受 (to accept something or someone readily or gladly)
	He embraces the new information age.
bracelet ['breɪslət]	*n.* 手镯 (a decorative band or chain usually worn on the wrist or arm)
	A gold bracelet dangled from her left wrist.

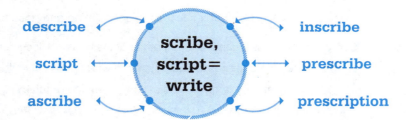

describe [dɪˈskraɪb]	*v.* 描写；描述 (to write or tell about something)
	① He described the house in perfect detail.
	② The witness wasn't able to describe the robber.
description [dɪˈskrɪpʃn]	*n.* 描述；形容 (a statement that tells you how something or someone looks, sounds)
	Reporters called the scene "a disaster area" and I think that was an accurate description.
script [skrɪpt]	*n.* 脚本；剧本 (the written form of a play or movie or the lines to be said by a performer)
	They stopped you as soon as you deviated from the script.
	v. 写剧本 (to write the script for a play, movie, television show, etc.)
	I scripted three episodes of the show.

inscribe [ɪnˈskraɪb]	*v.* 雕；刻 (to write or cut words, a name, etc. on something) They inscribed the monument with the soldiers' names.
inscription [ɪnˈskrɪpʃn]	*n.* 题词；献词 (words that are written on or cut into a surface) The painting had an inscription that read, "To my loving wife."
prescribe [prɪˈskraɪb]	*v.* 指定；规定 (to lay down a rule) We must follow the rules as prescribed by the government. *v.* 给……开药；开处方(to tell somebody to take a particular medicine or have a particular treatment; to write a prescription for a particular medicine, etc.) This drug should not be prescribed to children.
prescription [prɪˈskrɪpʃn]	*n.* 药方；处方 (a written message from a doctor that officially tells someone to use a medicine, therapy) The drug is only sold with a prescription.
ascribe [əˈskraɪb]	*v.* 把……归于 (to consider that something is caused by a particular thing or person) They ascribe most of their success to good timing and good luck.
subscribe [səbˈskraɪb]	*v.* 签署 (to write one's name underneath or at the end of a document) You'll receive a user name and password when you subscribe. *v.* 订阅 (to pay money to get a publication or service regularly) My main reason for subscribing to *New Scientist* is to keep abreast of advances in science.
transcribe [trænˈskraɪb]	*v.* 誊写；抄写 (to make a written copy of something) He transcribed all of his great-grandfather's letters.
circumscribe [ˈsɜːkəmskraɪb]	*v.* 约束；限制 (to limit or restrict somebody/something's freedom, rights, power, etc.) In the United States, nearly every action related to commercial aviation is circumscribed.
scribble [ˈskrɪbl]	*v.* 潦草地书写 (to write something quickly and in a way that makes it difficult to read) He scribbled down his phone number.

Unit 13

Bite系列

bite向bet转变，来自古代纵狗咬熊的游戏，人们把熊绑起来，作为诱饵（bait），鼓励和放纵多条恶狗去撕咬熊。后来演变为以bait（诱饵）怂恿某人去干坏事，abet（怂恿干坏事）也是来源于此。

bite [baɪt]	*v.* 咬 (to seize or cut into something with teeth) ① Some people bite their nails when they feel nervous. ② The patient had been bitten by a poisonous snake.
bait [beɪt]	*n.* 诱饵 (something that is used to attract fish or animals so they can be caught) Television programs are essentially bait to attract an audience for advertisements.
abet [əˈbet]	*v.* 教唆（犯罪）；煽动 (to help or encourage somebody to do something criminal or wrong) ① Their actions were shown to abet terrorism. ② His wife was sentenced to seven years imprisonment for aiding and abetting him.

Ush系列

rush [rʌʃ]	*v.* 猛冲；快速行进 (to do something very quickly or in a way that shows you are in a hurry) She rushed to close the window when she heard the rain.
blush [blʌʃ]	*v.* 脸红 (to become red in the face especially from shame, modesty or confusion) He blushed at the compliment.
gush [gʌʃ]	*v.* 喷涌；迸出 (to flow out very quickly and in large amounts) Water gushed from the fountain. *v.* 过分称赞；吹捧 (to speak in an extremely enthusiastic way) He gushed about his love for his wife.
flush [flʌʃ]	*v.* 奔流；冲刷 (to flow and spread suddenly and freely) She flushed the toilet and went back in the bedroom.

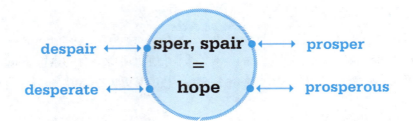

despair ← sper, spair → prosper
= hope
desperate ← → prosperous

prosper ['prɒspə]	*v.* 繁盛 (to become very active, healthy or strong) No crop can prosper in this heat. *v.* 成功；昌盛 (to become very successful usually by making a lot of money) He hopes his business will prosper.
prosperous ['prɒspərəs]	*adj.* 繁荣的；兴旺的 (having or showing success or financial good fortune) ① The company had a prosperous year. ② The place looks more prosperous than ever.
despair [dɪ'speə]	*n.* 绝望 (the feeling of no longer having any hope) A deep sense of despair overwhelmed him.
desperate ['despərət]	*adj.* 绝望的 (very sad and upset because of having little or no hope) The collapse of her business had made her desperate. *adj.* 急切的；极度渴望的 (showing great worry and loss of hope) They are in desperate need of financial assistance.

Spread系列

spread [spred]	*v.* 伸开；展开；蔓延 (to open or expand over a larger area) ① The newspaper was spread across his lap. ② The fire spread quickly through the building. *v.* (使) 传播 (to make something widely known) The use of computer technology has spread into all fields of work.
sprinkle ['sprɪŋkl]	*v.* 洒 (to spread small pieces or amounts of something over something) ① He sprinkled water on the plants. ② I sprinkled grass seed over the soil.

Unit 13

spray [spreɪ]	*v.* 喷；喷射 (to scatter or let something fall in a fine mist) ❶ She sprayed some perfume into the air. ❷ He sprayed the paint evenly over the surface.
sprawl [sprɔːl]	*v.* 伸开四肢坐 (to lie or sit with your arms and legs spread wide apart) The kids sprawled on the floor to watch TV. *v.* 杂乱无序地拓展 (to spread out unevenly) The city sprawls along the coastline.
disperse [dɪ'spɜːs]	*v.* (使) 分散；散开；驱散 (to move apart and go away in different directions; to make somebody/something to do this) ❶ The clouds dispersed. ❷ Police fired shots and used teargas to disperse the demonstrators.
sparse [spɑːs]	*adj.* 稀疏的；稀少的 (not thickly grown or settled) Many slopes are rock fields with sparse vegetation.
sprout [spraʊt]	*v.* 发芽；抽芽 (to grow, spring up or come forth) Potatoes will sprout in the bag if kept in a warm place. *v.* 迅猛发展 (to appear suddenly and in large numbers) More than a million satellite dishes have sprouted across the country.

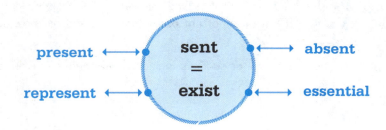

present ['preznt] *adj.* [prɪ'zent] *vt.*	*adj.* 出席的 (being in a particular place) All students are present. *v.* 提交 (to give something to someone in a formal way) The scientist presented his results to the committee. *adj.* 当前的 (relating to time that is not past or future) The minsters agreed that sanctions should remain in place for the present.
presentation [ˌprezn'teɪʃn]	*n.* 陈述；报告 (a formal talk, often in order to sell something or get support for a proposal) She will take your questions after she has made her presentation.

presence ['prezns]	*n.* 出席；存在 (someone or something that is seen or noticed in a particular place, area) The child is shy in the presence of strangers.
absent ['æbsənt]	*adj.* 缺席的 (not present) He has been absent from his desk for two weeks. *v.* 使离开 (to keep oneself away) He absented himself from the meeting.
absence ['æbsəns]	*n.* 缺席；缺勤 (a failure to be present at a usual or expected place) She returned to the company after a long absence. *n.* 不存在；缺乏 (the fact of somebody/something not existing or not being available; a lack of something) The products showed a remarkable absence of defects.
represent [,reprɪ'zent]	*v.* 代表 (to act or speak officially for someone or something) We elect men and women to represent us in Congress.
senator ['senətə]	*n.* 参议员 (a member of a senate) Senator Charles Schumer called on Facebook to change its privacy policy.
essential [ɪ'senʃl]	*adj.* 极其重要的；必不可少的 (extremely important or necessary) ❶ As a fighter pilot, he knows that good vision is essential. ❷ The essential problem with this plan is that it will cost too much. *n.* 要点；要素 (an important basic fact or piece of knowledge about a subject) The essentials for success include a willingness to work and the right attitude.
essence ['esns]	*n.* 本质；实质 (the most significant element, quality or aspect of a thing or person) The essence of love is unselfishness.

追根溯源

罗马神话中的花神叫做芙罗拉（Flora），相当于希腊神话中的克罗丽丝（Cloris）。她是女性祥和、青春、健康、性感和美好的代名词，世上对她女性之美的赞颂一直可以追溯到《荷马史诗》里。早在古罗马时花神就受到萨宾人的崇拜。后来意大利人把每年的4月28日至5月3日定为"花神节"。节日期间会举行非常放纵的竞技会，人们常用玫瑰花来装饰自己和动物。花神这个形象也一直以年轻美女手持花束的姿态出现。

据说，西风神泽费罗斯爱上了花神，在她身后紧追不舍。花神拼命奔跑，但最终没能逃脱，被西风神揽入怀中，从她口中溢出美丽的鲜花在大地上盛放。花神最后嫁给了西风神。结婚以后，西风神送给花神一座满是奇花异草的园子。春天到来的时候，花神和西风神亲密地手挽着手在园子里漫步，他们一路上走过的地方百花齐放，代表着春天的到来。

| floral | *adj.* 花的；花似的 (of or relating to flowers) |
| ['flɔːrəl] | The wine has a floral aroma. |

florid	*adj.* 红润的 (having a red or reddish color)
['flɒrɪd]	Tears were flowing over his florid face.
	adj. 过分装饰的；过多修饰的 (having too much decoration or detail)
	He gave a florid speech in honor of the queen's visit.

| flora | *n.* 植物群 (all the plants that live in a particular area, time, period or environment) |
| ['flɔːrə] | The variety of food crops and flora now exists in Dominica. |

flourish	*v.* 茁壮成长；健康幸福 (to grow well; to be healthy and happy)
['flʌrɪʃ]	Plants flourish in this rich soil.
	v. 繁荣；兴盛 (to develop quickly and be successful or common)
	Regional markets have flourished in recent years.

| flour | *n.* 面粉 (powder made from a grain especially wheat) |
| ['flaʊə] | They mill 1,000 tons of flour a day in every Australian state. |

Unit 13

锦囊妙记

hideous	*adj.* 极其丑陋的；可怕的 (very ugly or disgusting)
['hɪdiəs]	She saw a hideous face at the window and screamed.
	联想法 联想hide，把面孔遮住 (hide)的人是极其丑陋的 (hideous)。

stark	*adj.* 光秃秃的；荒凉的 (having few or no ornaments)
[stɑːk]	We were shocked by the stark, rocky landscape.
	adj. 赤裸裸的；真实而无法回避的 (real and impossible to avoid)
	She faced the stark reality of poverty.
	联想法 联想到star，星星的表面都是光秃秃的(stark)。

starch

[stɑːtʃ]

n. 淀粉 (a substance that is found in certain foods, such as bread, rice, and potatoes)

She reorganized her eating so that she was taking more fruit and vegetables and less starch, salt and fat.

v. 浆洗，使……变僵硬 (to make clothes, sheets, etc. stiff using starch)

He starches the collars of his shirts.

拆分法 star-start（开始），ch-吃，吃的是什么？都是淀粉(starch)。

mendacity

[men'dæsəti]

n. 虚伪，谎言 (lack of honesty)

Politicians are often accused of mendacity.

拆分法 men-男人，da-的，city-城市，男人的城市充满了虚伪与谎言(mendacity)。

mendacious

[men'deɪʃəs]

adj. 虚伪的 (not honest; likely to tell lies)

The newspaper story was mendacious and hurtful.

Unit 13

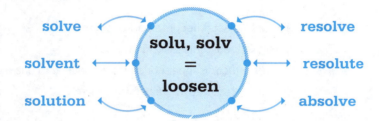

solve [sɒlv]	*v.* 解决 (to find a way to deal with and end a problem) I dreamed up a plan to solve both problems at once.
solution [sə'luːʃn]	*n.* 解决方案 (an answer to a problem) Although he has sought to find a peaceful solution, he is facing pressure to use greater military force.
solvent ['sɒlvənt]	*adj.* 有溶解能力的 (able to dissolve another substance,or be dissolved in another substance) Gasoline is a solvent liquid which removes grease spots. *adj.* 有清还债务能力的 (able to pay debts) He couldn't stay solvent after losing his business.
insolvent [ɪn'sɒlvənt]	*adj.* 无力偿付债务的 (not having enough money to pay debts) The bank was declared insolvent.
resolve [rɪ'zɒlv]	*v.* 解决 (to find an answer or solution to something) The brothers finally resolved their conflict. *v.* 决定；下定决心 (to make a definite and serious decision to do something) He resolved not to tell her the truth. *n.* 决心 (a strong determination to do something) His comments were intended to weaken her resolve but they only served to strengthen it.
resolution [ˌrezə'luːʃn]	*n.* 决议 (an opinion or decision formally expressed by a group of people) The meeting passed a resolution in favour of allowing women to join the society.

Unit 14

resolute ['rezəlu:t]	*adj.* 坚决的 (very determined) He described the situation as very dangerous and called for resolute action.
irresolute [ɪ'rezəlu:t]	*adj.* 犹豫不定的；无决断的 (not certain about what to do) We lay still a long time, very irresolute what course to take.
dissolve [dɪ'zɒlv]	*v.* 使溶解 (to make a solid become part of a liquid) The treatment is used to dissolve kidney stones. *v.* 消失；瓦解 (to end or disappear or cause something to end or disappear) Hopes for peace dissolved in renewed violence.
absolute ['æbsəlu:t]	*adj.* 绝对的；完全的 (total and complete) You can't predict the future with absolute certainty. *adj.* 专制的；独裁的 (having unlimited power) The country is ruled by an absolute dictator.
absolve [əb'zɒlv]	*v.* 免除责任；赦免罪行 (to make somebody free from guilt or responsibility) A police investigation yesterday absolved the police of all blame in the incident.

Sal系列

salmon ['sæmən]	*n.* 鲑鱼 (a large fish that is born in streams but that lives most of its life in the ocean and that is commonly used for food) Poachers have been netting salmon to supply the black market.
assault [ə'sɔ:lt]	*v.* 袭击 (to violently attack someone or something) **1** He was arrested for assaulting a police officer. **2** Enemy forces assaulted the city. *n.* 袭击 (a violent physical attack) She was injured in a brutal assault.
insult [ɪn'sʌlt] *vt.* ['ɪnsʌlt] *n.*	*v.* 侮辱；凌辱 (to do or say something that shows a lack of respect for someone) We were greatly insulted by his rudeness. *n.* 侮辱；凌辱 (a rude or offensive act or statement) The fans hurled insults at the referee as he walked off the field after the game.

desultory

['desəltri]

adj. 漫无目的的；无条理的；随意的 (marked by lack of definite plan, regularity, or purpose)

① They made a desultory discussion about the news of the day.

② He read the book in a desultory manner, skipping chapters as he pleased.

该词来自古罗马的骑术表演。骑师在表演时常常同时骑两匹以上的马，从一匹马跳跃至另一匹马，此类骑师在拉丁语中被称为dêsultor，即leaper（跳跃者），单词desultory就源于此，表示"随意的；无条理的"。

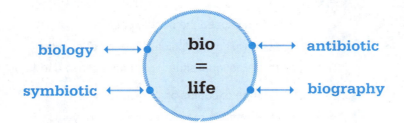

biology	*n.* 生物学 (a science that deals with things that are alive such as plants and animals)
[baɪ'ɒlədʒi]	The biology of these diseases is terribly complicated.
symbiotic	*adj.* 共生的 (used to describe a relationship between two different living creatures that live close together and depend on each other in particular ways, each getting particular benefits from the other)
[ˌsɪmbaɪ'ɒtɪk]	Fungi have a symbiotic relationship with the trees of these northwestern forests.
symbiosis	*n.* 共生关系 (the relationship between two different kinds of living things that live together and depend on each other)
[ˌsɪmbaɪ'əʊsɪs]	The bird lives in symbiosis with the hippopotamus.
antibiotic	*n.* 抗生素 (a drug that is used to kill harmful bacteria and to cure infections)
[ˌæntibaɪ'ɒtɪk]	The doctor put her on antibiotics.
biography	*n.* 传记 (the story of a real person's life written by someone other than that person)
[baɪ'ɒgrəfi]	A new biography of Abraham Lincoln was published.

Turb系列

disturb [dɪ'stɜːb]	*v.* 打扰；妨碍 (to worry or upset someone) She doesn't want to be disturbed while she's working.
disturbing [dɪ'stɜːbɪŋ]	*adj.* 烦扰的；令人不安的 (making you feel worried or upset) There are disturbing reports of killings at the two centres.
perturb [pə'tɜːb]	*v.* 使 (某人) 烦恼 (to cause someone to be worried or upset) Canadian and Mexican officials were initially perturbed by Trump's threats.
turbulent ['tɜːbjələnt]	*adj.* 湍急的；汹涌的 (moving in an irregular or violent way) Turbulent waters caused the boat to capsize. *adj.* 骚乱的；混乱的 (full of confusion, violence or disorder) The present international situation remains tense and turbulent.
turmoil ['tɜːmɔɪl]	*n.* 混乱；动荡 (a state of confusion or disorder) ① The country has been in turmoil for the past 10 year. ② Her marriage was in turmoil.

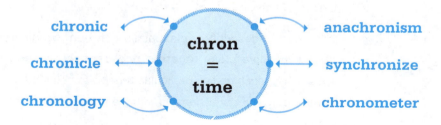

chronic ['krɒnɪk]	*adj.* 慢性的；长期的 (happening or existing frequently or most of the time) 10,000 deaths a year from chronic lung disease are attributable to smoking.
chronicle ['krɒnɪkl]	*n.* 编年史；年代记 (a description of events in the order that they happened) Her latest novel is a chronicle of life in a Devon village. *v.* 按时间顺序记录 (to describe a series of events in the order that they happened) The book chronicles the events that led to the American Civil War.

chronology [krə'nɒlədʒi]	*n.* 按事件发生的年代排列的顺序；年表 (the order in which a series of events happened; a list of these events in order) Historians seem to have confused the chronology of these events.
chronological [ˌkrɒnə'lɒdʒɪkl]	*adj.* 按时间顺序的 (arranged in the order that things happened or came to be) His art is displayed in roughly chronological order.
anachronism [ə'nækrənɪzəm]	*n.* 时代错误 (something that is mistakenly placed in a time where it does not belong in a story, movie, etc.) There are the truly strange anachronisms throughout the movie.
synchronize ['sɪŋkrənaɪz]	*v.* 使同步 (to happen at the same time) The sound and picture have to synchronize perfectly.
chronometer [krə'nɒmɪtə]	*n.* 精密计时器 (an accurate clock especially used in navigation) This would require having an infinitely precise chronometer at hand.

Labor系列

labor ['leɪbə]	*n.* 劳动 (physical or mental effort) Getting the job done will require many hours of difficult labor.
laboratory [lə'bɒrətri]	*n.* 实验室 (a room or building in which scientific experiments and tests are done) This was demonstrated in a laboratory experiment with rats.
laborious [lə'bɔːriəs]	*adj.* 费力的 (requiring much effort) Rebuilding was a slow and laborious task. *adj.* 勤劳的 (devoted to labor) The volunteers have been commendably laborious in their clean-up of the beach.
collaborate [kə'læbəreɪt]	*v.* 合作；协作 (to work with another person or group in order to achieve or do something) The two companies agreed to collaborate. *v.* 勾结；通敌 (to give help to an enemy who has invaded your country during a war) He was suspected of collaborating with the occupying army.

Unit 14

elaborate

[ɪˈlæbərət]

adj. 复杂的；精心制作的 (made or done with great care or with much detail)

1 The dancers were wearing elaborate costumes.

2 They made elaborate preparations for his visit.

v. 详细说明 (to give more details about something)

She was asked to say more about her earlier statements, but she declined to elaborate.

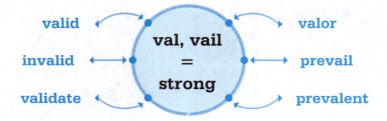

valor

[ˈvælə]

n. 勇猛 (courage or bravery)

The soldiers received the nation's highest award for valor.

valid

[ˈvælɪd]

adj. 正当的；合理的 (fair or reasonable)

She had a valid excuse for missing practice.

adj. 有法律效力的 (having legal force or effect)

The agreement is no longer valid under international law.

invalid

[ɪnˈvælɪd]

adj. 无效的 (having no force or effect)

The trial was stopped and the results declared invalid.

adj. 病人 (one who is sickly or disabled)

Her husband has become an invalid.

validate

[ˈvælɪdeɪt]

v. 使合法化 (to have legal force or effect)

The court validated the contract.

v. 证实 (to prove to be true, worthy or justified)

The decline in sales validated our concerns.

prevail

[prɪˈveɪl]

v. 获胜；占优势 (to defeat an opponent especially in a long or difficult contest)

1 Good will prevail over evil.

2 I do hope he will prevail over the rebels.

v. 流行；盛行 (to be or become usual, common or widespread)

| 1 | This mistaken belief still prevails in some parts of the country. |
| 2 | West winds prevail in that region. |

prevalent

['prevələnt]

adj. 流行的；盛行的 (generally or widely accepted, practiced or favored)

1 Those teaching methods are still prevalent at some school.

2 Smoking is becoming increasingly prevalent among younger women.

Red系列

ruby

['ruːbi]

n. 红宝石 (a deep red stone that is used in jewelry)

She is wearing a small ruby earring.

robust

[rəʊ'bʌst]

adj. 强健的 (strong and healthy)

She was almost 90, but still very robust.

adj. 坚定的 (strongly held and forcefully expressed)

A British Foreign Office minister has made a robust defence of the agreement.

corroborate

[kə'rɒbəreɪt]

v. 证实；支持 (to support with evidence)

The witnesses corroborated the policeman's testimony.

Scissor系列

scissors

['sɪzəz]

n. 剪刀 (a cutting instrument having two blades whose cutting edges slide past each other)

She picked up a pair of scissors from the windowsill.

scalpel

['skælpəl]

n. 外科手术刀 (a small knife with a thin, sharp blade that is used in surgery)

A scalpel and tweezers are the only tools needed.

sculpture

['skʌlptʃə]

n. 雕刻；雕塑 (a piece of art that is made by carving or molding clay, stone or metal)

He studied sculpture because he enjoyed working with clay.

v. 雕刻 (to make a work of art by shaping as stone, wood or metal)

The artist used a hammer and chisel to sculpture the horse out of ice.

Unit 14

scarce [skeəs]	*adj.* 缺乏的；罕见的 (very small in amount or number) Food was scarce during the war.
sculptor ['skʌlptə]	*n.* 雕刻家；雕塑家 (a person who makes sculptures) The sculptor rounded the clay into a sphere.
scarcity ['skeəsəti]	*n.* 不足；缺乏 (a very small supply) Scarcity of food forced the herds to move.
scar [skɑ:(r)]	*n.* 伤痕；伤疤 (a mark left on the skin after a wound heals) Her face was disfigured by a long red scar. *v.* 留下伤疤 (to mark with a scar) His arm was badly scarred after the accident.
carve [kɑ:v]	*v.* 切开；雕刻 (to cut with care or precision) ① We carved an ice sculpture. ② He carves his figures from white pine.

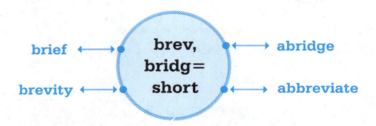

brief [bri:f]	*adj.* 短时间的；短暂的 (lasting only a short period of time) The meeting will be brief. *v.* 向……介绍基本情况 (to give somebody information or instructions about something) The President has been briefed by his advisers.
brevity ['brevəti]	*n.* 简练；简洁 (the use of few words to say something) The report is a masterpiece of brevity.
abbreviate [ə'bri:vieɪt]	*v.* 使简短；缩简 (to make a word, phrase or name shorter) He abbreviated his first name to Alec.
abridge [ə'brɪdʒ]	*v.* 减少；缩短 (to diminish or reduce something) ① The library's hours have been drastically abridged to cut costs. ② The new law might abridge our freedom of expression.

Claw系列

claw [klɔː]	*n.* 爪 (a sharp curved part on the toe of an animal) The eagle was carrying a mouse in its sharp claws. *v.* (用爪子或手指甲) 抓，撕 (to scratch, dig or pull with or as if with claws) She tried to claw his face with her fingernails.
clasp [klɑːsp]	*v.* 紧紧抓住 (to hold someone or something tightly with your hands or arms) She clasped her son in her arms. *v.* 扣住 (to fasten with or as if with a clasp) He clasped the keys to his belt. *n.* 扣钩；扣环 (a device for holding together objects or parts of something) Be careful that your clasp on the cat isn't too tight, or she could get hurt.
clutch [klʌtʃ]	*v.* 抓紧；紧握 (to hold onto someone or something tightly with your hand) **1** The child clutched her mother's hand firmly. **2** I had to clutch the counter to keep from falling.
clench [klentʃ]	*v.* 紧握；抓紧 (to hold something tightly) She had a gun clenched tightly in her hand.

Gra系列

grasp [grɑːsp]	*v.* 抓住 (to take and hold something with your hands) I grasped the end of the rope and pulled as hard as I could. *v.* 理解 (to understand something that is complicated or difficult) The Government has not yet grasped the seriousness of the crisis. *n.* 理解 (an understanding of something) The books on the top shelf are just beyond my grasp.
grab [græb]	*v.* 抓住；抓取 (to quickly take and hold someone or something with your hand) The little boy grabbed onto his mother's leg and wouldn't let go. *v.* 吸引……注意力 (to get the attention or interest of someone or something) I jumped on the wall to grab the attention.
grapple ['græpl]	*v.* 抓住；与……搏斗 (to hold and fight with another person) Passers-by grappled with the man after the attack. *v.* 努力解决问题 (to try hard to find a solution to a problem)

Unit 14

The economy is just one of several critical problems the country is grappling with.

grip [grɪp]	*v.* 握紧；抓牢 (to seize or hold something firmly) I gripped the door handle and pulled as hard as I could. *v.* 吸引住 (to get and hold the interest or attention of someone) ① The story really grips the reader. ② The scandal has gripped the nation.
grope [grəʊp]	*v.* 触摸；试探着前进 (to move along by feeling with the hands) We groped along the dark passage.

追根溯源

在罗马神话中，Mercury是众神的信使，也是旅行者、商人和盗贼的保护神，他以善辩、狡诈、行走快速著称。为了纪念这位众神中行走最快的神，古罗马人将绕太阳转动速度最快的行星即水星命名为Mercury。古代占星家认为命属水星宫的人，也像Mercury一样，生性反复无常，但却能言善辩、精明机智，所以mercurial 也被用来表示"多变的；机智的"。因Mercury也是商人的保护神，因此跟商业相关的词也来自他，例如，commerce（商业），commercial（商业的）。商人重利，因而延伸出mercenary（唯利是图的）一词。

Mercury ['mɜːkjəri]	*n.* 水星 (the planet that is closest to the sun) In the summer, the Mercury can reach over 100 degrees Fahrenheit.
mercurial [mɜːˈkjʊəriəl]	*adj.* (指人) 反复无常的 (changing moods quickly and often) The boss's mood is so mercurial that we never know how he's going to react to anything.
commerce ['kɒmɜːs]	*n.* 商业；贸易 (activities that relate to the buying and selling of goods and services) During the war, they laid an embargo on commerce with enemy countries.
commercial [kəˈmɜːʃl]	*adj.* 商业的；贸易的 (used in the buying and selling of goods and services) British Rail has indeed become more commercial over the past decade. *n.* 广告 (an advertisement on radio or television) The average American sees and hears thousands of commercial messages each day.

Unit 14

merchant [ˈmɜːtʃənt]	*n.* 商人；批发商 (someone who buys and sells goods especially in large amounts) Merchants traveled hundreds of miles to trade in the city.
merchandise [ˈmɜːtʃəndaɪs]	*n.* 商品；货物 (goods that are bought and sold) Merchandise can now circulate freely among the EU countries.
mercenary [ˈmɜːsənəri]	*adj.* 唯利是图的 (caring only about making money) His motives in choosing a career were purely mercenary. *n.* 雇佣兵 (a soldier who is paid by a foreign country to fight in its army) This was an army of foreign mercenaries.

锦囊妙记

felony [ˈfeləni]	*n.* 重罪 (a very serious crime) The crime is considered a felony under state law. 谐音法 felony-废了你！废了你当然要犯重罪(felony)！
attack [əˈtæk]	*v.* 攻击；进攻 (to act violently against someone or something) ① Troops attacked the fortress at dawn. ② The professor has been widely attacked for her position on the issue. 谐音法 a——，ttack-坦克，一辆坦克进行攻击(attack)。
weird [wɪəd]	*adj.* 怪诞的；奇异的 (unusual or strange) I had such a weird dream last night. 拆分法 we-我们，ird-bird（鸟），我们成了鸟人，很怪异(weird)！
drain [dreɪn]	*v.* 排水 (to remove liquid from something by letting it flow away or out) The river drains into a lake. *v.* 流干；排干 (to slowly make or become dry or empty) ① The swamp has been drained. ② Years of civil war have drained the country's resources. 拆分法 d-大，rain-雨，下大雨要排水(drain)。
denigrate [ˈdenɪɡreɪt]	*v.* 诋毁；贬低 (to make something seem less important or valuable) No one is trying to denigrate the importance of a good education. We all know that it is crucial for success. 联想法 de-down，nigr-nigger（黑鬼）：白人骂黑人是黑鬼，这当然是贬低(denigrate)和蔑称。

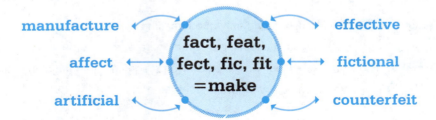

manufacture	fact, feat, fect, fic, fit =make	effective
affect		fictional
artificial		counterfeit

affect

[ə'fekt]

v. 影响 (to have an effect on somebody/something)

More than seven million people have been affected by drought.

v. 假装 (to pretend that a false behavior or feeling is natural or genuine)

She affected surprise upon hearing the news.

effect

[ɪ'fekt]

n. 影响；效果 (a change that results when something is done or happens)

Computers have had a profound effect on our lives.

infect

[ɪn'fekt]

v. 感染；传染 (to cause someone or something to become sick or affected by disease)

The virus has infected many people.

v. 使感染（某种感情）；影响 (to make somebody share a particular feeling)

Her enthusiasm infects the other players.

infectious

[ɪn'fekʃəs]

adj. 传染的；有传染性的 (passing from one to another in the form of a germ)

Infectious diseases are spreading among many of the flood victims.

effective

[ɪ'fektɪv]

adj. 有效的；起作用的 (producing a result that is wanted)

The project looks at how we could be more effective in encouraging students to enter teacher training.

adj. 生效的 (starting at a particular time)

The new rules will become effective immediately.

efficient

[ɪ'fɪʃnt]

adj. 有效率的 (capable of producing desired results without wasting materials, time or energy)

As we get older, our bodies become less efficient at burning up calories.

efficiency

[ɪˈfɪʃnsi]

n. 效率 (the ability to do something or produce something without wasting materials, time or energy)

1 Because of her efficiency, we got all the work done in a few hours.

2 The company is trying to lower costs and improve efficiency.

artificial

[ˌɑːtɪˈfɪʃl]

adj. 人造的；人工的 (not natural or real)

This product contains no artificial colors, natural substances are used.

proficient

[prəˈfɪʃnt]

adj. 精通的；熟练的 (very good at doing something)

1 He has become very proficient at computer programming.

2 She is proficient in two foreign languages.

benefit

[ˈbenɪfɪt]

n. 利益；好处 (a good or helpful result or effect)

There are many financial benefits to owning your own home.

v. 对……有益 (to be useful or profitable to somebody)

Some critics say that the tax cuts only benefit wealthy people.

beneficial

[ˌbenɪˈfɪʃl]

adj. 有利的；有益的 (producing good or helpful results or effects)

1 Some insects are harmful but others are beneficial.

2 He hopes the new drug will prove beneficial to many people.

benefactor

[ˈbenɪfæktə(r)]

n. 捐助者；赞助人 (someone who helps another especially by giving money)

With the help of a rich benefactor he set up a charity.

beneficiary

[ˌbenɪˈfɪʃəri]

n. 受益人 (someone or something that benefits from something)

Her husband was the chief beneficiary of her will.

manufacture

[ˌmænjuˈfæktʃə(r)]

v. 制造；生产 (to make into a product suitable for use)

The company manufactures wool and cotton clothing.

v. 捏造 (to invent a story, an excuse, etc. by using your imagination often in order to trick)

According to the prosecution, the officers manufactured an elaborate story.

n. 生产；制造 (the process of making products especially with machines in factories)

We're developing new methods of paper manufacture.

perfect

[ˈpɜːfɪkt]

adj. 完美的 (having no mistakes or flaws)

The church is a perfect example of medieval architecture.

defect ['di:fekt]	*n.* 瑕疵；毛病 (something that makes a thing imperfect) ① A slight defect lowered the diamond's value. ② Vanity and pride were his two worst character defects.
deficit ['defɪsɪt]	*n.* 不足额；赤字 (an amount of money that is less than the amount that is needed) The government is facing a deficit of $3 billion.
deficient [dɪ'fɪʃnt]	*adj.* 不足的；缺乏的 (not having enough of something that is important or necessary) Their food is deficient in vitamins. *adj.* 有缺陷的 (not good enough) Several bridges in the city are structurally deficient.
sufficient [sə'fɪʃnt]	*adj.* 足够的；充足的 (having or providing as much as is needed) ① There must be sufficient funds in your bank account to cover the check. ② Her explanation was not sufficient to satisfy the police.
insufficient [ˌɪnsə'fɪʃnt]	*adj.* 不足的；不够的 (not having or providing enough of what is needed) He decided there was insufficient evidence to justify criminal proceedings.
suffice [sə'faɪs]	*v.* 足够；充足 (to be or provide as much as is needed) ① No, you don't need to write a letter. A phone call will suffice. ② Suffice it to say that afterwards we never met again.
fiction ['fɪkʃn]	*n.* 小说；虚构的文学作品 (literary works invented by the imagination, such as novels or short stories) I prefer reading fiction to hearing about real events.
fictional ['fɪkʃənl]	*adj.* 虚构的 (not real or based on fact) The events in the horror movie seemed so real to some fans that they could not believe that the whole thing was fictional.
facilitate [fə'sɪlɪteɪt]	*v.* 促进；助长 (to make something easier) ① Cutting taxes may facilitate economic recovery. ② Her rise to power was facilitated by her influential friends.
facility [fə'sɪləti]	*n.* 设备 (something such as a building or large piece of equipment that is built for a specific purpose) Our hotel room had cooking facilities.

magnificent [mæg'nɪfɪsnt]	*adj.* 壮丽的；伟大的 (very beautiful or impressive)
	① He gave a magnificent performance.
	② We were impressed by the magnificent cathedrals of Europe.

magnify [mæg'nɪfɪsnt]	*v.* 放大 (to make something greater)
	The lens magnified the image 100 times.
	v. 加强；加剧 (to make something seem greater or more important than it is)
	I don't want to magnify the importance of these problems.

| **feat** [fiːt] | *n.* 功绩；伟业 (achievement that shows courage, strength or skill) |
| | A racing car is an extraordinary feat of engineering. |

| **defeat** [dɪ'fiːt] | *v.* 击败；战胜 (to win a victory over someone or something in a war, contest, game) |
| | We must be ready to defeat our enemies in battle. |

counterfeit ['kaʊntəfɪt]	*v.* 仿制；伪造 (to imitate or copy something especially in order to deceive)
	Modern money is difficult to counterfeit.
	adj. 仿造的；伪造的 (not genuine)
	The concert ticket is counterfeit.

| **feasible** ['fiːzəbl] | *adj.* 可行的 (possible to do or accomplish) |
| | This committee selected the plan that seemed most feasible. |

Behind系列

| **hind** [haɪnd] | *adj.* (动物的腿) 后面的 (the hind legs or feet of an animal with four legs are those at the back) |
| | Suddenly the cow kicked up its hind legs. |

hinder ['hɪndə(r)]	*v.* 阻碍；妨碍 (to make it difficult for somebody to do something or for something to happen)
	① Snow and high winds hindered our progress.
	② The country's economic growth is being hindered by the sanctions.

Trick系列

trick [trɪk]	**n.** 戏法；把戏 (an action that is meant to deceive someone) It was a trick to persuade her to give him money. **v.** 哄骗 (to deceive somebody with tricks) He tricked her by wearing a disguise.
betray [bɪ'treɪ]	**v.** 背叛 (to give information about a person, group, country, etc. to an enemy) They betrayed their country by selling its secrets to other governments.
treason ['triːzn]	**n.** 叛国（罪）；不忠 (the crime of betraying your country) Treason in this country is still punishable by death.
traitor ['treɪtə(r)]	**n.** 卖国贼；叛徒 (a person who is not loyal to his or her own country, friends) He was a traitor who betrayed his country by selling military secrets to the enemy.
treacherous ['tretʃərəs]	**adj.** 骗人的；不忠的 (not able to be trusted) He publicly left the party and denounced its treacherous leaders.
artifact ['ɑːtɪfækt]	**n.** 人工制品；手工艺品 (an object that is made by a person, especially something of historical or cultural interest) The caves contained many prehistoric artifacts.
artisan [ˌɑːtɪ'zæn]	**n.** 技工；工匠 (someone whose job requires skill with their hands) They sell rugs made by local artisans.
artistry ['ɑːtɪstri]	**n.** 艺术才能 (artistic ability or skill) We admired the singer's artistry.
artifice ['ɑːtɪfɪs]	**n.** 诡计 (dishonest or insincere behavior or speech that is meant to deceive someone) The whole story was just an artifice to win our sympathy.
artless ['ɑːtləs]	**adj.** 单纯的；自然的 (not false or artificial) Her simple artless charm won us over instantly.
artful ['ɑːtfl]	**adj.** 巧妙的 (performed with or showing art or skill) That kitchen gadget is an artful tool for extracting cherry pits. **adj.** 狡猾的；有手段的 (clever at taking advantage) The artful lawyer got the witness to admit he had been lying.

Unit 15

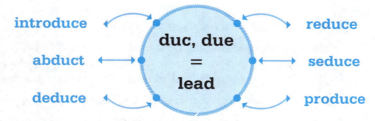

introduce [ˌɪntrəˈdjuːs]	*v.* 介绍 (to make someone known to someone else by name) Let me introduce myself, my name is John Smith. *v.* 引进 (to cause something to begin to be used for the first time) New computers have been introduced into the office. *v.* 提出 (to bring forward for discussion or consideration) He introduced several issues during the meeting.
introduction [ˌɪntrəˈdʌkʃn]	*n.* 介绍；引言 (the part of a book that leads up to and explains what will be found in the main part) In her introduction to the book she provides a summary of the ideas. *n.* 引进 (the action of bringing into use, making available) The plant is a new introduction to the garden.
reduce [rɪˈdjuːs]	*v.* 减少；缩小 (to make something smaller in size, amount or number) 1 The medicine reduces the risk of infection. 2 Her prison sentence was reduced from 15 years to 10 years.
reduction [rɪˈdʌkʃn]	*n.* 减少；降低 (the act of making something smaller or less) 1 Many companies have announced dramatic reductions in staff. 2 Many voters want to see some reduction of the deficit.
produce [prəˈdjuːs]	*v.* 生产 (to make something especially by using machines) Thousands of cars are produced here each year.
product [ˈprɒdʌkt]	*n.* 产品；结果 (something that is made or grown to be sold or used) 1 The company's newest product is selling well. 2 This book is the product of many years of hard work.
productive [prəˈdʌktɪv]	*adj.* 富有成效的；多产的 (producing or able to produce something especially in large amounts) 1 Some staff members are more productive than others. 2 I had a very productive day.

abduct

[æb'dʌkt]

v. 劫持；诱拐 (to lead a person away by force)

She was charged with abducting a six-month-old child.

conduct

[kən'dʌkt]*vt.*

['kɒndʌkt]*n.*

v. 引导；带领 (to guide or lead someone through or around a place)

Our guide slowly conducted us through the museum.

v. 组织；执行 (to plan and put into operation from a position of command)

The police are conducting an investigation into last week's robbery.

n. 行为；举止 (the way that a person behaves in a particular place or situation)

He has trouble understanding that other people judge him by his conduct.

conductor

[kən'dʌktə(r)]

n. 导体 (a material or object that permits an electric current to flow easily)

Metal is a good conductor of electricity.

n. 乐队指挥 (a person who stands in front of an orchestra, a group of singer etc., and directs their performance, especially somebody who does this as a profession)

She is the conductor of our school orchestra.

induce

[ɪn'djuːs]

v. 引诱；引起 (to cause someone or something to do something)

1 The advertisement is meant to induce people to eat more fruit.

2 Her illness was induced by overwork.

seduce

[sɪ'djuːs]

v. 诱惑；勾引 (to persuade someone to do something and especially to do something wrong)

1 She was seduced into crime.

2 The other team seduced him with a better offer.

deduce

[dɪ'djuːs]

v. 推论；推断 (to figure out something by using reason or logic)

1 From the height of the sun I deduced that it was about ten o'clock.

2 What can we deduce from the evidence?

subdue

[səb'djuː]

v. 征服；控制 (to get control of a violent or dangerous person or group by using force)

The troops were finally able to subdue the rebel forces after many days of fighting.

v. 抑制；压抑 (to get control of something, such as a strong emotion)

She struggled to subdue her fears.

Light系列

lightning
['laɪtnɪŋ]

n. 闪电；雷电 (the flashes of light that are produced in the sky during a storm)
One man died when he was struck by lightning.

adj. 闪电般的；迅速的 (moving or done very quickly)
Driving today demands lightning reflexes.

enlighten
[ɪn'laɪtn]

v. 启发；启蒙 (to give knowledge or understanding to someone)
The lecturer at the planetarium enlightened us about the latest astronomical discoveries.

highlight
['haɪlaɪt]

v. 使突出；强调 (to make or try to make people notice or be aware of someone or something)
The report highlights the major problems facing society today.

v. 将（文本的某部分）用彩笔做标记 (to mark part of a text with a special colored pen)
The students highlighted important vocabulary words in their textbooks.

v. 为……中最突出的事物 (to be a very interesting, exciting or important part of something)
Our trip was highlighted by a great jazz concert we attended.

n. 亮点 (a very interesting event or detail)
He mentioned the highlights of his trip.

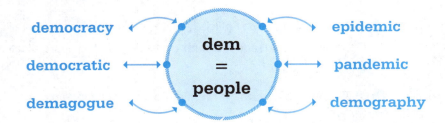

democracy ← → epidemic

democratic ← → pandemic

demagogue ← → demography

dem = people

democracy
[dɪ'mɒkrəsi]

n. 民主；民主国家 (a form of government in which people choose leaders by voting)
① The nation has chosen democracy over monarchy.
② In a democracy, every citizen should have the right to vote.

democratic
[ˌdemə'krætɪk]

adj. 民主的 (controlled by representatives who are elected by the people of a country; connected with this system)
The organization works to promote democratic reforms around the world.

epidemic [ˌepɪˈdemɪk]	*n.* 流行病 (a widespread outbreak of an infectious disease) A flu epidemic is sweeping through Moscow. *adj.* 传染性的 (spreading widely and affecting many people at the same time) The little girl's giggles were epidemic, and soon the entire gathering was laughing.
pandemic [pænˈdemɪk]	*n.* 大规模流行病 (an occurrence of a disease that affects many people over a very wide area) The 1918 flu was pandemic and claimed millions of lives.
demography [dɪˈmɒgrəfi]	*n.* 人口统计学 (the statistical study of human populations) Demography is the analysis of population variables.
demagogue [ˈdeməgɒg]	*n.* 煽动者；蛊惑民心的政客 (a political leader who tries to get support by making false claims and promises and using arguments based on emotion rather than reason) That politician is just a demagogue who preys upon people's fears and prejudices.

None系列

null [nʌl]	*adj.* 无效的 (having no legal or binding force) A spokeswoman said the agreement had been declared null and void.
annul [əˈnʌl]	*v.* 宣告无效；取消 (to say officially that something is no longer valid) Opposition party leaders are now pressing for the entire election to be annulled.
annihilate [əˈnaɪəleɪt]	*v.* 歼灭；毁灭 (to do away with entirely so that nothing remains) ① An atomic bomb can annihilate a city. ② The army was annihilated.
inane [ɪˈneɪn]	*adj.* 无意义的；愚蠢的 (with no meaning; very silly or stupid) She started asking me inane questions.
deny [dɪˈnaɪ]	*v.* 否认 (to say that something is not true) He denied the report that he would be quitting his job. *v.* 拒绝承认 (to refuse to accept or admit something) The government denies the basic freedoms of its citizens.

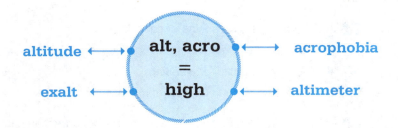

altitude ['æltɪtjuːd]	*n.* 高度；海拔高度 (the vertical elevation of an object above a surface) Some visitors find it difficult to adjust to the city's high altitude.
altimeter ['æltɪmiːtə(r)]	*n.* 高度计 (an instrument for measuring altitude) A barometric altimeter indicates height above sea level or some other selected elevation.
exalt [ɪgˈzɔːlt]	*v.* 颂扬；赞扬 (to praise someone or something highly) The essay exalts the simple beauty of the country.
acrobat ['ækrəbæt]	*n.* 杂技演员 (one that performs gymnastic feats requiring skillful control of the body) An acrobat has to be agile.
acrophobia [ˌækrəˈfəʊbɪə]	*n.* 恐高症 (abnormal fear or dread of being at a great height) She has acrophobia and always becomes dizzy in a high-rise elevator.

追根溯源

　　astonish从法语estoner发展而来，按字面意思讲，原有"雷击"之意，后引申为"使震惊；使惊呆"。英语中的两个词stun（击晕；使震惊）和astound（使震惊；使惊骇）也出自此词源，也含有"雷击"之意。Stunning是形容词，表示"令人震惊的"。

thunder ['θʌndə(r)]	*n.* 雷声 (the very loud sound that comes from the sky during a storm) ❶ Lightning flashed and thunder boomed. ❷ We could hear the rumble of thunder in the distance.
stun [stʌn]	*v.* 击晕 (to cause someone to suddenly become very dizzy) Sam stood his ground and got a blow that stunned him. *v.* 使震惊 (to surprise or upset someone very much) He was stunned by the news.

stunning ['stʌnɪŋ]	*adj.* 令人震惊的 (very surprising or shocking) Researchers have made a stunning discovery. *adj.* 极好的 (very beautiful or pleasing) Our room had a stunning view of the lake.
astonish [ə'stɒnɪʃ]	*v.* 使惊讶 (to cause a feeling of great wonder or surprise in someone) I was astonished to find a meteorite in my backyard.
astound [ə'staʊnd]	*v.* 使震惊 (to surprise or shock somebody very much) The magician will astound you with his latest tricks.
astounding [ə'staʊndɪŋ]	*adj.* 令人震惊的 (so surprising that it is difficult to believe) There was an astounding 20% increase in sales.

锦囊妙记

coast [kəʊst]	*n.* 海岸 (the land along or near a sea or ocean) He lives on the coast.
roast [rəʊst]	*v.* 烤；烘 (to cook food with dry heat in an oven or over a fire) ① The chicken is roasting in the oven. ② We roasted the peanuts over the fire.
toast [təʊst]	*n.* 干杯 (an act of drinking in honor of a person) He made a toast to the bride and groom. *n.* 烤面包 (sliced bread made crisp, hot, and brown by heat) I had toast for breakfast.
boast [bəʊst]	*v.* 吹嘘；炫耀 (to speak of oneself with excessive pride) He liked to boast that he was the richest man in town. *v.* 以……为傲 (to have something that is impressive and that you can be proud of) Our school boasts more top students than any other in the city.

串联记忆法：夏天的傍晚，一群人在海边(coast)，吃着烧烤(roast)， 喝着酒，干着杯 (toast)， 吹着牛(boast)!

Unit 15

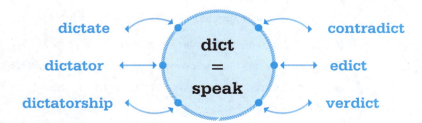

dictate	*v.* 口述 (to utter words to be transcribed)
[dɪkˈteɪt]	She's dictating a letter to her secretary.
	v. 支配；命令 (to say or state something with authority or power)
	You can't dictate what I can do.
dictator	*n.* 独裁者；专制者 (a person who rules a country with total authority and
[dɪkˈteɪtə]	often in a cruel or brutal way)
	The country was ruled by a military dictator.
dictatorship	*n.* 独裁；专政 (government by a dictator)
[ˌdɪkˈteɪtəʃɪp]	The country suffered for many years under his dictatorship.
predict	*v.* 预言；预测 (to say that something will or might happen in the future)
[prɪˈdɪkt]	① It's hard to predict how the election will turn out.
	② Many people predicted that the store would fail, but it has done very well.
prediction	*n.* 预测；预报 (an act of saying what will or might happen in the future)
[prɪˈdɪkʃn]	Journalists have begun making predictions about the winner of the
	coming election.
unpredictable	*adj.* 不可预测的 (impossible to predict)
[ˌʌnprɪˈdɪktəbl]	The king was a completely unpredictable tyrant.
verdict	*n.* 裁决；裁定 (the decision made by a jury in a trial)
[ˈvɜːdɪkt]	The jury reached a guilty verdict.
edict	*n.* 法令；告示 (an official order given by a person with power or by a
[ˈiːdɪkt]	government)
	The government issued an edict banning public demonstrations.

benediction [ˌbenɪ'dɪkʃn]	*n.* 祈祷；祝福 (a short blessing said especially at the end of a religious service) The priest offered a benediction for the missing children.
indict [ɪn'daɪt]	*v.* 控告；起诉 (to formally decide that someone should be put on trial for a crime) The grand jury is expected to indict him for murder.
indictment [ɪn'daɪtmənt]	*n.* 控诉 (the act of officially charging someone with a crime) The grand jury has handed down indictments against several mobsters. *n.* 谴责 (an expression or statement of strong disapproval) She intended the film to be an indictment of the media.
dedicate ['dedɪkeɪt]	*v.* 奉献；献身 (to commit to a goal or way of life) She vowed to herself that she would dedicate her life to scientific studies. *v.* (艺术作品) 献给 (something as a book or song is written or performed as a compliment to someone) This book is dedicated to the memory of my mother.
indicate ['ɪndɪkeɪt]	*v.* 表明 (to show that something exists or is true) ❶ The high fever indicates a serious condition. ❷ The map indicates where the treasure is buried.
indication [ˌɪndɪ'keɪʃn]	*n.* 指示；表明 (something, such as a sign or signal, that points out or shows something) Warm weather is an indication of spring.
contradict [ˌkɒntrə'dɪkt]	*v.* 反驳；驳斥 (to say the opposite of something that someone else has said) Donald Trump and his attorney general contradict each other on immigration policy.
contradictory [ˌkɒntrə'dɪktəri]	*adj.* 矛盾的；对立的 (containing or showing a contradiction) Contradictory predictions regarding stock prices were of no help to investors at all.
abdicate ['æbdɪkeɪt]	*v.* 放弃 (职责、权力等)；退位 (to give up a position of power or authority) The ruler was forced to abdicate.
vindicate ['vɪndɪkeɪt]	*v.* 证明……无辜 (to prove that somebody is not guilty when they have been accused of doing something wrong or illegal) The evidence will vindicate her.

Unit 16

	v. 证明……正确 (to prove that something is true or that you were right to do something, especially when other people had a different opinion) These discoveries vindicate their theory.
jurisdiction [,dʒʊərɪs'dɪkʃn]	*n.* 司法权；管辖权 (the power or right to make judgments about the law, to arrest and punish criminals) The court has jurisdiction over most criminal offenses.

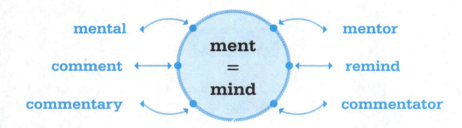

mental ['mentl]	*adj.* 内心的；精神的 (relating to the mind; spiritual) Attitudes to mental illness have shifted in recent years.
comment ['kɒment]	*v.* 评论 (to state your opinion or make a remark on something) When asked about his involvement in the scandal, he refused to comment. *n.* 评论 (a statement that expresses a personal opinion or belief) We've received positive comments from many of our readers.
commentary ['kɒməntri]	*n.* 实况解说；现场报道 (a spoken description of an event, such as a sports contest, as it is happening) The major television stations provided running commentaries on the election results. *n.* 注释 (a written explanation or criticism or illustration that is added to a book or other textual material) The book is a commentary on her experiences abroad.
commentator ['kɒmənteɪtə(r)]	*n.* 解说员；时事评论员 (a person who discusses important people and events on television, in newspapers) This might not be a good era for journalists, but it is a boom time for commentators.
mentor ['mentɔ:(r)]	*n.* 导师；指导者 (someone who teaches or gives help and advice to a less experienced and often younger person) After college, her professor became her close friend and mentor.

remind	*v.* 使想起；使记起 (to make someone think about something again)
[rɪ'maɪnd]	① She'll forget to call the doctor if you don't remind her.
	② I constantly have to be reminded how to pronounce her name.
reminiscent	*adj.* 使人想起的 (reminding you of someone or something else)
	The movie's style is reminiscent of old westerns.
[ˌremɪ'nɪsnt]	*adj.* 怀旧的 (having many thoughts of the past)
	I'm in a reminiscent mood.

Test系列

testify	*v.* 作证 (to make a formal statement of something sworn to be true)
['testɪfaɪ]	Two witnesses testified in court.
	v. 证实 (to show that something is true or real)
	Recent excavations testify to the presence of cultivated inhabitants on the hill during the Arthurian period.
testimony	*n.* 证词 (a statement made by a witness under oath especially in a court)
	There were contradictions in her testimony.
['testɪməni]	*n.* 证明 (evidence that something exists or is true)
	It is testimony to her courage and persistence that she worked for so long in the face of such adversity.
attest	*v.* 证明；证实 (to prove that something is true or real)
	① The certificate attests the authenticity of the painting.
[ə'test]	② I can attest to his innocence.

Able系列

apt	*adj.* 合适的；恰当的 (appropriate or suitable)
	"Stripe" is an apt name for the cat, since she has striped fur.
[æpt]	*adj.* 有……倾向的 (having a tendency to do something)
	① He is apt to become angry over small things.
	② That dog is apt to run off if you don't put him on a leash.

adapt

[ə'dæpt]

v. 使适应 (to change your behavior so that it is easier to live in a particular place or situation)

She has adapted herself to college life quite easily.

v. 使适合 (to change something so that it functions better or is better suited for a purpose)

The camera has been adapted for underwater use.

v. 改编 (to change a movie, book, play so that it can be presented in another form)

The movie was adapted from the book of the same title.

aptitude

['æptɪtjuːd]

n. 天资；天赋 (a natural ability to do something or to learn something)

The new test is supposed to measure the aptitudes of the students.

adept

[ə'dept]

adj. 熟练的；擅长的 (very good at something)

① He's adept in several languages.

② He is an adept guitar player.

inept

[ɪ'nept]

adj. 无能的；不称职的 (lacking skill or ability)

He was completely inept at sports.

Unit 16

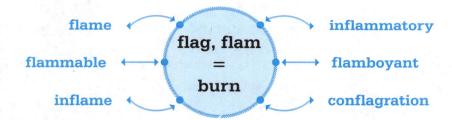

flame

[fleɪm]

n. 火焰 (the hot, glowing gas that can be seen when a fire is burning)

They tried to put out the fire, but the flames grew higher.

v. 燃烧；发出火焰 (to burn with or as if with a flame)

① The sun flamed through the clouds.

② His eyes flamed with anger.

flammable

['flæməbl]

adj. 易燃的；可燃的 (capable of being set on fire and of burning quickly)

These materials are highly flammable.

inflame

[ɪn'fleɪm]

v. 使发怒；激怒 (to cause a person or group to become angry or violent)

His comments have inflamed an already tense situation.

inflammable
[ɪnˈflæməbl]

adj. 可燃的 (capable of being set on fire and of burning quickly)

Paper is highly inflammable.

inflammatory
[ɪnˈflæmətri]

adj. 有煽动性的 (tending to excite anger or disorder)

He incited the mob with an inflammatory speech.

flamboyant
[flæmˈbɔɪənt]

adj. 火焰似的；过分华丽的 (richly colored and easily noticed)

His clothes were rather flamboyant for such a serious occasion.

flagrant
[ˈfleɪɡrənt]

adj. 骇人听闻的；公然的；罪恶昭彰的 (shocking because it is done in a very obvious way and shows no respect for people, laws, etc.)

The judge called the decision "a flagrant violation of international law".

conflagration
[ˌkɒnfləˈɡreɪʃn]

n. 大火 (灾) (a large destructive fire)

A conflagration in 1947 reduced 90 percent of the houses to ashes.

flare
[fleə(r)]

v. 闪耀；燃烧 (to burn with an unsteady flame)

Camp fires flared like beacons in the dark.

v. 发怒 (to express strong emotion such as anger)

She suddenly lost her temper with me and flared up.

Pro系列

prone
[prəʊn]

adj. 有……倾向的；可能的 (likely to do, have, or suffer from something)

He was prone to emotional outbursts under stress.

adj. 俯卧的 (lying with the front of your body facing downward)

Bob slid from his chair and lay prone on the floor.

approach
[əˈprəʊtʃ]

v. (在距离或时间上) 接近，靠近 (to come near to somebody/something in distance or time)

The cat approached the baby cautiously.

n. 靠近 (an act or instance of drawing near)

The quiet afternoon was interrupted by the approach of a motorboat.

n. 方法 (a way of doing or thinking about something)

She took the wrong approach in her dealings with them.

approachable
[əˈprəʊtʃəbl]

adj. 平易近人的；友善的 (friendly and easy to talk to)

We found him very approachable and easy to talk with.

proximity	*n.* 接近；邻近 (the state of being near)
[prɒkˈsɪməti]	The proximity of the curtains to the fireplace was a cause of concern for the safety inspector.
approximate	*adj.* 大约的；大概的 (nearly correct or exact)
[əˈprɒksɪmət]	This is the approximate location of the ancient city.
	v. 近似；接近 (to be very similar to but not exactly like something)
	I've finally found a vegetarian burger that approximates the taste of real beef.

Place系列

fireplace	*n.* 壁炉 (a specially built place in a room where a fire can be built)
[ˈfaɪəpleɪs]	A house with a fireplace has a stronger appeal to buyers.
replace	*v.* 替换；代替 (to take the place of something)
[rɪˈpleɪs]	Paper bags have been largely replaced by plastic bags.
	v. 放回原处 (to put something back in a former or proper place)
	He carefully replaced the vase on the shelf.
replaceable	*adj.* 可替换的；可替代的 (capable of being replaced)
[rɪˈpleɪsəbl]	A person, unlike a machine, is not replaceable.
displace	*v.* 取代；替换 (to take the job or position of someone or something)
[dɪsˈpleɪs]	Coal is to be displaced by natural gas and nuclear power.
	v. 使……流离失所 (to force people or animals to leave the area where they live)
	The hurricane displaced most of the town's residents.

Unit 16

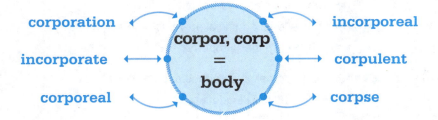

corporation	*n.* 公司 (a group of people acting as one body)
[ˌkɔːpəˈreɪʃn]	The local corporation has given permission for the work to proceed.

incorporate [ɪnˈkɔːpəreɪt]	*v.* 包含；吸收 (to include or be included as a part or member of a united whole) The new cars will incorporate a number of major improvements.
corporeal [kɔːˈpɔːriəl]	*adj.* 肉体的；物质的 (of the nature of the physical body; not spiritual) ① Every one has corporeal cravings such as hunger and thirst. ② He is very religious; corporeal world has little interest for him.
incorporeal [ˌɪnkɔːˈpɔːriəl]	*adj.* 无实体的；非物质的 (having no material body or form;immaterial) Ghosts are supposed to be incorporeal.
corpulent [ˈkɔːpjələnt]	*adj.* 肥胖的 (very fat) A corpulent, elegantly dressed opera singer came out and sang, and we knew it was over.
corpse [kɔːps]	*n.* 死尸；尸体 (a dead body, especially the dead body of a human) What she saw was just an unfeeling corpse.
corps [kɔːz]	*n.* 一群人 (a group of persons acting under one authority) The reporter is widely respected throughout the press corps.

Seek系列

seek [siːk(r)]	*v.* 寻找；探寻 (to search for someone or something) You should seek medical help immediately if you experience any chest pain or shortness of breath.
seize [siːz]	*v.* 抓住 (to get something in a forceful, sudden, or violent way) He seized the chance to present his ideas to his boss. *v.* 夺取；占领 (to attack and take control of a place by force or violence) The army has seized control of the city. *v.* 没收 (to use legal or official power to take something) The bank seized their property.
beseech [bɪˈsiːtʃ]	*v.* 恳求；乞求 (to ask in a serious and emotional way) We beseeched the king to let him live.
besiege [bɪˈsiːdʒ]	*v.* 包围；围攻 (to surround a city, building, with soldiers and try to take control) The army besieged the castle.

	v. 烦扰；纠缠 (to overwhelm with questions or requests)
	Customers have besieged the company with questions.

Ride系列

ridiculous	*adj.* 可笑的；荒谬的 (extremely silly or unreasonable)
[rɪ'dɪkjələs]	That's an absolutely ridiculous price for that sweater.
ridicule	*v.* 嘲笑；嘲弄 (to make fun of someone or something)
['rɪdɪkjuːl]	The other kids ridiculed him for the way he dressed.
	n. 嘲笑 (harsh comments made by people who are laughing at someone or something)
	She didn't show anyone her artwork for fear of ridicule.
deride	*v.* 嘲笑；愚弄 (to laugh at somebody/something in scorn)
[dɪ'raɪd]	People once derided the idea that man could fly.

Over系列

override	*v.* 优先；比……更重要 (to have more importance or influence than something)
[ˌəʊvə'raɪd]	These new rules override the old ones.
	v. 推翻；废除 (to make something no longer valid)
	The president vetoed the bill, and the Senate failed by a single vote to override his veto.
overthrow	*v.* 打倒；推翻 (to remove someone or something from power especially by force)
[ˌəʊvə'θrəʊ]	That government was overthrown in a military coup three years ago.
overcome	*v.* 战胜；克服 (to defeat someone or something)
[ˌəʊvə'kʌm]	① After a tough battle, they overcame the enemy.
	② She overcame a leg injury and is back running again.
overturn	*v.* (使) 翻转 (to turn something over)
[ˌəʊvə'tɜːn]	Waves overturned the boat.

	v. 推翻；颠覆 (to turn over or upside down)
	He accused his opponents of wanting to overturn the government.

overwhelm	*v.* 淹没 (to cover somebody/something completely)
[ˌəʊvəˈwelm]	The city was overwhelmed by the flooding caused by the hurricane.
	v. 压倒 (to cause someone to have too many things to deal with)
	They were overwhelmed with work.
	v. 压垮 (to defeat someone or something completely)
	The city was overwhelmed by the invading army.

overwhelming	*adj.* 势不可当的；压倒一切的 (very great or strong)
[ˌəʊvəˈwelmɪŋ]	① The vote was overwhelming—283 in favour, and only 29 against.
	② The overwhelming feeling is just deep, profound shock and anger.

Ddle系列

puddle	*n.* 水坑 (a very small pool of usually dirty or muddy water)
[ˈpʌdl]	I was wet and I must somewhere have stepped in a puddle.

paddle	*n.* 桨；短桨 (an instrument like an oar used in moving and steering a small boat)
[ˈpædl]	He used a piece of driftwood as a paddle.

waddle	*v.* (像鸭子一样) 摇摇摆摆地走 (to walk with short steps, swaying from side to side, like a duck)
[ˈwɒdl]	We waddle and hop and have lots of fun.

twaddle	*n.* 废话；蠢话 (foolish words or ideas)
[ˈtwɒdl]	We don't believe that twaddle anymore.

dawdle	*v.* 闲逛；游荡 (to spend time idly)
[ˈdɔːdl]	Don't dawdle, the young head is soon white.

muddle	*n.* 糊涂；困惑 (a state of confusion or disorder)
[ˈmʌdl]	His mind was in a muddle.
	v. 使糊涂 (to mix up something in a confused way)
	The drink muddled him and his voice became loud.

addle	*v.* 使糊涂；使混乱 (to make someone's mind or brain unable to think clearly)
[ˈædl]	It's a dangerous poison that's strong enough to addle the brain.

Donald（唐老鸭）真糊涂，遇到add（加法）就addle（糊涂），走起路来总waddle（摇摇摆摆），满嘴都是twaddle（废话），整天就知道dawdle（闲逛），拿起paddle（船桨），搅和puddle（水洼），沾满mud（泥浆），弄得一片muddle（混乱）。

追根溯源

古罗马人在占卜时，会用手或魔杖在空中划出一块区域，然后观察这片天空中所发生的事，如飞鸟从何方飞入。还有可能在地面上划出一块区域，然后在这个区域内进行占卜。temple一开始指的就是占卜时所划出的这样一片区域，后来引申为"寺庙；神殿"之意。占卜的人在划定的区域要一边观察鸟的飞行，一边沉思，contemplate就有了"注视；深思"的意思。

temple ['templ]	*n.* 庙宇；神殿 (a building for religious practice) We went to the temple of Atlantis and saw it by moonlight.
contemplate ['kɒntəmpleɪt]	*v.* 注视；凝视 (to look at somebody/something with careful and thoughtful attention) He stood there contemplating the stars in the sky. *v.* 深思熟虑 (to think deeply about something) He contemplated the meaning of the poem for a long time.
contemplation [ˌkɒntəm'pleɪʃn]	*n.* 深思熟虑 (the act of thinking deeply about something) She goes to the forest to spend time in contemplation of nature. *n.* 凝视 (the act of looking carefully at something) She was lost in quiet contemplation of the scene.

temple有一个同形同音异义词tempus，表示时间，temporary（临时的）和contemporary（当代的）均来自这个表示"时间"的词根。

temporary ['temprəri]	*adj.* 临时的；暂时的 (continuing for a limited amount of time; not permanent) ① The drug will give you temporary relief from the pain. ② His job here is only temporary.
contemporary [kən'temprəri]	*adj.* 当代的；现代的 (happening or beginning now or in recent times) The gallery holds regular exhibitions of contemporary art, sculpture and photography.

Unit 16

adj. 同时代的 (existing or happening in the same time period)

The book draws upon official records and the reports of contemporary witnesses.

n. 同代人；同辈人 (a person who lives at the same time or is about the same age as another person)

She is politically very different from most of her contemporaries.

锦囊妙记

obedience [ə'biːdɪəns]	*n.* 遵守；顺从 (the act of obeying) Children should learn obedience and respect for authority. 谐音法 obedience—偶必定死，若不服从(obedience)，偶必定死。
obedient [ə'biːdɪənt]	*adj.* 服从的；顺从的 (willing to do what someone tells you to do or to follow a law, rule) That boy is so obedient that he does everything the first time he is asked.
obsolete ['ɒbsəliːt]	*adj.* 过时的；废弃的 (making something old-fashioned or no longer useful) With technological changes many traditional skills have become obsolete. 谐音法 obsolete—偶不舍离它，虽然已经过时 (obsolete) 了，我恋旧，偶不舍离它。
vigilant ['vɪdʒələnt]	*adj.* 警惕的；警觉的 (very careful to notice any signs of danger or trouble) They were vigilant about protecting their children. 谐音法 vigilant—危机来的！危机要来了！一定要保持警惕 (vigilant)。
woeful ['woʊfl]	*adj.* 悲哀的；忧伤的 (very sad) The puppy had woeful eyes. *adj.* 糟糕的；严重的 (very bad or serious) The student's grades were woeful. 谐音法 woeful—呜呜！他在呜呜地哭，就是很悲伤啊 (woeful)!

Unit 16

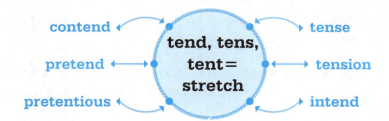

contend → tense

pretend → tension

pretentious → intend

tend, tens, tent = stretch

tense [tens]	*adj.* 令人紧张的 (showing or causing nervousness) This gesture of goodwill did little to improve the tense atmosphere at the talks. *v.* （使肌肉）拉紧，绷紧 (to make a muscle hard and tight) She tensed as the deadline grew near. *adj.* 肌肉紧张的 (not relaxed but hard and tight) My calf muscles are really tense.
tension ['tenʃn]	*n.* 紧张；不安 (a feeling of nervousness that makes you unable to relax) Political tensions in the region make it unstable.
intense [ɪn'tens]	*adj.* 强烈的；剧烈的 (very great in degree; very strong) ① He shielded his eyes from the intense flash of light. ② She has an intense dislike for her husband's friend.
intensify [ɪn'tensɪfaɪ]	*v.* 增强；加剧 (to become stronger or more extreme) ① Sunlight poured through the windows, intensifying the heat. ② They intensified their efforts to increase sales.
contend [kən'tend]	*v.* 争夺；竞争 (to compete with someone or for something) The team is expected to contend for the championship this year. *v.* 声称；主张 (to argue or state something in a strong and definite way) These people contend that they have earned the right to the land.
contentious [kən'tenʃəs]	*adj.* 争论激烈的 (involving a lot of arguing) After a contentious debate, members of the committee finally voted to approve the funding. *adj.* 有争议的 (likely to cause people to argue or disagree) The dispute involves one of the region's most contentious leaders.

Unit 17

intend

[ɪnˈtend]

v. 打算；计划 (to plan or want to do something)

① They intend to claim for damages against the three doctors.

② I didn't intend any disrespect.

intention

[ɪnˈtenʃn]

n. 意图；目的 (an aim or a plan)

① He has good intentions, but his suggestions aren't really helpful.

② She announced her intention to run for president.

intentional

[ɪnˈtenʃənl]

adj. 有意的；故意的 (done in a way that is planned or intended)

I apologize for the omission of your name from the list. It was not intentional.

extend

[ɪkˈstend]

v. 延伸；扩大 (to spread or stretch forth)

① The woods extend for miles to the west.

② The caves extend for some 18 kilometres.

extensive

[ɪkˈstensɪv]

adj. 广阔的；广大的；大量的 (large in size or amount)

① The story received extensive coverage in the *Times*.

② The storm caused extensive damage.

pretend

[prɪˈtend]

v. 假装；伪装 (to act as if something is true when it is not true)

① She looked like she was enjoying the party but she was just pretending.

② He pretended to make a phone call.

pretentious

[prɪˈtenʃəs]

adj. 爱炫耀的 (trying to appear better or more important than is really the case)

That pretentious couple always serves caviar at their parties, even though they themselves dislike it.

tentacle

[ˈtentəkl]

n. 触手；触角 (one of the long, flexible arms of an animal such as an octopus that are used for grabbing things and moving)

It has a round head, long tentacle, and a transparent white body.

n. 影响力 (power or influence that reaches into many areas)

The corporation's tentacles are felt in every sector of the industry.

Order系列

ordinary [ˈɔːdnri]	*adj.* 普通的；平常的 (normal or usual) ① I was an ordinary student. ② She gave a very ordinary speech.
extraordinary [ɪkˈstrɔːdnr]	*adj.* 非凡的 (very unusual; very different from what is normal or ordinary) ① The researchers made an extraordinary discovery. ② The task requires extraordinary patience and endurance.
ordinance [ˈɔːdɪnəns]	*n.* 条例；法令 (a law or regulation made by a city or town government) A local ordinance forbids all street parking during snowstorms.
coordinate [kəʊˈɔːdɪneɪt]	*v.* 使协调 (to bring something into common action, movement or condition) ① Officials visited the earthquake zone to coordinate the relief effort. ② Since his illness, he has had trouble coordinating his arms and legs.
subordinate [səˈbɔːdɪnət]	*adj.* 附属的；次要的 (less important than someone or something else) Your personal preferences are subordinate to these responsibilities. *n.* 下属 (someone who has less power or authority than someone else) She leaves the day-to-day running of the firm to her subordinates.
inordinate [ɪnˈɔːdɪnət]	*adj.* 过度的；无节制的 (going beyond what is usual, normal, or proper) They spend an inordinate amount of time talking.

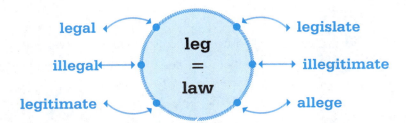

allege [əˈledʒ]	*v.* 断言；宣称 (to state without definite proof that someone has done something wrong or illegal) ① He alleged that the mayor has accepted bribes. ② You allege that she stole a large quantity of money. Do you have any proof?

allegation
[ˌælə'geɪʃn]

n. 指控；指责 (a statement saying that someone has done something wrong or illegal)

The police are investigating allegations that the mayor has accepted bribes.

legal
['li:gl]

adj. 合法的 (permitted by law)

The amount of alcohol in his blood exceeded the legal limit.

adj. 法律的 (relating to law)

She has many legal problems.

illegal
[ɪ'li:gl]

adj. 不合法的；违法的 (not allowed by the law)

In this state, it is illegal for anyone under the age of 21 to drink alcohol.

legalize
['li:gəlaɪz]

v. 使合法化 (to allow something by law)

The government has legalized the use of the new drug.

legislate
['ledʒɪsleɪt]

v. 立法；制定法律 (to make laws)

The government will legislate against discrimination in the workplace.

legislature
['ledʒɪsleɪtʃə(r)]

n. 立法机关 (a group of people with the power to make or change laws)

Our legislature passed a law requiring people to wear safety belts.

legislator
['ledʒɪsleɪtə(r)]

n. 立法者 (a person who makes laws especially for a political unit)

The legislators met in an all-night session to hammer out the details of the bill.

legislative
['ledʒɪslətɪv]

adj. 立法的 (relating to the action or process by which laws are made)

She is interested in the legislative process.

legitimate
[lɪ'dʒɪtɪmət]

adj. 合法的；合理的 (allowed according to rules or laws)

The government will not seek to disrupt the legitimate business activities.

illegitimate
[ˌɪlə'dʒɪtəmət]

adj. 不合法的 (not accepted by the law as rightful)

The election was dismissed as illegitimate by the opposition.

privilege
['prɪvəlɪdʒ]

n. 特权 (a right or benefit that is given to some people and not to others)

We had the privilege of being invited to the party.

v. 给予……特权 (to give an advantage that others do not have to)

The new tax laws unfairly privilege the rich.

Drip系列

drip [drɪp]	*v.* 滴出 (to fall in drops) Water dripped from a leak in the ceiling. *n.* 水滴；点滴 (a drop of liquid that falls from something) Water fell from the ceiling in a steady drip.
drench [drentʃ]	*v.* 使湿透 (to make someone or something completely wet) We were drenched by the sudden rainstorm.
drown [draʊn]	*v.* 淹死 (to die by being underwater too long and unable to breathe) She fell in the river and drowned. *v.* 淹没；浸没 (to cover something completely with a liquid) The food was drowned in sauce. *v.* (声音) 压过，淹没 (to be louder than other sounds so that you cannot hear them) The loud music drowned the sound of their conversation.
drizzle ['drɪzl]	*n.* 蒙蒙细雨 (rain that falls lightly in very small drops) It's raining, but it's only a drizzle. *v.* 下毛毛雨 (to rain in very small drops) It was beginning to drizzle, so she pulled on her hood.

Inhale与Exhale

inhale [ɪn'heɪl]	*v.* 吸入 (to take air, smoke, gas, etc. into your lungs as you breathe) He inhaled deeply and exhaled slowly, trying to relax.
exhale [eks'heɪl]	*v.* 呼气 (to breathe out the air or smoke, etc. in your lungs) Before answering, the suspect exhaled a cloud of cigarette smoke.

Oo系列

crook [krʊk]	*v.* 使成钩状；使弯曲 (to bend your finger, neck, or arm) He crooked his finger at us and led us to the table.

n. 骗子 (a dishonest person)

He thinks politicians are just a bunch of crooks.

hook

[hʊk]

v. 钩住 (to connect or attach something with a hook)

➊ The train cars were hooked together.

➋ I hooked a fish.

n. 钩子 (a curved or bent device for catching, holding or pulling something)

One of his jackets hung from a hook.

spoon

[spuːn]

n. 匙；小勺子 (a small shallow bowl with a relatively long handle)

He stirred his coffee with a spoon.

v. 用匙舀取 (to move or pick up food with a spoon)

He spooned the ice cream into a bowl.

loop

[luːp]

n. 圈；环 (a curved or circular shape in something long, for example in a piece of string)

The road went in a huge loop around the lake.

v. (使) 成环 (to form a circle or loop)

The road loops around the park.

cocoon

[kəˈkuːn]

n. 保护膜；防护层 (soft covering that wraps all around a person or thing and forms a protection)

The child was wrapped in a cocoon of blankets.

v. 把……紧紧包住 (to cover or protect someone or something completely)

She lay on the sofa, cocooned in blankets.

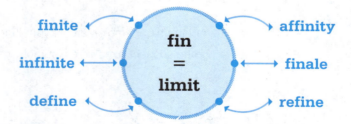

finite

[ˈfaɪnaɪt]

adj. 有限的 (having limits; limited)

➊ I was given a finite number of choices.

➋ The earth's supply of natural resources is finite.

infinite [ˈɪnfɪnət]	*adj.* 无限的；无穷的 (seeming to be without limits) ① She has infinite patience when she's dealing with children. ② The universe seems infinite.
infinitesimal [ˌɪnfɪnɪˈtesɪml]	*adj.* 极微小的 (immeasurably or incalculably small) The chance of winning is infinitesimal.
define [dɪˈfaɪn]	*v.* 阐明；明确；确定 (to describe or show something accurately) ① Her book aims to define acceptable social behavior. ② She believes that success should be defined in terms of health and happiness.
definite [ˈdefɪnət]	*adj.* 明确的 (clear in meaning) ① The teacher sets definite standards for her students. ② We'll need a definite answer by Tuesday.
definition [ˌdefɪˈnɪʃn]	*n.* 定义；规定 (an explanation of the meaning of a word) There is no general agreement on a standard definition of intelligence. *n.* 清晰度 (clearness of outline or detail) You can adjust the screen for better definition.
confine [kənˈfaɪn]	*v.* 限制；局限于 (to keep someone or something within limits) Health officials have successfully confined the epidemic to the local area. *v.* 监禁；关押 (to keep a person or animal in a place such as a prison) The accused was confined until the trial could take place.
confinement [kənˈfaɪnmənt]	*n.* 监禁；关押 (the state of being confined) She had been held in solitary confinement for four months.
refine [rɪˈfaɪn]	*v.* 提炼 (to bring to a pure state) Oil is refined to remove naturally occurring impurities. *v.* 改进；改善 (to improve something by making small changes) The inventor of the machine spent years refining the design.
finale [fɪˈnɑːli]	*n.* [乐]终曲；结局 (the last part of something, such as a musical performance, play) She sung a very difficult song for the finale.
affinity [əˈfɪnəti]	*n.* 密切关系；亲近 (a liking for or an attraction to something) ① They had much in common and felt a close affinity. ② Sam was born in the country and had a deep affinity with nature.

Unit 17

Slow系列

slacken ['slækən]	*v.* (使) 放慢；(使) 减弱 ① Inflationary pressures continued to slacken last month. ② As he began to relax, his grip on the steering wheel slackened.
slovenly ['slʌvnli]	*adj.* 懒散的；邋遢的 (messy or untidy) He dressed in a slovenly manner. *adj.* 疏忽的；马虎的 (done in a careless way) The officers were rather slovenly in their methods.
sloppy ['slɒpi]	*adj.* 马虎的；敷衍的 (careless in work or in appearance) He has little patience for sloppy work from colleagues.
sluggish ['slʌgɪʃ]	*adj.* 懒洋洋的；缓慢的 (markedly slow in movement, flow or growth) The sluggish pace of the project is worrisome.
sloth [sləʊθ]	*n.* 懒惰；倦怠 (the bad habit of being lazy and unwilling to work) He admitted a lack of motivation and a feeling of sloth.

Rise系列

horizon [hə'raɪzn]	*n.* 地平线 (the line where the earth seems to meet the sky) The sun rose slowly over the eastern horizon. *n.* 范围；眼界 (the limit or range of a person's knowledge, understanding, or experience) ① Reading broadens our horizons. ② These discoveries have opened up new horizons in the field of cancer research.
horizontal [ˌhɒrɪ'zɒntl]	*adj.* 水平的 (parallel to the ground) The board consists of vertical and horizontal lines.
arise [ə'raɪz]	*v.* 发生；出现 (to begin to occur or to exist) Mist arose from the valley. *v.* 起床 (to get up from sleep or after lying down) He arose at 6:30 a.m. as usual.

arouse [ə'raʊz]	*v.* 激起；引起 (感情，态度) (to make somebody have a particular feeling or attitude)
	① The report aroused a great deal of public interest.
	② There is nothing like a long walk to arouse the appetite.
origin ['ɒrɪdʒɪn]	*n.* 起源；根源 (the point or place where something begins or is created)
	The origins of human language remain a matter of considerable debate.
originate [ə'rɪdʒɪneɪt]	*v.* 起源于；来自 (to begin to exist)
	The custom is believed to have originated in the western U.S.
original [ə'rɪdʒənl]	*adj.* 最初的 (happening or existing first or at the beginning)
	Their original idea was to fix their old car, but they decided to buy a new one instead.
	adj. 独创的；新颖的 (not like others; new, different, and appealing)
	The car has a highly original design.
oriental [ˌɔːri'entl]	*adj.* 东方的 (relating to or coming from Asia and especially eastern Asia)
	Visitors can see a wide range of sets, from oriental gardens to a medieval town.
orientation [ˌɔːriən'teɪʃn]	*n.* 态度；观点；信仰 (a person's feelings, interests or beliefs)
	He makes no secret of his orientation.
	n. 指导；培训 (the process of giving people training and information about a new job, situation)
	These materials are used for the orientation of new employees.

追根溯源

　　在罗马神话中，天神宙斯（Zeus）被称为Jove，为了表示尊重，罗马人也称其为Jupiter（朱庇特），意思就是"诸神之父Jove"。八大行星当中体积最大的木星（Jupiter）就是以朱庇特的名字命名的。朱庇特天性风流，与无数仙女、凡人美女关系暧昧。古代占星家认为如果一个人命属木星宫，那么性格便会欢乐活泼。jovial（快乐的），jocund（欢乐的）和jocular（爱开玩笑的）这些词都来自Jove这个名字。

| **jovial** ['dʒəʊviəl] | *adj.* 快乐的；愉快的 (full of happiness and joy) |
| | The audience was in a jovial mood. |

jocund	*adj.* 欢乐的；愉快的 (full of joy)
['dʒɒkənd]	Her jocund character made her the most popular girl in the county.
jocular	*adj.* 爱开玩笑的；滑稽的 (liking to tell jokes)
['dʒɒkjələ(r)]	He is a jocular man who could make the most serious people smile.

　　在罗马神话中，萨图恩（Saturn）是农神，他展现出的形象就是在大地上不停地劳作、耕种。他不善言辞，给人一种忧郁的感觉。八大行星中的土星（Saturn）就是来自这位农神。占星家认为如果一个人命属土星宫，那么性格往往会比较忧郁，saturnine（忧郁的）一词便由此而来。人们为了纪念这位伟大的农神，星期六（Saturday）便以他的名字命名。

| **saturnine** | *adj.* 性格阴沉的；表情忧郁的(looking serious and threatening) |
| ['sætənaɪn] | He is saturnine in temperament. |

锦囊妙记

gallant	*adj.* 勇敢的 (behaving bravely and honorably in a dangerous or difficult situation)
['gælənt]	The gallant soldiers lost their lives so that peace might reign again.
	谐音法 ga-敢，当然是勇敢的(gallant)。
curse	*v.* 诅咒；咒骂 (to say rude things to somebody or think rude things about somebody/something)
[kɜːs]	He cursed his enemies.
	谐音法 curse-克死，咒骂一个人，不就是要克死(curse)一个人！
leisure	*n.* 闲暇；悠闲 (enjoyable activities that you do when you are not working)
['leʒə(r)]	I don't have much time for leisure.
	谐音法 lei-累，sure-当然，累！当然累！所以要休闲 (leisure)。
mature	*v.* 成熟 (to become fully developed)
[mə'tʃʊə(r)]	Girls mature earlier than boys both physically and mentally.
	adj. 成熟的 (having or showing the mental and emotional qualities of an adult)
	His parents didn't think he was mature enough to live on his own.
	联想法 ma-妈妈，妈妈孕育了你，当然很成熟(mature)！
immature	*adj.* 不成熟的 (not fully developed or grown)
[ˌɪmə'tjʊə(r)]	His teachers have complained about his immature behavior.

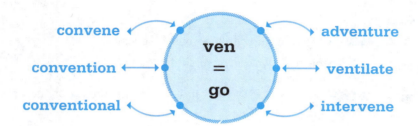

convene   ven = go   adventure

convention   ventilate

conventional   intervene

convene [kənˈviːn]	*v.* 召集；聚集 (to come together in a group for a meeting)
	❶ A panel of investigators was convened by the president to review the case.
	❷ This class convenes twice a week.
convention [kənˈvenʃn]	*n.* 会议 (a meeting of people for a common purpose)
	The Democratic National Convention will meet next week to announce their party's candidate for president.
	n. 惯例；习俗 (a custom or a way of acting or doing things that is widely accepted and followed)
	The president stressed the importance of observing the Geneva convention on human rights.
conventional [kənˈvenʃənl]	*adj.* 传统的 (used and accepted by most people; usual or traditional)
	His views on dating are more conventional than those of some of his friends.
	adj. 常规的 (common and ordinary; not unusual)
	We must reduce the danger of war by controlling nuclear, chemical and conventional arms.
covenant [ˈkʌvənənt]	*n.* 协议；协定 (a formal and serious agreement or promise)
	An international covenant on human rights.
revenue [ˈrevənjuː]	*n.* 税收；收入 (the total income produced by a given source)
	❶ Government officials have reported a decrease in revenue.
	❷ The factory lost revenue because of the strike by the workers.

Unit 18

avenue

['ævənjuː]

n. 林荫路；大街 (a broad passageway bordered by trees)

We drove down the avenue.

n. 手段；途径 (a way of achieving something or of reaching a goal)

We plan to pursue all available avenues to get our message to the public.

adventure

[əd'ventʃə(r)]

n. 冒险 (an exciting or dangerous experience)

The field trip was an adventure for the students.

adventurous

[əd'ventʃərəs]

adj. 爱冒险的；大胆的 (not afraid to do new and dangerous or exciting things)

The island attracts adventurous travelers.

venture

['ventʃə(r)]

v. 冒险 (to go somewhere that is unknown, dangerous, etc.)

It's important to plan carefully before venturing on a long journey.

v. 冒险尝试 (to start to do something new or different that usually involves risk)

The company is venturing into the computer software industry.

vent

[vent]

n. 通风孔 (an opening for the escape of a gas or liquid or for the relief of pressure)

Leave a vent open to let some moist air escape.

v. 发泄 (to express an emotion usually in a loud or angry manner)

He needs to vent his anger.

ventilate

['ventɪleɪt]

v. 使通风 (to allow fresh air to enter and move through a room, building, etc.)

She opened the windows to ventilate the room.

intervene

[ˌɪntə'viːn]

v. 阻碍；干涉 (to interfere with something so as to stop, settle, or change)

The military had to intervene to restore order.

contravene

[ˌkɒntrə'viːn]

v. 违反 (法律或规则) (to fail to do what is required by a law or rule)

1 The overcrowded dance club contravened safety regulations.

2 The unauthorized reproduction of the image contravenes copyright.

circumvent

[ˌsɜːkəm'vent]

v. 规避；逃避 (规则或限制) (to avoid being stopped by something, such as a law or rule)

1 He found a way to circumvent the law.

2 Military planners tried to circumvent the treaty.

Unit 18

inventory	*n.* 存货清单 (a complete list of the things that are in a place)
['ɪnvəntri]	We made an inventory of the library's collection.
	n. 库存 (a supply of goods that are stored in a place)
	The dealer keeps a large inventory of used cars and trucks.
advent	*n.* 出现；到来 (the arrival or coming of something)
['ædvent]	The leap forward in communication made possible by the advent of the mobile phone.

Experiment系列

experiment	*n.* 实验；试验 (a trial or test made to find out about something)
[ɪk'sperɪmənt]	Students will carry out simple laboratory experiments.
	v. 做实验 (to carry out experiments)
	The scientists have experimented on the tiny neck arteries of rats.
peril	*n.* 危险；冒险 (something that is likely to cause injury, pain, harm or loss)
['perəl]	People are unaware of the peril these miners face each day.
perilous	*adj.* 危险的；冒险的 (full of danger)
['perələs]	The journey through the jungle was perilous.
empirical	*adj.* 凭经验的；经验主义的 (originating in or based on observation or experience)
[ɪm'pɪrɪkl]	They collected plenty of empirical data from their experiments.
experience	*n.* 经验；体验 (direct observation of or participation in events as a basis of knowledge)
[ɪk'spɪəriəns]	He wrote about his experiences as a pilot.
	v. 感受；体验 (to undergo or live through)
	That was one of the worst days I've ever experienced.
expert	*n.* 专家；能手 (a person who has special skill or knowledge relating to a particular subject)
['ekspɜːt]	She was an acknowledged expert on child development.
	adj. 熟练的；经验丰富的 (having special skill or knowledge derived from training or experience)

① The company has become expert at adapting its products for new clients.

② We received some expert advice.

Dazzle系列

dazzle

['dæzl]

v. 使目眩 (to cause someone to be unable to see for a short time)

The desert sunlight dazzled us.

v. 使……惊异不已 (to surprise somebody by being or doing something special and unusual)

The magician's tricks dazzled the audience.

dazzling

['dæzlɪŋ]

adj. 耀眼的；光彩夺目的 (brilliantly or showily bright, colorful or impressive)

He has clear blue eyes and a dazzling smile.

dizzy

['dɪzi]

adj. 眩晕的 (having the feeling of spinning)

① The children were dizzy after spinning in circles.

② Complex math problems make me dizzy.

Swing系列

swing

[swɪŋ]

v. 摆动；摇荡 (to move backward and forward or from side to side while hanging from something)

① The monkeys were swinging from branch to branch high up in the trees.

② The clock's pendulum stopped swinging.

swirl

[swɜːl]

v. (使) 旋转 (to move in circles or to cause something to move in circles)

She smiled, swirling the wine in her glass.

n. 卷状的东西 (a twisting or swirling movement, form or object)

① A swirl of smoke rose from the chimney.

② They had eaten ice cream with chocolate swirls.

switch

[swɪtʃ]

n. 开关 (a small device that starts or stops the flow of electricity to something)

She flicked a switch and turned the lamp on.

v. (使) 转变 (to change or make something change from one thing to another)

He kept switching back and forth between topics.

swivel ['swɪvl]	*v.* (使) 旋转；转动 (to turn or make something turn around a fixed central point) She swiveled the chair around to face them. *v.* 转身；转动（身体、眼睛或头）(to turn or move your body, eyes or head around quickly to face another direction) He swiveled around to see who was behind him.

Twirl系列

twirl [twɜːl]	*v.* 快速转动 (to revolve rapidly) ① Several hundred people twirl around the ballroom dance floor. ② All around me leaves twirl to the ground. *n.* 旋转 (an act of turning or spinning around quickly) The twirl of the dancer's skirt mesmerized me.
whirlpool ['wɜːlpuːl]	*n.* 漩涡；涡流 (an area of water in a river, stream, etc., that moves very fast in a circle) The swimmer was caught in a whirlpool and nearly drowned.
twist [twɪst]	*v.* 扭成一束；搓，捻；绕 (to bend or turn something in order to change its shape) ① She twisted balloons into the shapes of different animals. ② He twists his lip into an odd expression when he's thinking. *n.* 蜿蜒；曲折 (a turn, curve, or bend in a road, river) The coastal road had many twists and turns.

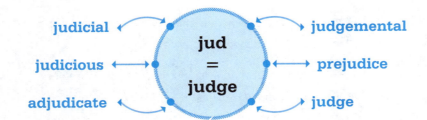

judicial ← jud = judge → judgemental

judicious ↔ jud = judge ↔ prejudice

adjudicate ← jud = judge → judge

judge [dʒʌdʒ]	*v.* 审判 (to decide whether somebody is guilty or innocent in a court) The jury will be asked to judge the defendant's guilt. *n.* 法官 (a person who has the power to make decisions on cases brought before a court of law) The judge sentenced him to five years in prison.

judgement ['dʒʌdʒmənt]	**n.** 判断；审判 (an opinion or decision that is based on careful thought) Don't rush to judgment without examining the evidence.
judgemental [dʒʌdʒ'mentl]	**adj.** 爱评头论足的 (tending to judge people too quickly and critically) He's judgmental about everyone except himself.
judicial [dʒu'dɪʃl]	**adj.** 司法的 (relating to courts of law or judges) Bias against women permeates every level of the judicial system.
judicious [dʒu'dɪʃəs]	**adj.** 明智的 (having or showing good judgment) The President authorizes the judicious use of military force to protect our citizens.
adjudicate [ə'dʒuːdɪkeɪt]	**v.** 判决；宣判 (to come to a judicial decision) The case was adjudicated in the state courts.
prejudice ['predʒudɪs]	**n.** 偏见；歧视 (an unfair feeling of dislike for a person or group because of race, sex or religion) The organization fights against racial prejudice.

Note系列

notice ['nəʊtɪs]	**n.** 通知 (a written or printed announcement) Please give us enough notice to prepare for your arrival. **v.** 注意 (to become aware of something or someone by seeing, hearing) You didn't notice that I got my hair cut.
notify ['nəʊtɪfaɪ]	**v.** 通知；布告 (to tell someone officially about something) Please notify the school of your new address.
notation [nəʊ'teɪʃn]	**n.** 记号 (a system of marks, signs, figures, or characters that is used to represent information) Music has a special system of notation.
denote [dɪ'nəʊt]	**v.** 预示；是……的征兆 (to show, mark, or be a sign of something) A star on the map denotes a capital.
notable ['nəʊtəbl]	**adj.** 值得注意的 (unusual and worth noticing) The proposed new structure is notable not only for its height, but for its shape.

	adj. 著名的 (very successful or respected)
	She became quite a notable director in the thirties and forties.
notorious	*adj.* 臭名昭著的 (well-known or famous especially for something bad)
[nəʊˈtɔːriəs]	He caught the villain, who turned out to be a very notorious criminal.

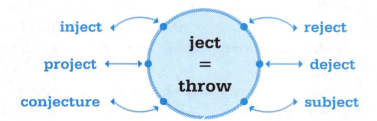

abject	*adj.* 悲惨绝望的；凄惨的 (terrible and without hope)
[ˈæbdʒekt]	They live in abject misery.
	adj. 下贱的；卑躬屈节的 (without any pride or respect for yourself)
	She thought he was an abject coward.
deject	*v.* 使沮丧；使灰心 (to lower the spirits of somebody; to dishearten)
[dɪˈdʒekt]	He was dejected by his misfortune and was unsure on how to proceed next.
reject	*v.* 拒绝接受；不予考虑 (to refuse to believe, accept, or consider something)
[rɪˈdʒekt]	❶ The college rejects hundreds of applicants each year.
	❷ My teacher rejected my excuse for being late.
inject	*v.* 注射 (to put a drug or other substance into a person's or an animal's body using a syringe)
[ɪnˈdʒekt]	The technique consists of injecting healthy cells into the weakened muscles.
	v. (给……) 添加；增加 (某品质) (to add a particular quality to something)
	He tried to inject confidence into his brother.
eject	*v.* 喷出；排出 (to push something out suddenly and with a lot of force)
[iˈdʒekt]	The burning house ejected yellow flames into the night sky.
	v. 驱逐；逐出 (to force somebody to leave a place)
	They were ejected from their house for not paying the rent.

Unit 18

subject

['sʌbdʒɪkt] *n.*

[səb'dʒekt] *v.*

n. 主题；话题 (the person or thing discussed)

If you're interested in linguistics, I know an excellent book on the subject.

n. 学科 (an area of knowledge that is studied in school)

Chemistry was my favorite subject in high school.

v. 受……支配 (to bring a country or group of people under control or rule)

Peoples subjected themselves to the emperor.

---

project

['prɒdʒekt] *n.*

[prə'dʒekt] *v.*

n. 项目；计划 (a plan or scheme to do something)

Money will also go into local development projects in China.

v. 预测；预计 (to plan, calculate, or estimate something for a time in the future)

He projected next year's costs as being slightly higher than this year's.

v. 投射 (to make light, an image, etc. fall onto a flat surface or screen)

The machine projects motion pictures on a screen.

---

conjecture

[kən'dʒektʃə(r)]

n. 猜测 (an opinion or conclusion based on guesswork)

The biography includes conjectures about the writer's earliest ambitions.

v. 猜测 (to form an opinion or idea without proof or sufficient evidence)

Some have conjectured that the distant planet could sustain life.

---

interject

[ˌɪntə'dʒekt]

v. (突然) 插入；插话 (to interrupt what someone else is saying with a comment, remark)

① "That's an interesting idea," he interjected, "but I don't think you've considered all of the details."

② He listened thoughtfully, interjecting only the odd word.

---

trajectory

[trə'dʒektəri]

n. 轨迹；弹道 (the curved path along which something such as a rocket moves through the air or through space)

① It is not difficult to sketch the subsequent trajectory.

② My career seemed to be on a downward trajectory.

Frac系列

fracture

['fræktʃə(r)]

n. 破裂；断裂 (a crack or break in something hard, such as bone)

She suffered a wrist fracture when she slipped on the ice.

v. (使) 折断；破碎 (to break or crack; to make something break or crack)

Their happiness was fractured by an unforeseen tragedy.

| **fractious** | *adj.* 易怒的；急躁的 (full of anger and disagreement) |
| ['frækʃəs] | The fractious crowd grew violent. |

fragment	*n.* 碎片；片段 (a broken part or piece of something)
['frægmənt]	① The dish lay in fragments on the floor.
	② I could only hear fragments of their conversation.
	v. (使) 碎裂；(使) 破裂 (to break or make something break into parts or pieces)
	These issues are fragmenting our society.

fragile	*adj.* 易碎的；脆弱的 (easily broken or damaged; very delicate)
['frædʒaɪl]	① Her health has always been very fragile.
	② The fragile economies of several southern African nations could be irreparably damaged.

| **infringe** | *v.* 违背；触犯 (法规) (to do something that does not obey or follow a rule, law, etc.) |
| [ɪn'frɪndʒ] | They claim that his use of the name infringes their copyright. |

Cherry系列

cherish	*v.* 珍惜 (to remember or hold an idea, belief, etc. in a deeply felt way)
['tʃerɪʃ]	I will always cherish that memory.
	v. 珍爱 (to feel or show great love for someone or something)
	He genuinely loved and cherished her.

| **charity** | *n.* 慈善机构 (an organization for helping people in need) |
| ['tʃærəti] | The dinner was held to raise funds for several charities. |

charitable	*adj.* 仁慈的；慈善的 (done or designed to help people who are poor, sick)
['tʃærətəbl]	① He performs charitable work to help the poor.
	② She makes a charitable donation every year.

caress	*v.* 爱抚；抚摸 (to touch someone or something in a gentle way)
[kə'res]	① She caressed the baby's cheek.
	② A warm breeze caressed her face.

Wrench系列

wrench [rentʃ]	*v.* 猛拉；猛拧 (to twist or pull somebody/something suddenly and violently) **1** He felt two men wrench the suitcase from his hand. **2** She wrenched herself from his grasp. *n.* 扳手 (a tool used in turning nuts or bolts) I had to run around to several shops to get that wrench.
wriggle ['rɪgl]	*v.* 扭动；蠕动 (to twist from side to side with small quick movements like a worm) The snake wriggled across the path and went underneath a bush.
wrestle ['resl]	*v.* 摔跤；扭斗 (to fight someone by holding and pushing) They'll be wrestling each other for the championship. *v.* 奋力对付；努力处理；全力解决 (to struggle to deal with something that is difficult) He's wrestling with a problem.
wrangle ['ræŋgl]	*n.* 争吵；争论 (an argument that is complicated and continues over a long period of time) They had a bitter wrangle over custody of their children.
wrap [ræp]	*v.* 包；裹 (to cover something by folding a piece of material around it) They were busy wrapping presents late on Christmas Eve.
wreath [ri:θ]	*n.* 花圈 (an arrangement of flowers and leaves, especially in the shape of a circle, placed on graves, etc. as a sign of respect for somebody who has died) The President laid a wreath on the hero's grave.
wrist [rɪst]	*n.* 手腕 (the joint between the hand and the arm) Hanging from his right wrist is a heavy gold bracelet.

Lift系列

lift [lɪft]	*v.* 举起；抬起 (to raise from a lower to a higher position) **1** He lifted his pen from the paper. **2** The balloon lifted into the sky.

aloft [əˈlɒft]	*adv.* 在空中；在高处 (in the air)
	① The balloon stayed aloft for days.
	② He held the trophy proudly aloft.
lofty [ˈlɒfti]	*adj.* （思想，目标等）崇高的；高尚的 (of a thought, an aim, etc. deserving praise because of its high moral quality)
	He set lofty goals for himself as a teacher.
	adj. 高傲的 (showing a proud and superior attitude)
	She showed a lofty disregard for their objections.

追根溯源

　　在罗马神话中，俄普斯（Ops）是播种和丰产女神，也是农神萨图恩（Saturn）的妻子。在古罗马神庙中，俄普斯往往和农神萨图恩一道接受人们的祭祀。每年8月25日是俄普斯(Ops)的节日，人们在收获完毕后举行感恩庆祝。Ops是丰产女神，她的名字自然就成为了表示"丰富的"词根，opulent（富裕的）和copious（大量的）便由此而来。

opulent [ˈɒpjələnt]	*adj.* 富裕的 (having or showing much wealth)
	The opulent mansion is filled with priceless art and antiques.
opulence [ˈɒpjələns]	*n.* 富裕；富饶 (state of being wealthy)
	In some parts of the city nearly unimaginable opulence can be found side by side with nearly unthinkable poverty.
copious [ˈkəʊpiəs]	*adj.* 大量的；多产的 (very large in amount or number)
	① The storm produced a copious amount of rain.
	② She sat in the front row and took copious notes during the lecture.

　　在希腊神话中，坦塔罗斯（拉丁语Tantalus，希腊语Tantalos）为希腊神话中主神宙斯之子，起初甚得众神的宠爱，获得别人不易得到的极大荣誉，例如，能参观奥林匹亚山众神的集会和宴会。坦塔罗斯因此变得骄傲自大，侮辱众神。有一次，为了试探众神是否真的知晓一切而邀请众神来家中做客，他杀死了自己的儿子，并将其做成一道美食来款待众神。众神看出了他的伎俩，没有吃。坦塔罗斯最终受到了众神的严惩，他被绑在深水当中，水波刚好触到他的下巴，他的额头上荡着鲜美的水果，可是当他渴了想喝水时，一低头，水便迅速下降，无法喝到；当他饿了想吃水果时，一抬头，果实便迅速上升，无法吃到，他因此而饱受折磨。人们借用他的名字Tantalus创造了表示"引诱"之意的tantalize一词，意指激起一个人对某事的渴望而不予满足。

tantalize	*v.* 逗弄；引诱 (to cause someone to feel interest or excitement about something that is very attractive)
['tæntəlaɪz]	**①** The boy would come into the room and tantalize the dog with bone.
	② She was tantalized by the possibility of earning a lot of money quickly.

锦囊妙记

languid	*adj.* 疲倦的；没精打采的 (having very little strength, energy, or activity)
['læŋgwɪd]	His languid manner annoys me when there's work to be done.
	谐音法 languid–懒鬼的，懒鬼看起来总是疲倦的，没精打采的 (languid)。
languor	*n.* 懒散；倦怠 (weakness or weariness of body or mind)
['læŋgə(r)]	They enjoyed the languor brought on by a hot summer afternoon.
	谐音法 languor–懒鬼，当然是懒散，倦怠 (languor)。
languish	*v.* 变得衰弱 (to be or become feeble, weak or enervated)
['læŋgwɪʃ]	Older people, especially, were languishing during the prolonged heat wave.
coward	*n.* 胆小鬼；懦夫 (someone who is too afraid to do what is right or expected)
['kaʊəd]	The soldiers who ran as soon as the first shots were fired were branded as cowards.
	谐音法 coward–靠我的，遇到事，只知道靠我的，当然是懦夫(coward)！
cower	*v.* 畏缩 (to move back or bend your body down because you are afraid)
['kaʊə(r)]	**①** The thunder made our dog cower.
	② They cowered at the sight of the gun.
	谐音法 cower–靠我！只知道靠我，当然是胆怯畏缩(cower)!

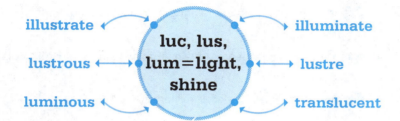

lucid	*adj.* 清楚的 (very clear and easy to understand)
['luːsɪd]	His explanation was lucid and to the point.
elucidate	*v.* 阐明；解释 (to explain or clarify something)
[i'luːsɪdeɪt]	When asked for details about his contract, he declined to elucidate.
translucent	*adj.* 半透明的；透亮的 (not transparent but clear enough to allow rays of light to pass through)
[træns'luːsnt]	We could see shapes moving on the other side of the translucent window, but we couldn't tell what they were.
luminous	*adj.* 发光的 (producing or seeming to produce light)
['luːmɪnəs]	I looked up at the night sky and marveled at the millions of luminous stars.
illuminate	*v.* 阐明；解释 (to make something easy to understand)
[ɪ'luːmɪneɪt]	The professor illuminates confusing parts of the novel for the students.
lustre	*n.* 光泽；光辉 (a shine or soft glow)
['lʌstə(r)]	Gold retains its lustre for far longer than other metals.
lustrous	*adj.* 柔软光亮的 (soft and shining)
['lʌstrəs]	Lustrous silver jewelry adorned her neck.
illustrate	*v.* 说明 (to give examples in order to make something easier to understand)
['ɪləstreɪt]	He illustrated his lecture with stories of his own experiences in the field.
	v. 给……加插图 (to decorate a story, book with pictures)
	He has illustrated the book with colorful photographs.

illustration

[ˌɪlə'streɪʃn]

n. 说明 (an example or instance used to make something clear)

The speech included illustrations of his successes.

n. 插图 (a picture or diagram that explains or decorates something)

The dictionary has color illustrations.

illustrious

[ɪ'lʌstriəs]

adj. 著名的；杰出的 (very famous and much admired because of what you have achieved)

1 William Shakespeare remains England's most illustrious playwright and poet.

2 He has had an illustrious military career.

illusion

[ɪ'luːʒn]

n. 错觉；幻想 (something that is false or unreal but seems to be true or real)

The video game is designed to give the illusion that you are in control of an airplane.

illusory

[ɪ'luːsəri]

adj. 虚幻的 (based on something that is not true or real)

It seemed to an idealistic and illusory dream.

lacklustre

['læklʌstə(r)]

adj. 无趣味的；枯燥乏味的 (lacking excitement or interest)

The actor gave a lacklustre performance.

luxury

['lʌkʃəri]

n. 奢侈品 (something that is expensive and not necessary)

He spent a fortune on expensive wines and other luxuries.

luxurious

[lʌg'ʒuəriəs]

adj. 奢侈的；豪华的 (very comfortable and expensive)

It is one of the country's most luxurious resorts.

Appear系列

appear

[ə'pɪə(r)]

v. 出现；显现 (to come into sight)

1 Stars appeared in the sky.

2 The first dinosaurs appeared around 215 million years ago.

disappear

[ˌdɪsə'pɪə(r)]

v. 不见；消失 (to stop being visible; to pass out of sight)

The sun disappeared behind a cloud.

v. 灭绝 (to stop existing)

Dinosaurs disappeared long ago.

apparent	*adj.* 清楚的；明显的 (easy to see or understand)
[əˈpærənt]	From the beginning, it was apparent that she was not an ordinary child.
transparent	*adj.* 透明的 (clear enough or thin enough to be seen through)
[trænsˈpærənt]	❶ Windows are made of transparent materials like glass or clear plastic.
	❷ The transparent ocean was so clear, you could see the fish swimming.
	adj. 透明的；清楚的 (easily detected or seen through)
	We are now striving hard to establish a transparent parliamentary democracy.

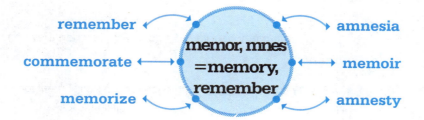

remember — amnesia

commemorate — memoir

memorize — amnesty

memor, mnes
=memory,
remember

remember	*v.* 记得；记起 (to bring back to your mind a fact, piece of information, etc. that you knew)
[rɪˈmembə(r)]	I remember my first day of school like it was yesterday.
memorize	*v.* 记住；熟记 (to learn something so well that you are able to remember it perfectly)
[ˈmeməraɪz]	He studied the map, trying to memorize the way.
memory	*n.* 记忆力 (the power or process of remembering what has been learned)
[ˈmeməri]	He began to lose his memory as he grew older.
	n. 回忆；往事 (the things learned and kept in the mind)
	The happiness of those times is still vivid in my memory.
commemorate	*v.* 纪念；庆祝 (to mark by some ceremonies; to celebrate)
[kəˈmeməreɪt]	Each year on this date we commemorate our ancestors with a special ceremony.
memorial	*n.* 纪念碑；纪念物 (a statue, stone, etc. that is built in order to remind people of an important past event or of a famous person who has died)
[məˈmɔːriəl]	Building a memorial to Columbus has been his lifelong dream.

immemorial [ˌɪmə'mɔːriəl]	*adj.* 无法追忆的；远古的 (very old or ancient; from a time so long ago that it cannot be remembered) ① Stories passed down from time immemorial. ② It has remained virtually unchanged since time immemorial.
memoir ['memwɑː(r)]	*n.* 回忆录；自传 (an account of the personal experiences of an author) He has just published a memoir in honour of his captain.
memento [mə'mentəʊ]	*n.* 遗物；纪念品 (something that is kept as a reminder of a person, place or thing) It was a memento of our trip.
amnesia [æm'niːziə]	*n.* 遗忘症；记忆缺失 (an abnormal and usually complete loss of one's memory) It is sad that many people have got amnesia when they come out from disasters.
amnesty ['æmnəsti]	*n.* 大赦；特赦 (a warrant granting release from punishment for an offense) The government gave amnesty to all political prisoners.

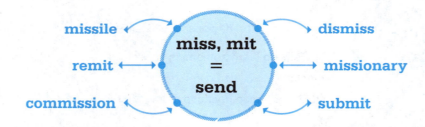

missile ['mɪsaɪl]	*n.* 导弹 (any object or weapon that is thrown at a target or shot from an engine, etc.) Missile launches and nuclear tests are banned by the U.N. Security Council.
dismiss [dɪs'mɪs]	*v.* 解雇 (to end the employment or service of someone) Several employees were recently dismissed. *v.* 解散 (to cause or allow someone to leave) The students were dismissed early because of the snowstorm. *v.* 不考虑；不理会 (to decide not to think about or consider something or someone) I don't think we should dismiss the matter lightly.

remit ['riːmɪt]	*v.* 汇款 (to send money as a payment) Many immigrants regularly remit money to their families.
remittance [rɪ'mɪtns]	*n.* 汇款 (an amount of money that is sent as a payment for something) Remittance can be made by check or credit card.
mission ['mɪʃn]	*n.* 使命 (a special assignment given to a person or group) He regards it as his mission to help the cause of world peace. *n.* 代表团 (a group of people sent by a government to represent it in a foreign country) He is a senior member of a diplomatic mission.
missionary ['mɪʃənri]	*n.* 传教士 (a Christian who has been sent to a foreign country to teach people about Christianity) An American missionary was released today after more than two months of captivity.
commission [kə'mɪʃn]	*n.* 委员会 (a group of persons directed to perform some duty) Both states set up commissions to examine their public schools. *v.* 任命；委任 (to appoint or assign to a task or function) The king commissioned the artist to paint his portrait. *n.* 佣金 (a percentage of the money received from a total paid to the agent) He gets a commission for each car he sells.
submit [səb'mɪt]	*v.* 提交 (to leave to the judgment or approval of someone else) 1 I'm submitting a plan for consideration. 2 Photographs submitted for publication will not be returned. *v.* 顺从；服从 (to yield to the authority, control, or choice of another) The students must submit themselves to the disciplines at school.
submissive [səb'mɪsɪv]	*adj.* 顺从的；唯命是从的 (willing to obey someone else) Most doctors want their patients to be submissive.
emit [i'mɪt]	*v.* 发出；发射 (to send light, energy, etc. out from a source) The telescope can detect light emitted by distant galaxies.
emission [i'mɪʃn]	*n.* 排放物 (something sent out or given off) For environmental safety we must seek to reduce the factory's emission of fumes and smoke.

emissary
['emɪsəri]

n. (外交上的) 使者 (a person who is sent on a mission to represent another person or organization)

She acted as the president's personal emissary to the union leaders.

promise
['prɒmɪs]

v. 允诺；许诺 (to state that something will or will not be done)

The governor promised that the prisoners would receive a fair trial.

compromise
['kɒmprəmaɪz]

v. 折中解决；妥协 (to settle by agreeing that each side will change or give up some demands)

The two sides were unwilling to compromise.

v. 损害 (to damage or weaken something)

We can't reveal that information without compromising national security.

intermittent
[ˌɪntə'mɪtənt]

adj. 间歇的；断断续续的 (stopping and starting at irregular intervals)

1 The patient was having intermittent pains in his back.

2 After three hours of intermittent rain, the game was abandoned.

transmit
[træns'mɪt]

v. 传输；传送 (to send or convey from one person or place to another)

Mosquitoes transmit disease to humans.

transmission
[træns'mɪʃn]

n. 播送；传送 (process of sending electrical signals to a radio, television,computer)

The equipment is used for the transmission of television signals.

admit
[əd'mɪt]

v. 许可进入 (to allow somebody/something to enter a place)

Journalists are rarely admitted to the region.

v. 承认 (to agree, often unwillingly, that something is true)

I am willing to admit that I do make mistakes.

admission
[əd'mɪʃn]

n. 准许进入 (the act of admitting or allowing something)

He submitted an application for admission to the school.

n. 承认；坦白 (a statement in which somebody admits that something is true, especially something wrong or bad that they have done)

By his own admission, he evaded taxes as a Florida real-estate speculator.

permit
[pə'mɪt] v.

['pɜːmɪt] n.

v. 许可；准许 (to allow something to happen)

1 The judge permitted the release of the prisoner.

2 Smoking is not permitted in the building.

n. 许可证；执照 (license granted by one having authority)

The majority of foreign nationals working here have work permits.

Unit 19

permission

[pə'mɪʃn]

n. 准许；许可 (the approval of a person in authority)

1 They got permission from the city to build an apartment complex.

2 The teacher gave me her permission to go home early.

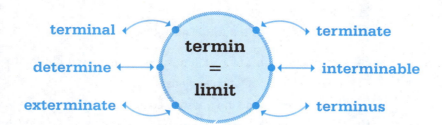

terminal

['tɜ:mɪnl]

adj. 晚期的 (approaching death, fatal)

Downie, 53, who was diagnosed with terminal brain cancer in December 2015, died on Tuesday night surrounded by his children and family.

n. 航站楼 (station where transport vehicles load or unload passengers or goods)

Passengers from all terminals at the airport fled in a panic over erroneous reports of an additional airport shooter.

terminate

['tɜ:mɪneɪt]

v. 结束；使终结 (to end; to make something end)

His contract terminates at the end of the season.

terminable

['tɜ:mɪnəbl]

adj. 有期限的；可终止的 (able to be terminated)

The contract was terminable by either party.

terminus

['tɜ:mɪnəs]

n. 终点 (the end of a travel route such as a rail or bus line)

We arrived at the terminus.

interminable

[ɪn'tɜ:mɪnəbl]

adj. 冗长的；无止境的 (seeming to have no end)

Winter seems interminable and summer seems too short.

determine

[dɪ'tɜ:mɪn]

v. 查明；测定；准确算出 (to discover the facts about something; to calculate something exactly)

Police determined the cause of the accident.

v. 决定 (to come to a decision)

The new policy will be determined by a special committee.

exterminate

[ɪk'stɜ:mɪneɪt]

v. 消灭；根除 (to destroy or kill a group of animals, people, etc. completely)

The invaders nearly exterminated the native people.

sacred

['seɪkrɪd]

adj. 神圣的 (worthy of religious worship)

They'll make jokes about anything. Nothing is sacred to those guys.

adj. 不可侵犯的 (highly valued and important)

① He said the unity of the country was sacred.

② We have a sacred duty to find out the truth.

sacrifice

['sækrɪfaɪs]

n. 牺牲；献祭 (an act of killing a person or animal in a religious ceremony as an offering to please a god)

The villagers hoped the gods would accept their sacrifice.

v. 以 (人或动物) 作为祭献 (to offer as a sacrifice)

The ancient ritual involved sacrificing an animal.

v. 牺牲；奉献 (to give up something especially for the sake of something or someone else)

They sacrificed their lives for their country.

sanctity

['sæŋktəti]

n. 圣洁；神圣 (state of being holy, very important, or valuable)

He has violated, in cold blood, the sanctity of a human heart.

sanctuary

['sæŋktʃuəri]

n. 避难所；庇护所 (a place that provides safety or protection)

The refugees found sanctuary when they crossed the border.

sanctify

['sæŋktɪfaɪ]

v. 使神圣 (to make something holy)

The constitution sanctified the rights of the people.

desecrate

['desɪkreɪt]

v. 亵渎；玷污 (to treat a sacred place or sacred object shamefully or with great disrespect)

① She shouldn't have desecrated the picture of a religious leader.

② The earth is to be honored; it is not to be desecrated.

consecrate

['kɒnsɪkreɪt]

v. 把……奉为神圣 (to officially make something, such as a place or building, holy through a special religious ceremony)

They planned to consecrate the altar in the new church with great ceremony.

sanctimonious

[ˌsæŋktɪ'məʊniəs]

adj. 假装圣洁的 (pretending to be morally better than other people)

You do not have to be so sanctimonious to prove that you are devout.

Unit 19

Break系列

breach [briːtʃ]	_v._ 违反；破坏 (to not keep to an agreement or not keep a promise) The newspaper breached the code of conduct on privacy. _n._ 违反；破坏 (a failure to act in a promised or required way) Many people consider her decision to be a breach of trust.
brittle ['brɪtl]	_adj._ 易碎的 (easily broken or cracked) These incidents suggest the peace in North Korean is still brittle.
debris ['debriː]	_n._ 碎片；残骸 (the pieces that are left after something has been destroyed) After the earthquake, rescuers began digging through the debris in search of survivors.

Caper系列

caper ['keɪpə(r)]	_v._ 跳跃；雀跃 (to jump around in a lively way) As summer drew to a close, the children spent their days wistfully capering on the beach.
capricious [kə'prɪʃəs]	_adj._ 变化无常的；任性的 (changing often and quickly) The court ruled that the punishment was arbitrary and capricious.

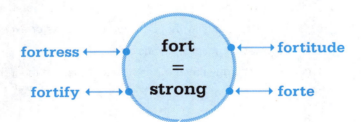

fortress ['fɔːtrəs]	_n._ 堡垒；要塞 (a place that is protected against attack) After a long fight, they managed to take the fortress.
fortify ['fɔːtɪfaɪ]	_v._ 加强；增强 (to make someone or something stronger) ❶ Support for his theories has been fortified by the results of these experiments. ❷ He took a deep breath to fortify himself before stepping onto the stage.

fortitude

['fɔ:tɪtjuːd]

n. 坚韧；刚毅 (mental strength and courage that allows someone to face danger, pain)

She has endured disappointments with fortitude and patience.

forte

['fɔ:teɪ]

n. 特长；专长 (something in which a person shows special ability)

Music is my forte.

追根溯源

　　在古希腊神话中，海神波塞冬（Poseidon）的威严可与大地无穷无尽的生命力及洪水相匹敌，被称为大海的宙斯，其地位和力量之高，仅次于天父宙斯。海王星以他的罗马名涅普顿（Neptune）命名。希腊语词根posis便来自波塞冬（Poseidon），表示"威力强大"，potent（强有力的）和potential（有潜力的）都来源于此。

potent

['pəʊtnt]

adj. 有效的；强有力的 (very effective)

The drug is extremely potent, but causes unpleasant side effects.

impotent

['ɪmpətənt]

adj. 无力的；虚弱的 (lacking power or strength)

The aggression of a bully leaves people feeling hurt, angry and impotent.

potential

[pə'tenʃl]

adj. 潜在的；有可能的 (existing in possibility)

Critics say the factory poses a potential threat to the environment.

n. 潜力 (an ability or quality that can lead to success or excellence)

❶ She has great potential as a musician.

❷ The new technology has the potential to transform the industry.

Lunar系列

lunar

['luːnə(r)]

adj. 月球的 (of or relating to the moon)

The astronauts piloted their craft down to the lunar surface.

lunatic	*adj.* 疯狂的；精神错乱的 (affected with a severely disordered state of mind)
['luːnətɪk]	He hatched a lunatic plot to overthrow the government.
	在西方一直广泛流传着这样一种说法：精神病与月的盈亏有关，在月亮逐渐变圆之时，精神病患者会随之变得更加狂乱。意为"疯子"的lunatic一词正是基于这一说法而产生的。

锦囊妙记

stoic	*adj.* 坚忍的；苦修的 (showing no emotion especially when something bad is happening)
['stəʊɪk]	He had a stoic expression on his face.
	联想法 sto—stone，一个人像石头一样无情，就是坚忍的(stoic)。
hermit	*n.* 隐士 (a person who lives alone, away from people and society)
['hɜːmɪt]	The cave was inhabited by a hermit.
	谐音法 hermit—何觅他，觅不到了，因为他归隐了(hermit)。
aghast	*adj.* 惊呆的；吓呆的 (struck with terror, surprise or horror)
[ə'gɑːst]	The news left her aghast.
	联想法 ghast—ghost，见到鬼了，当然是吓呆了(aghast)。
ghastly	*adj.* 可怕的 (very shocking or horrible)
['gɑːstli]	When he heard the news, his face took on a ghastly expression.
	联想法 联想ghost!

Unit 19

Unit
20

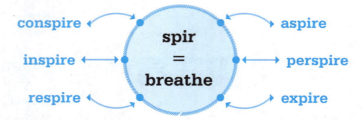

spirit ['spɪrɪt]	**n.** 精神；心灵 (the force within a person that is believed to give the body life, energy and power) ① The human spirit is virtually indestructible. ② Yoga is very healthy for both body and spirit.
spiritual ['spɪrɪtʃuəl]	**adj.** 精神的；心灵的 (relating to a person's spirit) Doctors must consider the emotional and spiritual needs of their patients. **adj.** 宗教的 (relating to religion or religious beliefs) I regularly consult our priest about spiritual matters.
dispiriting [dɪ'spɪrɪtɪŋ]	**adj.** 令人沮丧的 (lowering someone's spirits) It's very dispiriting to be out of a job.
conspire [kən'spaɪə(r)]	**v.** 密谋；共谋 (to secretly plan with someone to do something that is harmful or illegal) They conspired with the terrorists to overthrow the government.
conspiracy [kən'spɪrəsi]	**n.** 阴谋 (a secret plan made by two or more people to do something that is harmful or illegal) The CIA uncovered a conspiracy against the government.
inspire [ɪn'spaɪə(r)]	**v.** 鼓舞；激励 (to make someone want to do something) ① He inspired generations of future scientists. ② Her courage has inspired us. **v.** 给予……灵感 (to cause something to occur or to be created or done) Her first novel was inspired by her early childhood.
inspirational [ˌɪnspə'reɪʃənl]	**adj.** 鼓舞人心的 (providing inspiration) He also travels the world as an inspirational speaker.

Unit 20

inspiration [ˌɪnspəˈreɪʃn]	*n.* 灵感 (something that moves someone to act, create or feel an emotion) **1** His paintings take their inspiration from nature. **2** While deciding on a costume, I had an inspiration.
aspire [əˈspaɪə(r)]	*v.* 渴望；立志 (to want achieve something, such as a particular career or level of success) She aspired to the position of president.
aspiration [ˌæspəˈreɪʃn]	*n.* 强烈的愿望 (a strong desire to achieve something) She left home with aspirations for a better life.
aspiring [əˈspaɪərɪŋ]	*adj.* 有志气的；有抱负的 (desiring and working to achieve a particular goal) Aspiring musicians need hours of practice every day.
expire [ɪkˈspaɪə(r)]	*v.* 失效 (to no longer be valid after a period of time) He continued to live in the States after his visa had expired. *v.* 断气 (to die) He endured excruciating agonies before he finally expired.
expiration [ˌekspəˈreɪʃn]	*n.* 满期；截止 (the end of something that lasts for a certain period of time) Check the expiration date on your passport.
respire [rɪˈspaɪə(r)]	*v.* 呼吸 (to breathe in and out) **1** Fish use their gills to respire. **2** Different parts of a plant respire at different rates.
respiration [ˌrespəˈreɪʃn]	*n.* 呼吸 (the act or process of breathing) The doctor checked his heartbeat and respiration.
respiratory [rəˈspɪrətri]	*adj.* 呼吸的 (relating to breathing) If you smoke then the whole respiratory system is constantly under attack.
respite [ˈrespaɪt]	*n.* 喘息；缓解 (a period of rest or relief) **1** The bad weather has continued without respite. **2** Devaluation would only give the economy a brief respite.
perspire [pəˈspaɪə(r)]	*v.* 出汗；流汗 (to give off salty liquid through the skin) I was nervous and I feel myself start to perspire.
perspiration [ˌpɜːspəˈreɪʃn]	*n.* 汗水；出汗 (the clear liquid that forms on your skin when you are hot or nervous) His hands were wet with perspiration.

Unit 20

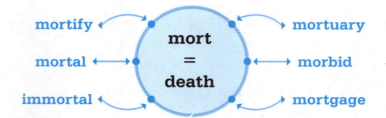

mortal	adj. 终有一死的 (certain to die)
['mɔːtl]	Every living creature is mortal.
	adj. 致命的 (possibly causing death)
	He suffered a mortal wound in the battle.
immortal	adj. 不死的；永恒的 (not capable of dying; living forever; eternal)
[ɪ'mɔːtl]	A person's soul is said to be immortal.
	n. 不朽的作家 (a person of lasting fame)
	Shakespeare is one of the immortals.
mortify	v. 使受辱 (to cause someone to feel very embarrassed and foolish)
['mɔːtɪfaɪ]	Jane mortified her family by leaving her husband.
mortuary	n. 停尸房；太平间 (a room in a hospital where dead bodies are kept before
['mɔːtʃəri]	they are buried)
	The bodies were taken to a mortuary.
morbid	adj. 病态的 (relating to unpleasant subjects such as death)
['mɔːbɪd]	She reads the account of the murder with a morbid interest.
moribund	adj. 濒死的；垂死的 (no longer active or effective; close to failure)
['mɒrɪbʌnd]	The actor is trying to revive his moribund career.
mortgage	n. 抵押 (a legal agreement in which a person borrows money to buy
['mɔːgɪdʒ]	property such as a house and pays back the money over a period of
	years)
	He will have to take out a mortgage in order to buy the house.
	v. 抵押 (to give someone a legal claim on property that you own in
	exchange for money that you will pay back over a period of years)
	She mortgaged her house in order to buy the restaurant.

Cover系列

recover [rɪˈkʌvə(r)]	*v.* 恢复健康；康复 (to become healthy after an illness or injury) He had a heart attack but is recovering well. *v.* 找回；寻回；找到 (to get back or find something that was lost, stolen or missing) The program helps users recover computer files that have been deleted.
discover [dɪˈskʌvə(r)]	*v.* 发现 (to see, find or become aware of something for the first time) Several new species of plants have recently been discovered.
discovery [dɪˈskʌvəri]	*n.* 发现；发觉 (something seen or learned for the first time) Scientists announced the discovery of a new species of plant.
uncover [ʌnˈkʌvə(r)]	*v.* 揭露；发现 (to find or become aware of something that was hidden or secret) ❶ Archaeologists uncovered the ruins of an ancient city. ❷ We shoveled away the dirt to uncover the treasure.
recuperate [rɪˈkuːpəreɪt]	*v.* 恢复；复原 (to return to normal health or strength after being sick, injured) It takes a long time to recuperate after major surgery.
covert [ˈkʌvət]	*adj.* 隐蔽的；不公开的 (made or done secretly) He has taken part in a number of covert military operations.
overt [əʊˈvɜːt]	*adj.* 明显的；公然的 (easily seen; not secret or hidden) They focus on overt discrimination rather than insidious aspects of racism.

Unit 20

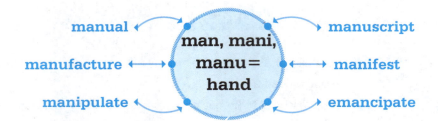

manual ['mænjuəl]	*adj.* 手工的 (relating to using the hands)
	He has a collection of old-fashioned manual typewriters.
	adj. 体力的 (doing or involving hard physical work)
	She spent the summer doing manual labor on her uncle's farm.
	n. 手册 (a small book that gives useful information about something)
	We lost the instruction manual and couldn't put our bikes together.
manufacture [ˌmænjuˈfæktʃə(r)]	*v.* 制造；生产 (to make into a product suitable for use)
	This firm manufactures cars at the rate of two hundred per day.
	v. 捏造；虚构 (to create something, such as a false story or explanation by using your imagination)
	He manufactures excuses for being absent.
manipulate [məˈnɪpjuleɪt]	*v.* 操作；处理 (to operate, use or move something with the hands or by mechanical means)
	The mechanical arms are manipulated by a computer.
	v. (暗中) 控制；操纵；影响 (to control or influence somebody/something, often in a dishonest way so that they do not realize it)
	The candidates tried to manipulate public opinion.
manipulative [məˈnɪpjələtɪv]	*adj.* 控制的；善于摆布 (他人) 的 (skilfull at influencing somebody or forcing somebody to do what you want, often in an unfair way)
	The worker was promoted despite aggressive and manipulative behavior.
manifest [ˈmænɪfest]	*adj.* 明白的；明显的 (easy to detect or recognize)
	His love for literature is manifest in his large library.
	v. 显示；表明 (to make evident or certain by showing or displaying)
	Their religious beliefs are manifested in every aspect of their lives.
manure [məˈnjʊə(r)]	*n.* 肥料 (material that fertilizes land)
	The farmer is putting manure on his fields.
	v. 给……施肥 (to put manure on or in soil to help plants grow)
	The farmer has been manuring the fields.

manuscript ['mænjuskrɪpt]	*n.* 手稿；原稿 (the original copy of a play, book, piece of music, etc., before it has been printed) The library owns the author's original manuscript.
emancipate [ɪ'mænsɪpeɪt]	*v.* 解放；解脱 (to free someone from someone else's control or power) **1** That war preserved the Union and emancipated the slaves. **2** He felt the only way to emancipate himself from his parents was to move away.
emancipation [ɪ,mænsɪ'peɪʃn]	*n.* 解放 (an act of setting someone free from control or slavery) They discussed the role that the emancipation of slaves played in the nation's history.

Am系列

amity ['æməti]	*n.* 和睦；友好 (a friendly relationship between people or countries) He wished to live in amity with his neighbor.
amicable ['æmɪkəbl]	*adj.* 友好的；温和的 (showing a polite and friendly desire to avoid disagreement and argument) They reached an amicable agreement.
amiable ['eɪmiəbl]	*adj.* 和蔼可亲的；温和的 (friendly and pleasant) **1** Everyone knew him as an amiable fellow. **2** She had an amiable conversation with her friend.
amorous ['æmərəs]	*adj.* 多情的；爱情的 (showing strong feelings of sexual attraction or love) Male birds engage in amorous behavior—nest-building, singing, showing off their finery—in order to attract females.

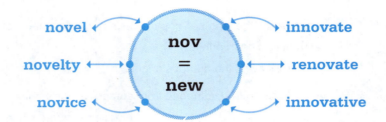

novel ['nɒvl]	**n.** (长篇) 小说 (a long story usually about imaginary characters and events) The scriptwriter helped him to adapt his novel for the screen. **adj.** 新奇的 (new and different from what is already known) She has suggested a novel approach to the problem.
novelty ['nɒvlti]	**n.** 新奇；新奇的事物 (something that is new or unusual) Eating shark meat is a novelty to many people.
novice ['nɒvɪs]	**n.** 初学者；新手 (a person who has just started learning or doing something) He's a novice in cooking.
innovate ['ɪnəveɪt]	**v.** 改革；创新 (to do something in a new way) We must constantly adapt and innovate to ensure success in a growing market.
innovative ['ɪnəveɪtɪv]	**adj.** 革新的；创新的 (having new ideas about how something can be done) He was one of the most creative and innovative engineers of his generation.
renovate ['renəveɪt]	**v.** 翻新；修复 (to put something in good condition again) The entire house is being renovated.
renovation [ˌrenə'veɪʃn]	**n.** 翻新；修复 (the act or process of repairing and painting an old building, piece of furniture, etc. so that it is in good condition again) The cinema will reopen next week after the renovation.

Join系列

joint [dʒɔɪnt]	**adj.** 共同的；联合的 (combining the work of two or more people or groups of people) The joint effect of wind and rain caused erosion.

Unit 20

	n. 关节 (a point where two bones meet in the body) Her joints ache if she exercises.
adjoin [ə'dʒɔɪn]	*v.* 邻近；毗连 (to be next to or joined to something) The two rooms adjoin each other.
adjacent [ə'dʒeɪsnt]	*adj.* 邻近的；毗邻的 (next to or near something) My sister sleeps in the adjacent room.
juncture ['dʒʌŋktʃə(r)]	*n.* 关头；关键时刻 (an important point in a process or activity) Negotiations between the countries reached a critical juncture.
adjunct ['ædʒʌŋkt]	*n.* 附件；附属物 (a thing that is added or attached to something larger or more important) Massage therapy can be used as an adjunct along with the medication.

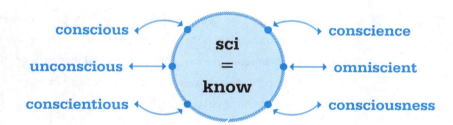

conscious ['kɒnʃəs]	*adj.* 有意识的 (awake and able to understand what is happening around you) She was fully conscious throughout the operation.
consciousness ['kɒnʃəsnəs]	*n.* 意识 (the condition of being mentally awake and active) Following surgery, she slowly regained consciousness. *n.* 观念，态度 (knowledge that is shared by a group of people) He hopes that he can raise public consciousness of the disease.
unconscious [ʌn'kɒnʃəs]	*adj.* 失去知觉的；无意识的 (not awake especially because of an injury, drug) She was unconscious for three days after the accident.
conscience ['kɒnʃəns]	*n.* 良心；道德心 (a sense of right and wrong and a feeling that what is right should be done) ① Her conscience told her to tell the truth. ② Democracy depends on the conscience of the voters.

conscientious [ˌkɒnʃi'enʃəs]	*adj.* 认真负责的 (very careful about doing what you are supposed to do) ① She has always been a very conscientious worker. ② He was conscientious about following the doctor's orders.
omniscient [ɒm'nɪsiənt]	*adj.* 无所不知的 (having unlimited understanding or knowledge) There's so many movies that show the CIA is omniscient and far more efficient than it really is.
subconscious [ˌsʌb'kɒnʃəs]	*n.* 潜意识 (the part of your mind that contains feelings that you are not aware of) A person's behavior can be influenced by urges that exist only in the subconscious.

Max系列

magnitude ['mægnɪtjuːd]	*n.* 巨大；重大；重要性 (the great size or importance of something; the degree to which something is large or important) Ministers underestimated the magnitude of the task confronting them. *n.* (地震) 级数 (a number that shows the power of an earthquake) The San Francisco earthquake of 1906 had a magnitude of 8.3.
magnify ['mægnɪfaɪ]	*v.* 加强；加大 (to make something greater) ① A microscope magnifies an object seen through it. ② Poverty and human folly magnify natural disasters. *v.* 夸大 (to make something seem more important or serious than it really is) The problem has been magnified by rumors.
magnate ['mægneɪt]	*n.* 富豪；巨头 (a person who has great wealth and power in a particular business or industry) He is a rich shipping magnate.
magnet ['mægnət]	*n.* 有吸引力的事物 (something or someone that attracts people or things) Lower interest rates are acting like a magnet, dragging consumers back to the shops.
magnetic [mæg'netɪk]	*adj.* 有磁性的；有吸引力的 (having a great power to attract people) The prosperous German economy have magnetic effect on would-be immigrants.

climax
['klaɪmæks]

n. 高潮 (the most interesting and exciting part of something)

At the novel's climax, the main character finds herself face to face with the thief.

v. 达到顶点或高潮 (to reach the most exciting or important part in something)

The movie climaxes with a fantastic chase scene.

Volun系列

volunteer
[ˌvɒlənˈtɪə(r)]

n. 志愿者；义务工作者 (a person who does work without getting paid to do it)

She now helps in a local school as a volunteer three days a week.

v. 自愿去做；主动提供 (to offer to do something without being forced to or without getting paid to do it)

The room was quiet; no one volunteered any further information.

volition
[vəˈlɪʃn]

n. 意志；意愿 (the power to make your own choices or decisions)

We like to think that everything we do and everything we think is a product of our volition.

volatile
['vɒlətaɪl]

adj. 易变的；不稳定的 (likely to change in a very sudden or extreme way)

1. There have been riots before and the situation is volatile.
2. He has a volatile temper.
3. It's thought that the blast occurred when volatile chemicals exploded.

malevolent
[məˈlevələnt]

adj. 恶毒的；心肠坏的 (having or showing a desire to cause harm to another person)

The wicked old woman gave a malevolent smile.

benevolent
[bəˈnevələnt]

adj. 乐善好施的 (kind and generous)

He belonged to several benevolent societies and charitable organizations.

Verb系列

verbal
['vɜːbl]

adj. 言语的；口头的 (relating to or consisting of words)

1. He scored well on the verbal section of the test.
2. He leveled a verbal assault against his Democratic opponents.

verbose

[vɜːˈbəʊs]

adj. 冗长的；啰唆的 (containing more words than necessary)

1 He is a verbose speaker.

2 She has a verbose writing style.

reverberate

[rɪˈvɜːbəreɪt]

v. 回响 (to reflect or be reflected many times)

1 Thunder reverberated in the mountains.

2 My voice reverberated throughout the room.

v. （事情、思想等）产生巨大反响 (to have a strong effect on people for a long time or over a large area)

The news sent shock waves through the community that have continued to reverberate to this day.

追根溯源

　　普罗透斯（Proteus)是希腊神话中的一个早期海神，是荷马所称的"海洋老人"之一。普罗透斯的名字来自希腊语protos（第一）。他有预测未来的能力，但只向能逮住他的人透露预言。为了避免被人逮住，他拥有随意改变自己形状的神力。普罗透斯居住在尼罗河三角洲海岸外的法罗斯岛上，以放牧海兽为生。英语词根proto表示"最初的"。prototype（原型），protagonist（主角），protein（蛋白质）和protocol（草案）都来自这一词源。

prototype

[ˈprəʊtətaɪp]

n. 原型 (an original model on which something is patterned)

1 They tested the prototype of the car.

2 He is developing a prototype for his invention.

n. 模范；典型 (a standard or typical example)

He is the prototype of a conservative businessman.

protein

[ˈprəʊtiːn]

n. 蛋白质 (a substance found in foods such as meat, milk, eggs and beans that is an important part of the human diet)

Fish is a major source of protein for the working man.

protocol

[ˈprəʊtəkɒl]

n. 礼仪 (a system of rules that explain the correct conduct and procedures to be followed in formal situations)

They did not follow the proper diplomatic protocols.

n. 草案 (a document that describes the details of a treaty or formal agreement between countries)

There are also protocols on the testing of nuclear weapons.

protagonist	*n.* 主人公；主角 (the main character in a novel, play, movie)
[prə'tægənɪst]	At the end of the story, the protagonist emerges as a powerful pugilist.
	n. 提倡者；拥护者 (an active supporter of a policy or movement, especially one that is trying to change something)
	She was a leading protagonist in the civil rights movement.

锦囊妙记

elated	*adj.* 兴高采烈的 (very happy and excited)
[ɪ'letɪd]	She was elated upon learning that she had been accepted by her first-choice college.
	谐音法 e-out (出来)，la-啦啦，啦啦队出来了，非常地兴高采烈 (elated)。
zealous	*adj.* 热心的；热情的 (showing a strong and energetic desire to get something done or see something succeed)
['zeləs]	The police were zealous in their pursuit of the criminals.
blatant	*adj.* 公然的；明目张胆的 (very obvious and offensive)
['bleɪtnt]	He showed a blatant disregard for the safety of other drivers.
	谐音法 bla-吧啦，吧啦！在公众场合吧啦吧啦说个不停！真是明目张胆 (blatant)。
assassinate	*v.* 暗杀；行刺 (to murder a usually important person by a surprise or secret attack)
[ə'sæsɪneɪt]	They discovered a secret plot to assassinate the governor.
	拆分法 ass-驴子，ass-驴子，in-在屋里，ate-吃，两头驴子在屋里遭到暗杀 (assassinate)，被吃掉了！

Unit 21

impede ⟷ pedestrian

impediment ⟷ **ped, pod = foot** ⟷ pedal

expedite ⟷ centipede

---

impede

[ɪmˈpiːd]

v. 阻碍；妨碍 (to slow the movement, progress or action of someone or something)

1 The soldiers could not impede the enemy's advance.

2 Fallen rock is impeding the progress of rescue workers.

---

impediment

[ɪmˈpedɪmənt]

n. 妨碍；阻止 (something that makes it difficult to do or complete something)

The new taxes were a major impediment to economic growth.

---

expedite

[ˈekspədaɪt]

v. 加快进展 (to cause something to happen faster)

We have developed rapid order processing to expedite deliveries to customers.

---

expedition

[ˌekspəˈdɪʃn]

n. 考察；远征 (a journey especially by a group of people for a specific purpose such as to explore a distant place)

An avid mountain climber, always on an expedition to some far-off corner of the world.

n. 远征队 (a group of people who travel together to a distant place)

Forty-three members of the expedition were killed.

---

pedal

[ˈpedl]

n. 踏板；脚蹬子 (a flat piece of metal, rubber, etc., that you push with your foot to make a machine move, work, or stop)

The harder the brake pedal is pressed, the greater the car's deceleration.

v. 骑自行车 (to ride a bicycle to a particular place)

He was pedaling as fast as he could.

---

pedestrian

[pəˈdestriən]

n. 步行者；行人 (a person who is walking)

The car slid off the road and almost hit a group of pedestrians.

	adj. 平淡无奇的 (not interesting or unusual)
	His style is so pedestrian that the book is really boring.
centipede ['sentɪpiːd]	*n.* 蜈蚣 (a small creature that is like an insect and that has a long, thin body and many legs)
	A centipede snaked swiftly away.
podiatrist [pə'daɪətrɪst]	*n.* 足病医生 (a specialist in care for the feet)
	He goes to the podiatrist to have his feet treated.
tripod ['traɪpɒd]	*n.* [摄]三脚架 (a three-legged stand as for a camera)
	A tripod will be useful to align and steady the camera.

Cur系列

accurate ['ækjərət]	*adj.* 精确的；准确的 (free from mistakes or errors)
	This may provide a quick and accurate way of monitoring the amount of carbon dioxide in the air.
accuracy ['ækjərəsi]	*n.* 精确性 (freedom from mistakes)
	① Each experiment is performed twice to ensure accuracy.
	② The police questioned the accuracy of his statement.
inaccurate [ɪn'ækjərət]	*adj.* 有错误的；不精密的 (not correct or exact)
	The reports were based on inaccurate information.
secure [sɪ'kjʊə(r)]	*v.* 使安全 (to make something safe by guarding or protecting it)
	We must secure the country's borders.
	adj. 安全的 (providing protection from danger or harm)
	Being home made me feel secure.
security [sɪ'kjʊərəti]	*n.* 安全；保证 (the state of being protected or safe from harm)
	① The college failed to provide adequate security on campus after dark.
	② We must insure our national security.

Unit 21

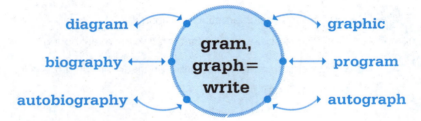

diagram ['daɪəɡræm]	*n.* 图表；图解 (a drawing that explains or shows the parts of something) This diagram shows how the clock operates.
biography [baɪ'ɒɡrəfi]	*n.* 传记 (the story of a real person's life written by someone other than that person) An unauthorized biography of the actor gave him some serious headaches.
autobiography [ˌɔːtəbaɪ'ɒɡrəfi]	*n.* 自传 (the biography of a person written by that person) I read her autobiography last year.
autograph ['ɔːtəɡrɑːf]	*n.* 亲笔签名 (a famous person's signature, especially when somebody asks them to write it) There were several autograph seekers outside the theatre.
program ['prəʊɡræm]	*v.* 编程 (to give a computer a set of instructions) He programmed the computer to calculate his monthly expenses and earnings. *n.* 计划；方案 (a plan of things that are done in order to achieve a specific result) ❶ The president accused the committee for the delay in passing his program. ❷ The reform program has brought unacceptably high unemployment and falling wages.
telegraph ['telɪɡrɑːf]	*n.* 电报 (an old-fashioned system of sending messages over long distances by using wires and electrical signals) I sent the message by telegraph. *v.* 发电报 (to send a message by telegraph) He telegraphed a message to her.
topography [tə'pɒɡrəfi]	*n.* 地形学 (the features, such as mountains and rivers, in an area of land) A map of the topography of the coastline shows a significant loss of wetlands.

Unit 21

graphic ['græfɪk]	*n.* 形象的 (shown or described in a very clear way) The report offered many graphic details about the devastating earthquake.
calligraphy [kə'lɪgrəfi]	*n.* 书法 (beautiful and artistic handwriting) Her calligraphy was the clearest I'd ever seen.

Spond系列

respond [rɪ'spɒnd]	*v.* 回答；响应 (to say something in return) The teacher asked a question, but the student didn't respond.
response [rɪ'spɒns]	*n.* 反应；回答 (something that is said or written as a reply to something) When I told him my plan, I wasn't expecting such an enthusiastic response.
responsible [rɪ'spɒnsəbl]	*adj.* 尽责的 (able to be trusted to do what is right or to do the things that are expected or required) She is a very responsible worker. *adj.* 负有责任的 (getting the credit or blame for acts or decisions) You are responsible for the damage.
irresponsible [ˌɪrɪ'spɒnsəbl]	*adj.* 不负责任的 (not thinking enough about the effects of what you do; not showing a feeling of responsibility) She made irresponsible comments that helped cause the riot.
correspond [ˌkɒrə'spɒnd]	*v.* 与……通信 (to write to someone or to each other) We corresponded regularly. *v.* 符合；与……一致 (to be similar or equal to something) Her finished sculpture did not correspond to how she had imagined it.
spontaneous [spɒn'teɪniəs]	*adj.* 自发的；自然的 (done or said in a natural and often sudden way and without a lot of thought or planning) The comment was completely spontaneous.

Unit 21

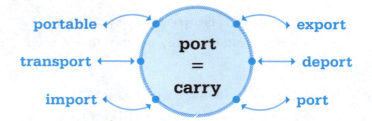

portable ['pɔːtəbl]	**adj.** 手提的；轻便的 (capable of being carried or moved about) **Portable** devices such as MP3 players are becoming increasingly popular.
export [ɪk'spɔːt] v. ['ekspɔːt] n.	**v.** 出口；输出 (to send a product to be sold in another country) The nation **exports** beef and coffee. **n.** 出口 (a product that is sent to another country to be sold there) Ghana's main **export** is cocoa.
import [ɪm'pɔːt] v. ['ɪmpɔːt] n.	**v.** 进口 (to bring a product into a country to be sold) A dealer **imports** cars from Italy to the U.S. **n.** 进口 (a product brought into a country to be sold there) My car is an **import** from Italy.
deport [dɪ'pɔːt]	**v.** 驱逐 (to force a person who is not a citizen to leave a country) Thousands of immigrants had been illegally **deported**.
deportation [ˌdiːpɔː'teɪʃn]	**n.** 驱逐出境；放逐 (the removal from a country of a person who is not a citizen) Immigration officers tried to serve her with a **deportation** order.
transport ['trænspɔːt]	**v.** 运送；运输 (to carry someone or something from one place to another) ① There's no petrol, so it's very difficult to **transport** goods. ② The illness was first **transported** across the ocean by European explorers.
transportation [ˌtrænspɔː'teɪʃn]	**n.** 交通；运输 (a system for moving passengers or goods from one place to another) Campuses are usually accessible by public **transportation**.
port [pɔːt]	**n.** 港口 (a place as a harbor where ships can find shelter from a storm) The ship came into **port**.

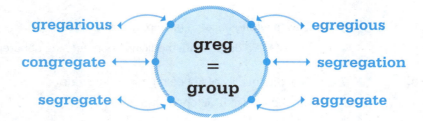

greg = group

gregarious ← | → egregious

congregate ← | → segregation

segregate ← | → aggregate

gregarious [grɪ'geərɪəs]	*adj.* 爱交际的；合群的 (enjoying the company of other people) A gregarious child who ran up to every person on the playground and wanted to be their friend.
congregate ['kɒŋgrɪgeɪt]	*v.* 使集合；聚集 (to bring or come together in a group, crowd, or assembly) Young people often congregate in the main square in the evenings.
segregate ['segrɪgeɪt]	*v.* 分离；隔离 (to separate groups of people because of their particular race, religion) The civil rights movement fought against practices that segregated blacks and whites.
segregation [ˌsegrɪ'geɪʃn]	*n.* 分离；隔离 (the practice or policy of separating a race, class or group from the rest of society) They fought to end the segregation of public schools.
egregious [ɪ'gri:dʒɪəs]	*adj.* 极坏的；极糟的 (outstandingly bad) The student's theme was marred by a number of egregious errors in spelling.
aggregate ['ægrɪgət]	*adj.* 总计的；合计的 (formed by adding together two or more amounts) The university receives more than half its aggregate income from government sources. *v.* 使聚集；使积聚 (to collect or gather into a mass or whole) The particles of sand aggregated into giant dunes.

Unit 21

Fall系列

false [fɔ:ls]	*adj.* 不正确的；虚假的 (not true or accurate) Indicate whether each of the following statements is true or false.
falsify ['fɔ:lsɪfaɪ]	*v.* 篡改；伪造 (to make something false) They were caught falsifying their records.

fallacy ['fæləsi]	*n.* 谬误；谬见 (a wrong belief; a false or mistaken idea) The fallacy of their ideas about medicine soon became apparent.
falsehood ['fɔːlshʊd]	*n.* 谎言；假话 (the quality of not being true or accurate) She called the verdict a victory of truth over falsehood.
fault [fɔːlt]	*n.* 缺点；缺陷 (a weakness in character) Forgetfulness is my worst fault. *n.* 过错；责任 (responsibility for something wrong) She committed too many faults to win the match.
default [dɪ'fɔːlt]	*v.* 未履行任务或责任 (to fail to fulfill a contract, agreement or duty) The credit card business is down, and more borrowers are defaulting on loans.
foible ['fɔɪbl]	*n.* 小缺点；小癖好 (a minor fault in someone's character or behavior) We could tolerate my uncle's foibles because we loved him dearly.

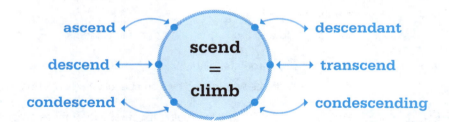

ascend [ə'send]	*v.* 上升；登高 (to go up or to climb up; to rise or move toward the sky) ① She believed that when she died, her soul would ascend to heaven. ② We ascended the hill. *v.* 职位上升 (to rise to a higher or more powerful position in a government or company) Abraham Lincoln ascended to the presidency in 1861.
descend [dɪ'send]	*v.* 下来；下降 (to go or move from a higher to a lower place or level) The airplane will descend to a lower altitude soon. *v.* 堕落；沦落 (to sink in dignity or respectability) I never thought they would descend to cheating. *v.* 源于 (to come down from an earlier time) The custom descends from ancient times.

descendant [dɪ'sendənt]	*n.* 后代；后裔 (someone who is related to a person or group of people who lived in the past) Many people in this area are descendants of German immigrants. *n.* 后代 (a plant or animal that is related to a particular plant or animal that lived long ago) Recent evidence supports the theory that birds are the modern descendants of dinosaurs.
condescend [ˌkɒndɪ'send]	*v.* 屈尊；俯就 (to do something that you usually do not do because you believe you are too important to do it) These two great commanders did not condescend to fight in person.
condescending [ˌkɒndɪ'sendɪŋ]	*adj.* 高傲的 (showing that you believe you are more intelligent or better than other people) His comments were offensive and condescending to us.
transcend [træn'send]	*v.* 超越 (to rise above or go beyond the limits of something) She was able to transcend her own suffering and help others.
transcendent [træn'sendənt]	*adj.* 卓越的；至高无上的 (far better or greater than what is usual) The star player's transcendent performance helped the team to a surprise victory.

Agon系列

agony ['ægəni]	*n.* 极大的痛苦 (great physical or mental pain) A new machine may save thousands of animals from the agony of drug tests.
agonizing ['ægənaɪzɪŋ]	*adj.* 痛苦难忍的 (very mentally or physically painful) He now faced an agonizing decision about his immediate future.
antagonize [æn'tægənaɪz]	*v.* 使成为敌人 (to cause someone to feel hostile or angry) Her comments antagonized many people.
antagonist [æn'tægənɪst]	*n.* 敌手；反对者 (a person who opposes another person) He had never previously lost to his antagonist.

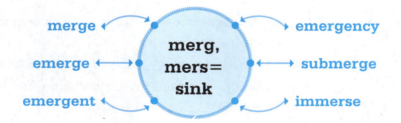

merge [mɜːdʒ]	*v.* 合并 (to cause to unite, combine, or coalesce) The two banks merged to form one large institution. *v.* 融合 (to be combined or blended into a single unit) She merged into the crowd and disappeared.
emerge [i'mɜːdʒ]	*v.* 出现；浮现 (to come up to the surface of or rise from water) ① The swimmer emerged from the water. ② The growing corruption has emerged in the past few years.
emergent [i'mɜːdʒənt]	*adj.* 紧急的 (arising unexpectedly) Since it was not seen as an emergent problem, it was continually put off. *adj.* 新生的 (newly formed or prominent) Emergent democracies created markets that were ripe for exploitation.
emergency [i'mɜːdʒənsi]	*n.* 紧急情况 (an unexpected situation that requires immediate action) ① Her quick thinking in an emergency saved the baby's life. ② He has the ability to deal with emergencies quickly.
submerge [səb'mɜːdʒ]	*v.* 淹没；沉没 (to place under the surface of a liquid, especially water) The river burst its banks, submerging an entire village.
immerse [ɪ'mɜːs]	*v.* 浸没 (to plunge into something as a fluid that surrounds or covers) She immersed the vegetables in boiling water. *v.* 沉迷……中 (to become completely involved with) She had immersed herself in writing short stories.

追根溯源

　　在希腊神话中，战神阿瑞斯（Ares）是主神宙斯和天后赫拉的儿子，爱神阿芙洛狄忒的情人，掌管战争。他相貌英俊，孔武有力，性格残暴好斗，象征着战争的野蛮杀戮。在罗马神话中他被称为马尔斯（Mars）。因为罗马人崇尚武力，所以战神在罗马神话中地位极高，火星（Mars）和三月（March）都以他的名字命名。单词march还表示"进军"，因为古罗马人认为三月份是进军打仗的好季节。从战神的名字中还产生了martial（战争的）， march（行军）等单词。

march [mɑːtʃ]	*v.* 行军；进军 (to move along with a steady regular step especially with others) A Scottish battalion was marching down the street.
martial ['mɑːʃl]	*adj.* 军事的；战争的 (relating to war or soldiers) The paper was actually twice banned under the martial regime.

infant（婴儿）和infantry（步兵）来自同一拉丁词根in-not, fan-phon-speak，通过词根意思来看，不会说话的人当然是婴儿（infant）。用infantry表示"步兵"，因为昔日步兵地位低于骑兵，步兵往往是由那些太年轻而无经验的人充当，有"军中婴儿"之意。

infant ['ɪnfənt]	*n.* 婴儿；幼儿 (a child in the first period of life) He showed us a picture of his infant daughter.
infancy ['ɪnfənsi]	*n.* 婴儿期 (the first part of a child's life) She was often sick during her infancy.
infantry ['ɪnfəntri]	*n.* 步兵 (soldiers trained, armed and equipped to fight on foot) He joined the infantry after leaving school.

锦囊妙记

bully ['bʊli]	*v.* 恐吓；威逼 (to frighten, hurt or threaten a smaller or weaker person) ① I asked her if she was bullied by the other children. ② She used to bully me into doing her schoolwork. 联想法 bull-公牛，一个长得像公牛一样的人，强壮又凶狠，所以容易欺负（bully）弱小。
ebullient [ɪ'bʌliənt]	*adj.* 热情奔放的；精力充沛的 (lively and enthusiastic) The Prime Minister was a fiery, ebullient, quick-witted man. 联想法 e-out，bull-公牛，像西班牙的斗牛奔跑出来一样，热情奔放，精力充沛（ebullient）。

exuberant [ɪɡˈzjuːbərənt]	*adj.* 繁茂的；生气勃勃的 (existing in large amounts; very plentiful) Exuberant crowds rushed to greet the returning Olympic champions. **联想法** ex-out，uber-打车软件，打车软件在世界各地发展迅速，一片繁茂，生气勃勃 (exuberant)。
exotic [ɪɡˈzɒtɪk]	*adj.* 异国的；奇异的 (very different, strange or unusual) Consumers are increasingly interested in the authentically exotic tastes. *n.* 外来物 (a plant or animal that does not live or grow naturally in a particular area) Some native species are being crowded out by exotics. **联想法** EXO-韩国的组合，对于中国人来说，当然是外来的 (exotic)。
vomit [ˈvɒmɪt]	*v.* 呕吐 (to bring food from the stomach back out through the mouth) The dog vomited on the floor. **谐音法** vomit-我呕！我呕就是我呕吐 (vomit)！

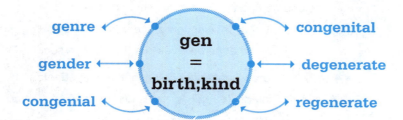

genre → gen = birth;kind ← congenital
gender ↔ ↔ degenerate
congenial ← → regenerate

genre [ˈʒɒrə]	*n.* 类型；种类 (kind, category or sort, especially of literary or artistic work) My favorite music genre is blues.
gender [ˈdʒendə(r)]	*n.* 性别 (a person's gender is the fact that they are male or female) Women are sometimes denied opportunities solely because of their gender.
congenial [kənˈdʒiːniəl]	*adj.* 意气相投的 (alike or sympathetic in nature, disposition or tastes) A congenial college makes me work more efficiently. *adj.* 友善的；宜人的 (existing together in harmony) ① We studied in the congenial atmosphere of the library. ② She was congenial and easygoing.
genocide [ˈdʒenəsaɪd]	*n.* 种族屠杀 (the deliberate killing of people who belong to a particular racial, political or cultural group) They've launched a campaign of genocide against the immigrants.
generate [ˈdʒenəreɪt]	*v.* 生产；引起 (to produce something or cause something to be produced) ① This business should generate a lot of revenue. ② His theories have generated a great deal of interest among other scientists.
generation [ˌdʒenəˈreɪʃn]	*n.* 一代人 (a group of people born and living during the same time) We need to preserve these resources for future generations. *n.* 产生 (the act or process of producing or creating something) Japan has announced plans for a sharp rise in its nuclear power generation.

Unit 22

degenerate
[dɪ'dʒenəreɪt]

v. 使退化；恶化 (to become worse, weaker, less useful)
Inactivity can make your joints stiff, and the bones may begin to degenerate.

v. 退化；堕落 (to sink into a low intellectual or moral state)
The debate degenerated into a shouting match.

adj. 堕落的；退化的 (having low standards of behaviour or morality)
He criticizes what he believes is a degenerate society.

regenerate
[rɪ'dʒenəreɪt]

v. 使再生 (to grow again after being lost, damaged, etc.)
The lizard is able to regenerate its tail.

v. 振兴；复兴 (to restore to original strength)
The government will continue to try to regenerate inner city areas.

genuine
['dʒenjuɪn]

adj. 真正的 (actual, real or true)
Tests proved that the letter was genuine, and not a forgery.

adj. 真诚的 (sincere and honest)
He has always shown a genuine concern for poor people.

genius
['dʒiːniəs]

n. 天才 (a very smart or talented person)
Albert Einstein and Isaac Newton were great scientific geniuses.

ingenious
[ɪn'dʒiːniəs]

adj. 聪明的 (very smart or clever)
She was ingenious at finding ways to work more quickly.

adj. 巧妙的 (marked by originality, resourcefulness, and cleverness)
The director used ingenious devices to keep the audience in suspense.

ingenuous
[ɪn'dʒenjuəs]

adj. 天真无邪的 (showing innocence and childlike honesty)
I'm not so ingenuous as to believe everything he says.

progeny
['prɒdʒəni]

n. 子孙；后裔 (a person who comes from a particular parent or family; descendant)
Many Americans are the progeny of immigrants.

homogeneous
[ˌhɒmə'dʒiːniəs]

adj. 由同类事物（或人）组成的 (made up of the same kind of people or things)
Japan is a wealthy, homogeneous, developed nation with a stable political system.

Option系列

option ['ɒpʃn]	*n.* 选择 (the power or right to choose) Children have an option between milk and juice.
optional ['ɒpʃənl]	*adj.* 可选择的 (left to choice; not required) Jackets are required at the restaurant, but ties are optional.
optimal ['ɒptɪməl]	*adj.* 最佳的；最优的 (most desirable or satisfactory) Under optimal conditions, these plants grow quite tall.

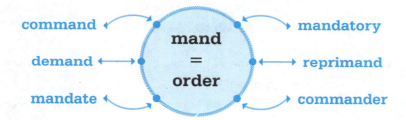

command ← mand = order → mandatory
demand ← mand = order → reprimand
mandate ← mand = order → commander

demand [dɪ'mɑːnd]	*v.* 要求 (to say in a forceful way that something must be done or given to you) ① The reporter demanded to see the documents. ② The customer demanded a refund. *n.* 要求 (a forceful statement in which you say that something must be done or given to you) The workers said they would not end the strike until their demands were met.
command [kə'mɑːnd]	*v.* 指挥 (to give someone an order) Military leaders commanded the troops to open fire. *v.* 控制 (to have authority and control over a group of people or something) The company commands much power and influence in the business world.
commander [kə'mɑːndə(r)]	*n.* 指挥官；司令官 (a person who is in charge of a group of people) ① He said 14 police were killed, including both commanders of the checkpoints. ② The president is ultimately responsible because he's the Commander in Chief of the world's most powerful military.

mandate ['mændeɪt]	*v.* 强制执行 (to officially require something) The law mandates that every car have seat belts. *n.* 授权；命令 (an official order given to somebody to perform a particular task) They carried out the governor's mandate to build more roads.
mandatory ['mændətəri]	*adj.* 强制的；命令的 (required by a law or rule) The tests are mandatory for all students wishing to graduate.
reprimand ['reprɪmɑːnd]	*v.* 谴责；惩戒 (to speak in an angry and critical way to someone who has done something wrong) The soldiers were severely reprimanded.

Reptile系列

reptile ['reptaɪl]	*n.* 爬行动物 (any animal that has cold blood and skin covered in scales, and that lays eggs) Insects provide a food source for many birds, amphibians, bats and reptiles, while plants rely on insects for pollination.
creep [kriːp]	*v.* 悄悄地缓慢行走；蹑手蹑脚地移动 (of people or animals, to move slowly, quietly and carefully, because you do not want to be seen or heard) I caught him creeping down the stairs to the kitchen.
surreptitious [ˌsʌrəp'tɪʃəs]	*adj.* 鬼鬼祟祟的 (done, made, or acquired by stealth) ① He made a surreptitious entrance to the club through the little door in the brick wall. ② His surreptitious behaviour naturally aroused suspicion.

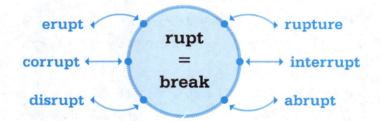

rupture ['rʌptʃə(r)]	*n.* (关系的)破裂，决裂；绝交 (the ending of agreement or of good relations between people, countries, etc.)

Unit 22

The incidents have not yet caused a major rupture in the political ties between countries.

disrupt

[dɪsˈrʌpt]

v. 扰乱；使中断；打乱(to make it difficult for something to continue in the normal way)

1 The weather disrupted our travel plans.

2 The strike canceled hundreds of flights, shut down public offices and severely disrupted local transportation.

disruptive

[dɪsˈrʌptɪv]

adj. 破坏的；扰乱的 (preventing something from continuing or operating in a normal way)

Alcohol can produce violent, disruptive behavior.

interrupt

[ˌɪntəˈrʌpt]

v. 打断 (to stop suddenly, as a conversation, activity, or relationship)

1 His dinner was interrupted by a phone call.

2 Every summer periods of cool weather occasionally interrupt the intense heat.

corrupt

[kəˈrʌpt]

adj. 堕落的；道德败坏的 (dishonest, evil or immoral)

The country's justice system is riddled with corrupt judges who accept bribes.

v. 使腐化；使堕落 (to make or become evil or bad)

He was corrupted by the bad influence of two friends.

corruption

[kəˈrʌpʃn]

n. 腐败；贪污 (dishonest or illegal behavior especially by powerful people, such as government officials or police officers)

There are rumors of widespread corruption in the city government.

corruptible

[kəˈrʌptəbl]

adj. 易腐蚀的；易腐败的 (capable of being corrupted)

The body is corruptible but the spirit is incorruptible.

erupt

[ɪˈrʌpt]

v. 爆发；喷发 (to send out rocks, ash, lava, etc., in a sudden explosion)

1 The volcano erupted with tremendous force.

2 A bitter dispute has erupted among the members of the team.

eruption

[ɪˈrʌpʃn]

n. 喷发；爆发 (the sudden occurrence or appearance of something)

The temple was destroyed in the violent eruption of the volcano.

abrupt

[əˈbrʌpt]

adj. 突然的；意外的 (happening without warning)

There was an abrupt change in the weather.

bankrupt ['bæŋkrʌpt]	*adj.* 破产的；倒闭的 (unable to pay debts)
	If the firm cannot sell its products, it will go bankrupt.
	v. 使破产；使倒闭 (to cause a person, business, etc. to be unable to pay debts)
	Several bad investments bankrupted him.

Flect系列

reflect [rɪˈflekt]	*v.* 反射 (to throw back light or sound)
	A polished surface reflects light.
	v. 认真思考；沉思 (to think seriously and carefully about)
	Before I decide, I need time to reflect.
reflective [rɪˈflektɪv]	*adj.* 反射的 (capable of reflecting light, images, or sound waves)
	Avoid pans with a shiny, reflective base as the heat will be reflected back.
	adj. 反思的 (thinking carefully about something)
	She was in a very reflective mood.
flexible [ˈfleksəbl]	*adj.* 灵活的；易弯曲的；可变动的 (easily changed; able to change or to do different things)
	❶ She's been doing exercises to become stronger and more flexible.
	❷ Our schedule for the weekend is very flexible.
deflect [dɪˈflekt]	*v.* 使歪斜；使转向 (to cause something that is moving to change direction)
	❶ The goalie deflected the ball with his hands.
	❷ They are trying to deflect attention from the troubled economy.

Unit 22

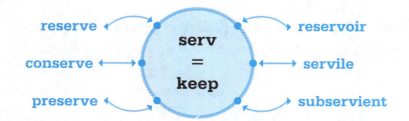

reserve [rɪ'zɜːv]	*v.* 保留；留出 (to make arrangements so that you will be able to use or have something, such as a room, table, or seat, at a later time) She usually reserved her best dishes for very important dinners. *n.* 储备 (a supply of something that is stored so that it can be used at a later time) He had to call upon his inner reserves of strength to keep going.
reservation [ˌrezə'veɪʃn]	*n.* 保留；预订 (an act of setting something aside for future use) We made dinner reservations at the restaurant for 6 o'clock.
reserved [rɪ'zɜːvd]	*adj.* 矜持的；内敛的 (restrained in words and actions) She is a very reserved young woman.
unreserved [ˌʌnrɪ'zɜːvd]	*adj.* 未保留的；坦率的 (not limited in any way) I have nothing but unreserved admiration for him.
reservoir ['rezəvwɑː(r)]	*n.* 蓄水池(a place, such as a part of a machine, where a liquid is stored) The villagers piped in drinking water from the reservoir.
conserve [kən'sɜːv]	*v.* 保护；保存 (to keep something in a safe condition) We need to conserve our natural resources.
conservative [kən'sɜːvətɪv]	*adj.* 保守的 (believing in the value of established and traditional practices in politics and society) She is a liberal Democrat who married a conservative Republican.
preserve [prɪ'zɜːv]	*v.* 保护 (to keep somebody/something safe from injury, harm or destruction) ❶ These laws are intended to help preserve our natural resources. ❷ The fossil was well preserved.
servile ['sɜːvaɪl]	*adj.* 过分屈从的 (very obedient and trying too hard to please someone) ❶ He was subservient and servile. ❷ An honest judge cannot be servile to public opinion.

subservient [səb's3:viənt]	*adj.* 屈从的；恭顺的 (very willing or too willing to obey someone else) She refused to take a subservient role in their marriage.

Author系列

author ['ɔ:θə(r)]	*n.* 授权；批准 (a person who writes books or the person who wrote a particular book) I enjoyed the book, but I can't remember the name of the author.
authorize ['ɔ:θəraɪz]	*v.* 授权；批准 (to give official approval for something) The city council authorized the sale of the land.
authorization [,ɔ:θəraɪ'zeɪʃn]	*n.* 授权；批准 (an official form of approval for something) You may not enter the security area without authorization.
authority [ɔ:'θɒrəti]	*n.* 权威 (power to exercise control) The boss is not popular but his authority is unquestioned. *n.* 官方；当局 (a government agency or public office responsible for an area of regulation) State authorities are investigating the disputed election.
authoritative [ɔ:'θɒrətətɪv]	*adj.* 权威的 (having or showing impressive knowledge about a subject) ① The book is an authoritative guide to the city's restaurants. ② Her smile was warm but authoritative.
authoritarian [ɔ:,θɒrɪ'teəriən]	*adj.* 专制的；独裁的 (requiring people to obey rules or laws; not allowing personal freedom) Senior officers could be considering a coup to restore authoritarian rule.
authentic [ɔ:'θentɪk]	*adj.* 真正的；可信的 (true and accurate) Experts have confirmed that the signature on the letter is authentic.
authenticate [ɔ:'θentɪkeɪt]	*v.* 鉴别；鉴定 (to prove or serve to prove to be real, true, or genuine) The signature has been authenticated.

dialogue ['daɪəlɒg]	*n.* 对话 (a conversation between two or more people) ① The two parties have been in constant dialogue with each other. ② The best part of the book is the clever dialogue.
prologue ['prəʊlɒg]	*n.* 序言；开场白 (an introduction to a book or play) A drama begins with a prologue, but the prologue is not the climax.
epilogue ['epɪlɒg]	*n.* 后记；收场白 (a concluding part added to a literary work) The play ended with a humorous epilogue.
monologue ['mɒnəlɒg]	*n.* (戏剧中的) 独白 (a long speech made by one actor in a play, film, etc., especially when alone) He ignored the question and continued his monologue.
soliloquy [sə'lɪləkwi]	*n.* (戏剧中的) 独白 (a long, usually serious speech that a character in a play makes to an audience) The professional actor can recite any Shakespearean soliloquy from memory.
eloquent ['eləkwənt]	*adj.* 雄辩的；有口才的 (fluent and persuasive) He was an eloquent speaker who captivated the audience.
loquacious [lə'kweɪʃəs]	*adj.* 爱说话的；多嘴的 (talking easily and often) I enjoy listening to my loquacious friend talk about her passions.
eulogy ['juːlədʒi]	*n.* 颂词；颂文 (a formal speech or piece of writing praising a person or thing, especially a person who has recently died) He delivered a moving eulogy at his father's funeral.
eulogize ['juːlədʒaɪz]	*v.* 称赞；颂扬 (to say or write good things about someone or something) He was eulogized at his funeral as a great actor and a good friend.
somniloquy [sɒm'nɪləkwi]	*n.* 梦话 (the action or habit of talking in one's sleep) Sleep talking, sometimes called somniloquy, might wake up the person next to you, but it's harmless.

Unit 22

Culp系列

culprit ['kʌlprɪt]	*n.* 犯人；罪犯 (one accused of or charged with a crime) The police caught the culprit a mere two blocks from the scene of the crime.
culpable ['kʌlpəbl]	*adj.* 应受谴责的 (deserving condemnation or blame as wrong or harmful) They held her culpable for the accident.
exculpate ['ekskʌlpeɪt]	*v.* 开脱；使无罪 (to prove that someone is not guilty of doing something wrong) The court exculpated him after a thorough investigation.

追根溯源

在古罗马时期，巫师通过观看鸟的飞行来占卜凶吉。在auspice 中，aus来自拉丁词根avis，有"鸟"的意思，spic来自词根，spect有"观看"的意思。后来，auspice的含义变为"吉兆"，随后又发展出"赞助；举办"的意思，可以理解为上天的吉兆就是老天的支持和赞助。用鸟占卜吉凶的巫师被称为augur，而augury自然就有了"占卜"之意。

auspice ['ɔːspɪs]	*n.* 预兆；吉兆 (a prophetic sign, especially a favorable sign) He interpreted the teacher's smile as an auspice that he would get an A on his presentation.
auspicious [ɔː'spɪʃəs]	*adj.* 吉祥的；有希望的 (showing or suggesting that future success is likely) The publication of my first book was an auspicious beginning of my career.
inauspicious [ˌɪnɔː'spɪʃəs]	*adj.* 不祥的；凶兆的 (not showing or suggesting that future success is likely) Despite its inauspicious beginnings, the company eventually became very profitable.
auspices ['ɔːspɪsɪz]	*n.* 主办；赞助 (kindly endorsement and guidance) The examination was held under the auspices of the government.
augury ['ɔːgjʊri]	*n.* 预兆；征兆 (a sign of what will happen in the future) Some people believe that a broken mirror is an augury of seven years' bad luck.

Unit 22

inaugurate

[ɪ'nɔ:gjəreɪt]

v. 举行就职典礼 (to introduce someone, such as a newly elected official) into a job or position with a formal ceremony)

He was inaugurated as president.

v. 开创；创始 (to bring about the beginning of something)

The company will inaugurate a new plan.

古罗马人就职时，往往会先进行占卜，占得吉兆才会举行就职仪式。所以表示就职的英语单词inaugurate就来自拉丁语，由in（into，入职）+augur（augury，预兆）+后缀-ate构成，字面意思就是"占卜取得吉兆后就职"。

锦囊妙记

ominous

['ɒmɪnəs]

adj. 不祥的，坏兆头的 (suggesting that something bad is going to happen in the future)

Any new gun control measure in the United States advances against an ominous reality, of a country already flooded with guns.

联想法 o-哦，mi-米，no-没有了，看看米缸，哦！米没了，这是个坏兆头(ominous)。

flaunt

[flɔ:nt]

v. 炫耀 (to show something in a very open way so that other people will notice)

She liked to flaunt her wealth by wearing furs and jewelry.

联想法 fl-fly（飞），aunt-姑姑，会飞的姑姑爱炫耀 (flaunt)。

daunt

[dɔ:nt]

v. 使气馁；恐吓 (to make someone afraid or less confident)

The dangers didn't daunt them.

联想法 d-打，aunt-姑姑，打姑姑就是恐吓 (daunt)。

flair

[fleə(r)]

n. 天资；天分 (an unusual and appealing quality or style)

She has a flair for acting.

联想法 fl-fly，air-空中，能在空中飞当然是一种天分(flair)。

hover

['hɒvə(r)]

v. 盘旋；徘徊 (to float in the air without moving in any direction)

Watch as the hummingbird hovers over the flowers.

联想法 over-在上面，看到鸟儿在头上徘徊 (hover)。

Unit 23

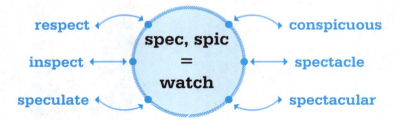

respect ← → conspicuous

inspect ← → → spectacle

spec, spic = watch

speculate ← → → spectacular

respect [rɪ'spekt]	*v.* 尊重 (to feel admiration for someone or something) The students respect the principal for his honesty. *n.* 尊重 (a feeling of admiring someone or something that is good, valuable or important) Despite our differences, I have enormous respect for him.
expect [ɪk'spekt]	*v.* 期望；预料 (to think that something will probably or certainly happen) It's expected that the new products will be available next month.
inspect [ɪn'spekt]	*v.* 检查；检验 (to look at something carefully in order to learn more about it, to find problems) ➊ She had the car inspected by a mechanic before she bought it. ➋ After the storm, we went outside to inspect the damage. *v.* 检阅；视察 (to officially visit a school, factory, etc. in order to check that rules are being obeyed and that standards are acceptable) The president inspected the troops.
inspector [ɪn'spektə(r)]	*n.* 检查员；视察员 (a person whose job is to inspect something) The regime has barred inspectors from inspecting military sites.
speculate ['spekjuleɪt]	*v.* 思索；猜测 (to think about something and make guesses about it) She could only speculate about her friend's motives. *v.* 投机 (to invest money in ways that could produce a large profit but that also involve a lot of risk) Big farmers are moving in, not in order to farm, but in order to speculate with rising land prices.

spectacle [ˈspektəkl]	*n.* 奇观；壮观 (something that attracts attention because it is very unusual or very shocking)
	The royal wedding was a great spectacle.
	n. 眼镜 (a pair of lenses set into a frame and worn over the eyes)
	He peered through his spectacles.
spectacular [spekˈtækjələ(r)]	*adj.* 场面富丽的；壮观的 (causing wonder and admiration; very impressive)
	The autumn foliage was spectacular.
	n. 壮观场面 (something that is spectacular)
	The World Cup is one of the world's great sporting spectaculars.
spectator [spekˈteɪtə(r)]	*n.* 观众；旁观者 (a person who watches an event, show, game, activity)
	① The accident attracted a large crowd of spectators.
	② The spectators lining the road cheered the racers on.
prospect [ˈprɒspekt] *n.* [prəˈspekt] *v.*	*n.* 前景；期望 (something that is waited for or expected)
	① There was no prospect that the two parties would reach an agreement anytime soon.
	② I chose to work abroad to improve my career prospects.
	v. 勘探；勘察 (to explore especially for mineral deposits)
	The companies are prospecting for oil not far from here.
suspect [səˈspekt] *vt.* [ˈsʌspekt] *n.*	*v.* 怀疑；感觉有问题；不信任 (to be suspicious about something; to not trust something)
	I have reason to suspect her sincerity when she makes promises like that.
	n. 嫌疑人 (a person who is believed to be possibly guilty of committing a crime)
	She is a possible suspect in connection with the kidnapping.
suspicious [səˈspɪʃəs]	*adj.* 可疑的；猜疑的 (causing a feeling that something is wrong or that someone is behaving wrongly)
	We were instructed to report any suspicious activity in the neighborhood.
conspicuous [kənˈspɪkjuəs]	*adj.* 易见的；明显的；惹人注意的 (easy to see or notice; likely to attract attention)
	① There were a number of conspicuous changes to the building.
	② The sign was placed in a very conspicuous spot.
	③ She felt very conspicuous in her pink coat.

retrospect [ˈretrəspekt]	*n.* 回顾；回想 (a looking back on things past) In retrospect, we should have saved more money for college.
retrospective [ˌretrəˈspektɪv]	*adj.* 回顾的；怀旧的 (relating to the past or something that happened in the past) The museum is having a retrospective exhibit of the artist's early works.
introspection [ˌɪntrəˈspekʃn]	*n.* 反省；内省 (an examination of one's own thoughts and feelings) He had always had his moments of quiet introspection.
perspective [pəˈspektɪv]	*n.* 观点 (the angle or direction in which a person looks at an object) He says the death of his father 18 months ago has given him a new perspective on life.
circumspect [ˈsɜːkəmspekt]	*adj.* 谨慎小心的 (thinking carefully about possible risks before doing or saying something) She has a reputation for being quiet and circumspect in investigating charges of child abuse.
perspicacious [ˌpɜːspɪˈkeɪʃəs]	*adj.* 有洞察力的 (showing an ability to notice and understand things that are difficult or not obvious) He is one of the most perspicacious and perceptive historians of that period.
despise [dɪˈspaɪz]	*v.* 鄙视；看不起 (to dislike and have no respect for somebody/something) She was despised as a hypocrite.
despicable [dɪˈspɪkəbl]	*adj.* 可鄙的 (very bad or unpleasant; deserving to be despised) The Minister said the bombing was a despicable crime.

Terror系列

terror [ˈterə(r)]	*n.* 恐怖 (a very strong feeling of fear) The sound of guns being fired fills me with terror.
terrorist [ˈterərɪst]	*n.* 恐怖分子 (a terrorist is a person who uses violence, especially murder and bombing, in order to achieve political aims) We were told that we were attacked because the terrorists hate our freedoms and democracy.

terrify ['terɪfaɪ]	*v.* 使恐怖；使惊吓 (to cause someone to be extremely afraid) The thought of dying alone terrifies her.
terrible ['terəbl]	*adj.* 可怕的；糟糕的 (very shocking and upsetting) Tens of thousands people suffered terrible injuries in the world's worst industrial disaster.
terrifying ['terɪfaɪŋ]	*adj.* 可怕的 (causing great fear) I still find it terrifying to find myself surrounded by large numbers of horses.
terrific [tə'rɪfɪk]	*adj.* 异乎寻常的 (very unusual) ① The car was going at terrific speed. ② The storm caused terrific damage. *adj.* 极好的 (extremely good) He is a terrific athlete and a brilliant jumper.
deter [dɪ'tɜː(r)]	*v.* 阻止；制止 (to cause someone to decide not to do something) Supporters of the death penalty argue that it would deter criminals from carrying guns.
deterrent [dɪ'terənt]	*n.* 制止物；威慑物 (a thing that makes someone decide not to do something) The alarm is a deterrent against theft.

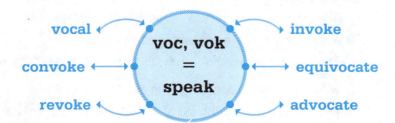

vocal ['vəʊkl]	*adj.* 发声的；嗓音的 (produced by the voice) She loved singing as a child and started vocal training at 12. *adj.* 直言的 (expressing opinions in a public and forceful way) He has been very vocal in his displeasure over the results.
vocalist ['vəʊkəlɪst]	*n.* 声乐家；歌手 (a person who sings) The pianist had to tailor his style to suit the vocalist's distinctive voice.

convoke

[kən'vəʊk]

v. 召集，召开 (会议) (to call a group of people to a formal meeting)

The king convoke parliament to cope with the impending danger.

evoke

[ɪ'vəʊk]

v. 唤起 (to bring a memory, feeling, image, etc. into the mind)

The old house evoked memories of his childhood.

evocative

[ɪ'vɒkətɪv]

adj. 唤起的 (bringing thoughts, memories or feelings into the mind)

1 The taste of the cakes was evocative of my childhood.

2 Her story is sharply evocative of Italian rural life.

revoke

[rɪ'vəʊk]

v. 撤销；取消 (to officially cancel something so that it is no longer valid)

My driver's license was revoked.

irrevocable

[ɪ'revəkəbl]

adj. 不能取消的；不可改变的 (not capable of being changed)

She has made an irrevocable decision.

provoke

[prə'vəʊk]

v. 挑衅；激怒 (to cause a person or animal to become angry, violent)

The animal will not attack unless it is provoked.

v. 激起 (to cause the occurrence of a feeling or action)

His remarks provoked both tears and laughter.

provocative

[prə'vɒkətɪv]

adj. 挑衅的；煽动性的；激起争端的 (intended to make people angry or upset; intended to make people argue about something)

His behavior was called provocative and antisocial.

invoke

[ɪn'vəʊk]

v. 援用；援引 (to refer to something in support of your ideas)

The judge invoked an international law that protects refugees.

v. 祈求 (to ask for aid or protection as in prayer)

The great magicians of old always invoked their gods with sacrifice.

advocate

['ædvəkeɪt]

v. 提倡；拥护 (to support something publicly)

1 Malala survived the attack, after successful surgery in England, and continued to advocate for girls education.

2 He advocates traditional teaching methods.

n. 提倡者 (a person who argues for or supports a cause or policy)

He was a strong advocate of free market policies and a multi-party system.

vocation

[vəʊ'keɪʃn]

n. 职业；使命 (a strong desire to spend your life doing a certain kind of work, such as religious work)

1 It was her vocation to be an actress.

2 He never felt a real sense of vocation.

equivocate [ɪˈkwɪvəkeɪt]	*v.* 含糊其词；支吾；搪塞 (to use unclear language especially to deceive or mislead someone) The applicant seemed to be equivocating when we asked him about his last job.
unequivocal [ˌʌnɪˈkwɪvəkl]	*adj.* 不含糊的；明确的 (very strong and clear; not showing or allowing any doubt) Her answer was an unequivocal yes.

Hilary系列

hilarious [hɪˈleəriəs]	*adj.* 欢闹的；非常滑稽的 (very funny) She gave us a hilarious account of her first days as a teacher.
exhilarate [ɪgˈzɪləreɪt]	*v.* 使高兴；使兴奋 (to cause someone to feel very happy and excited) The climactic moment of commencement ceremonies usually exhilarates graduates and proud parents alike.
calorie [ˈkæləri]	*n.* 大卡 (a unit of heat used to indicate the amount of energy that foods will produce in the human body) A glass of wine does have quite a lot of calories.
nonchalant [ˈnɒnʃələnt]	*adj.* 漠不关心的；冷淡的 (having a relaxed manner free from concern or excitement) He was surprisingly nonchalant about winning the award.

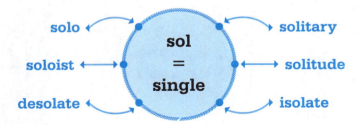

solo [ˈsəʊləʊ]	*n.* 独唱；独奏 (a piece of music that is performed by one singer or musician) She left the band last year and started a solo career.

soloist ['səʊləʊɪst]	*n.* 独奏者 (a person who performs a solo) The strings provided a melodic background to the passages played by the soloist.
sole [səʊl]	*adj.* 单独的；唯一的 (only or single) ① The sole aim of the program is to help the poor. ② She was the sole survivor of the tragedy.
isolate ['aɪsəleɪt]	*v.* 使隔离；使孤立 (to separate somebody/something physically or socially from other people or things) ① These policies will only serve to isolate the country politically and economically. ② When he wants to work, he isolates himself in his office and won't talk to anyone.
isolation [ˌaɪsə'leɪʃn]	*n.* 孤独；孤立状态 (the state of being alone or lonely) Many deaf people have feelings of isolation and loneliness.
solitary ['sɒlətri]	*adj.* 独处的；独居的 (without anyone or anything else) Most cats are solitary creatures. *adj.* 单个的；唯一的 (separate from other people or things) A solitary house stood on top of the cliff.
solitude ['sɒlɪtjuːd]	*n.* 单独；孤独 (a state or situation in which you are alone usually because you want to be) He enjoyed the peace and solitude of the woods.
desolate ['desələt]	*adj.* 荒凉的；无人居住的 (empty and without people, making you feel sad or frightened) A desolate house was abandoned many years ago.

Nose系列

nostril ['nɒstrəl]	*n.* 鼻孔 (one of the two openings of the nose) My left nostril is stuffed up.
sneeze [sniːz]	*v.* 打喷嚏 (to force the breath out in a sudden and noisy way) She was constantly sneezing and coughing.

snore [snɔː(r)]	*v.* 打呼噜 (to breathe noisily while sleeping) His mouth was open, and he was snoring. *n.* 打呼噜 (an act or sound of breathing with a rough hoarse noise while sleeping) His loud snore kept me awake.
sniff [snɪf]	*v.* 闻；嗅 (to breathe air in through the nose in order to discover or enjoy the smell of something) He held the flower up to his nose and sniffed. *v.* 轻蔑；蔑视 (to say with scorn) Foreign Office sources sniffed at reports that British troops might be sent. *n.* 闻；嗅 (act of drawing air into the nose in short breaths) He took a sniff of the pie.

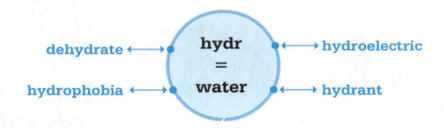

hydrant ['haɪdrənt]	*n.* 消防栓 (a water device to put out fire) It is not lawful to park in front of a hydrant.
hydrophobia [ˌhaɪdrə'fəʊbiə]	*n.* 恐水病；狂犬病 (extreme fear of water, which happens with rabies infection in humans) Symptoms are varied and occasionally dramatic, such as the fear of swallowing water known as hydrophobia.
hydroelectric [ˌhaɪdrəʊɪ'lektrɪk]	*adj.* 水力发电的 (generating electricity by conversion of the energy of running water) ① This machine uses the hydroelectric power. ② Plans are being drawn up to build a hydroelectric station here.
dehydrate [diː'haɪdreɪt]	*v.* 使 (食物) 脱水 (to remove water or moisture from something, such as food) Salt dehydrates the meat and keeps it from spoiling.

v. (身体) 失水，脱水；使 (身体) 脱水 (to lose too much water from your body; to make a person's body lose too much water)

Athletes drink lots of water so they don't dehydrate.

Mini系列

minuscule ['mɪnəskjuːl]	**adj.** 极小的；微小的 (very small) Public health officials have claimed that the chemical is harmless in such minuscule amounts.
diminish [dɪ'mɪnɪʃ]	**v.** 减少；缩减；减弱 (to become or to make something become smaller, weaker, etc.) The strength of the army was greatly diminished by outbreaks of disease.
diminutive [dɪ'mɪnjətɪv]	**adj.** 极小的；小型的 (very small) She noticed a diminutive figure standing at the entrance.
miniature ['mɪnətʃə(r)]	**adj.** 小型的；微小的 (very small) The little boy looks like a miniature version of his father.
minister ['mɪnɪstə(r)]	**n.** 大臣；部长 (a government official at the head of a section of government activities) The British ministers were present at the international peace conference.
administer [əd'mɪnɪstə(r)]	**v.** 管理；治理 (国家) (to manage the operation of something, such as a company or government) The plan calls for the UN to administer the country until elections can be held.
administration [əd,mɪnɪ'streɪʃn]	**n.** 政府 (the government of a country) ① Her lecture compared the policies of this administration to the previous one. ② The drug has been approved by the U.S. Food and Drug Administration.

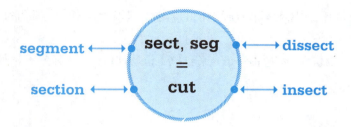

insect ['ɪnsekt]	*n.* 虫；昆虫 (a small animal that has six legs and a body formed of three parts and that may have wings) Many kinds of insect find their mates by scent.
bisect [baɪ'sekt]	*v.* 二等分 (to divide something into two equal parts) The city is bisected by the highway.
section ['sekʃn]	*n.* 部分 (one of the parts that form something) The dictionary includes a section on signs and symbols.
dissect [dɪ'sekt]	*v.* 解剖 (to cut up a dead person, animal or plant in order to study it) We dissected a frog in science class.
dissection [daɪ'sekʃn]	*n.* 解剖 (the act of cutting something or taking something apart for examination) Researchers need a growing supply of corpses for dissection.
segment ['segmənt]	*n.* 部分；段落 (one of the parts into which something can be divided) She cleaned a small segment of the painting. *v.* 分割；划分 (to divide something into parts) Market researchers have segmented the population into different age groups.
sectarian [sek'teəriən]	*adj.* 宗派的；派系的 (relating to religious or political sects and the differences between them) The country was split along sectarian lines.

Unit 23

追根溯源

　　大地女神盖亚受孕，诞生了三位复仇女神，在罗马神话中被称为Furia。她们的形象为三个身材高大的女性，头上长着蛇发，眼中流出血泪，双肩生有翅膀，手执火把和蝮蛇鞭。她们永不停息地追逐杀人凶手，尤其是谋杀血亲的人，使他们受到良心的煎熬，直到丧失理智。为了避免激怒她们，凡人不敢直呼她们的名字，只能称她们为"温和的人"（the kindly ones）。

罗马神话中，复仇女神的名字Furia来自拉丁语动词furere（狂怒），英语单词fury（狂怒）与其同源。

fury ['fjʊəri]	*n.* 狂怒 (violent anger) She screamed, her face distorted with fury and pain.
furious ['fjʊəriəs]	*adj.* 狂怒的；暴怒的 (very angry) She's furious at how slowly the investigation is proceeding.
infuriate [ɪn'fjʊərieɪt]	*v.* 使大怒；激怒 (to make someone very angry) I was infuriated by his arrogance.

锦囊妙记

trivial ['trɪviəl]	*adj.* 琐碎的；无价值的 (of little worth or importance) Don't get angry about trivial matters. 联想法 tri-three, 一生二，二生三，一过三就变得多而琐碎 (trivial)。
trifling ['traɪflɪŋ]	*adj.* 微不足道的 (having little value or importance) He worries about trifling details. 联想法 记忆方法同上。
trite [traɪt]	*adj.* 陈腐的；老一套的 (not interesting or effective because of being used too often) That argument has become trite. 联想法 tri-三，三角恋剧情太老套了 (trite)。
intricate ['ɪntrɪkət]	*adj.* 错综复杂的 (having many closely combined parts or elements) He knows his way around the intricate maze of European law。 联想法 in-进入，tri-三，三角恋，进入三角恋关系，相当错综复杂(intricate)。
extricate ['ekstrɪkeɪt]	*v.* 使摆脱困难 (to free from a trap or difficulty) She hasn't been able to extricate herself from her legal problems. 联想法 ex-out，tri-三角恋，从三角恋的纠缠中脱身 (extricate)。

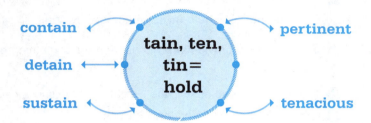

contain ← → pertinent

detain ← → **tain, ten, tin= hold**

sustain ← → tenacious

contain [kən'teɪn]	v. 包含；容纳 (to have something inside) This glass contains water. v. 遏制 (to keep something within limits) State health officials have succeeded in containing the virus.
container [kən'teɪnə(r)]	n. 容器 (an object such as a box or bottle that can hold something) The tea leaves come in a small metal container.
obtain [əb'teɪn]	v. 获得；得到 (to gain or get something usually by effort) He obtained a large sum of money by buying and selling houses.
obtainable [əb'teɪnəbl]	adj. 可获得的；可取得的 (If something is obtainable, it is possible to get or achieve it) The dried herb is obtainable from health shops.
attain [ə'teɪn]	v. 达到；获得 (to succeed in getting or doing something) This kind of tree can attain a height of 20 feet within just a few years.
attainment [ə'teɪnmənt]	n. 成就；造诣 (condition of having gotten or done something difficult) Her scientific attainments have made her quite well-known in the field of biology.
retain [rɪ'teɪn]	v. 保留；保持 (to continue to have or use something) ① The TV show has retained its popularity for many years. ② The interior of the shop still retains a nineteenth-century atmosphere.
retention [rɪ'tenʃn]	n. 保持；保留 (the state of being retained) They say the herb promotes memory retention.

Unit 24

detain [dɪˈteɪn]	*v.* 保留；保持 (to continue to have or use something) **1** They were detained by the police for questioning. **2** He claimed he had been illegally detained.
detention [dɪˈtenʃn]	*n.* 拘留；扣押 (the act of keeping someone in a prison or similar place) The prisoner was held in detention before trial.
sustain [səˈsteɪn]	*v.* 维持；支撑 (to provide what is needed for something or someone to exist, continue) **1** The roof, unable to sustain the weight of all the snow, collapsed. **2** Hope sustained us during that difficult time.
sustainable [səˈsteɪnəbl]	*adj.* 可持续的 (able to be used without being completely used up or destroyed) To be sustainable they have to think about the future and manage the waste and the sewage water.
sustenance [ˈsʌstənəns]	*n.* 营养；养料 (something such as food that keeps someone or something alive) Tree bark provides deer with sustenance in periods of drought.
tenacious [təˈneɪʃəs]	*adj.* 坚韧不拔的 (not easily stopped or pulled apart; firm or strong) **1** She is very tenacious and will work hard and long to achieve objectives. **2** The company has a tenacious hold on the market.
tenacity [təˈnæsəti]	*n.* 坚韧；坚毅 (the quality or state of being persistent) The athletes displayed great tenacity throughout the contest.
tenable [ˈtenəbl]	*adj.* 守得住的；可防守的 (capable of being defended against attack or criticism) The soldiers' encampment on the open plain was not tenable, so they retreated to higher ground.
abstain [əbˈsteɪn]	*v.* 戒除 (to keep oneself from doing something) He abstained from alcohol. *v.* 弃权 (to choose not to do or have something) Ten members voted for the proposal, six members voted against it, and two abstained.
tenant [ˈtenənt]	*n.* 房客；佃户 (a person or business that rents property from its owner) A tenant is now leasing the apartment.

continue

[kən'tɪnjuː]

v. 继续；持续 (to do something without stopping)

1. The weather continued hot and sunny.

2. The traditions will continue only as long as the next generations keep them alive.

continuous

[kən'tɪnjuəs]

adj. 连续的；持续的 (happening or existing without a break or interruption)

1. Residents report that they heard continuous gunfire.

2. The batteries provide enough power for up to five hours of continuous use.

continent

['kɒntɪnənt]

n. 大陆 (one of the main landmasses of the globe)

Dinosaurs evolved when most continents were joined in a single land mass.

pertain

[pə'teɪn]

v. 关于；有关 (to relate to someone or something)

His remark did not pertain to the question.

pertinent

['pɜːtɪnənt]

adj. 有关的；恰当的；相宜的 (appropriate to a particular situation)

He impressed the jury with his concise, pertinent answers to the attorney's questions.

impertinent

[ɪm'pɜːtɪnənt]

adj. 无礼的；莽撞的 (rude and showing a lack of respect)

I don't like strangers who ask impertinent questions.

maintain

[meɪn'teɪn]

v. 保持 (to cause something to exist or continue without changing)

1. He has found it difficult to maintain a healthy weight.

2. The police say that they will do whatever is necessary to maintain law and order.

v. 保养 (to keep something in good condition by making repairs, correcting problems)

It was obvious that the house had been poorly maintained.

maintenance

['meɪntənəns]

n. 维持；保持 (the act of providing basic and necessary support)

The building has suffered from years of poor maintenance.

entertain

[ˌentə'teɪn]

v. 热情款待 (to have people as guests in your home or in a public place such as a restaurant)

They like to entertain their friends at their home.

v. 使有兴趣；使快乐 (to provide amusement for someone by singing or acting)

1. Our father entertained us with stories.

2. Jugglers were on hand to entertain the crowd.

entertainment [ˌentəˈteɪnmənt]	*n.* 娱乐；消遣 (amusement or pleasure that comes from watching a performer playing a game) They played games in the evening for entertainment.

Nect系列

connect [kəˈnekt]	*v.* 连接；联结 (to become joined) 1 The bedroom connects to the kitchen. 2 There's no evidence connecting the company directly to the scandal.
connection [kəˈnekʃn]	*n.* 连接；联系 (something that joins or connects two or more things) The state plans to improve roads that serve as connections between major highways.
disconnect [ˌdɪskəˈnekt]	*v.* 切断；断开 (to separate something from something else) 1 Our landlord threatened to disconnect our electricity. 2 We were talking on the phone but suddenly we got disconnected.

Last系列

elastic [ɪˈlæstɪk]	*n.* 橡皮筋 (material that can be stretched) She wrapped an elastic around the cards. *adj.* 有弹性的；有弹力的 (capable of resuming original shape after stretching or compression) Rubber is an elastic material.
elasticity [ˌiːlæˈstɪsəti]	*n.* 弹性；弹力 (state of being easily stretched) Daily facial exercises help her to retain the skin's elasticity.
plastic [ˈplæstɪk]	*n.* 塑料 (a light strong material that is produced by chemical processes and can be formed into shapes when heated) The toy was made of plastic. *adj.* 塑料的 (made of plastic) She hiked down to the tree with a shovel and started digging for the plastic box holding the coins.

adj. 可塑的 (capable of being made into different shapes)

The mud is smooth, gray, soft, and plastic as butter.

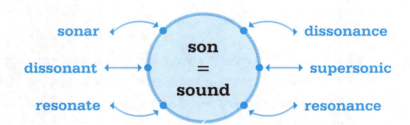

sonar ['səʊnɑː(r)]	*n.* 声呐装置 (a device used for finding things that are underwater by using sound waves) They detected the submarine by using sonar.
resonate ['rezəneɪt]	*v.* 回响；回荡 (to continue to produce a loud, clear and deep sound for a long time) The siren resonated throughout the city.
resonance ['rezənəns]	*n.* 共鸣；反响 (the power to bring images, feelings, etc. into the mind of the person reading or listening; the images, etc. produced in this way) His story didn't have much resonance with the audience.
dissonant ['dɪsənənt]	*adj.* 不和谐的；刺耳的 (not in harmony) His voice is drowned by the dissonant scream of a siren outside.
dissonance ['dɪsənəns]	*n.* 不和谐音；不一致 (lack of agreement) There is dissonance between what we are told and what we see with our own eyes.
supersonic [ˌsuːpə'sɒnɪk]	*adj.* 超音速的 (faster than the speed of sound) He joined the air force at 21 and began flying supersonic jet fighters.

Unit 24

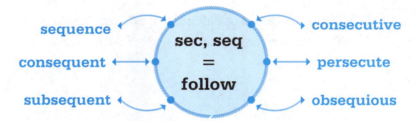

sequence ['siːkwəns]	**n.** 数列；序列 (the order in which things happen or should happen) **1** The chronological sequence gives the book an element of structure. **2** The project is nothing less than mapping every gene sequence in the human body.
sequential [sɪ'kwenʃl]	**adj.** 按次序的 (arranged in a particular order) The magician put the cards in sequential order.
subsequent ['sʌbsɪkwənt]	**adj.** 后来的；随后的 (coming later or after) The rate of population growth reached a peak in 1999 and declined in subsequent years.
consecutive [kən'sekjətɪv]	**adj.** 连续的；不间断的 (following one after the other in a series) It rained for three consecutive days.
consequent ['kɒnsɪkwənt]	**adj.** 随之发生的 (happening as a result of a particular action or set of conditions) Weather forecasters predict heavy rains and consequent flooding.
consequence ['kɒnsɪkwəns]	**n.** 结果；成果 (something that happens as a result of a particular action or set of conditions) **1** Some say many jobs will be lost as a consequence of the trade agreement. **2** The slightest error can have serious consequences. **n.** 重要性 (real importance) His promotion is of no consequence to me.
consequential [ˌkɒnsɪ'kwenʃl]	**adj.** 重要的；意义重大的 (be important or significant) There have been several consequential innovations in their computer software.
sequel ['siːkwəl]	**n.** 续集；续篇 (a book, movie, etc., that continues a story begun in another book, movie) **1** The new film is a sequel to the very successful comedy that came out five years ago. **2** He is busy writing the book's sequel.

persecute ['pɜːsɪkjuːt]	*v.* (尤指宗教或政治信仰的) 迫害 (to treat someone cruelly or unfairly especially because of race, religious or political beliefs) The country's leaders relentlessly persecuted those who fought against the regime.
persecution [ˌpɜːsɪ'kjuːʃn]	*n.* 迫害 (the act of continually treating somebody in a cruel and harmful way) The girls have managed to avoid religious persecution.
obsequious [əb'siːkwiəs]	*adj.* 卑躬屈膝的；谄媚的 (attempting to win favor from influential people by flattery) She's constantly followed by obsequious assistants who will do anything she tells them to.

Tech系列

technology [tek'nɒlədʒi]	*n.* 技术 (the use of science in solving problems as in industry or engineering) The government is developing innovative technologies to improve the safety of its soldiers.
technician [tek'nɪʃn]	*n.* 技术员 (a person whose job relates to the practical use of machines or science in industry) They hired a technician to help maintain the office's computers.
technical ['teknɪkl]	*adj.* 技术的 (having special knowledge especially of a mechanical or scientific subject) You have any problems with your new computer, we offer 24-hour technical support.
technique [tek'niːk]	*n.* 技巧；技能 (a way of doing something by using special knowledge or skill) The players need to practice in order to improve their technique.

Count系列

count [kaʊnt]	*v.* 数数 (to say numbers in order) She can count up to 10 in Italian. *v.* 计算总数 (to add people or things together to find the total number) She began to count up how many guests they had to invite.

account

[əˈkaʊnt]

n. 账户 (a record of money received and money paid out)

We opened new accounts at a bank last week.

v. 解释；说明 (to give an explanation of something)

This basic utilitarian model gives a relatively unsophisticated account of human behaviour.

accountant

[əˈkaʊntənt]

n. 会计员 (someone whose job is to keep the financial records of a business or person)

Then he moved to Virginia to live with his parents and work as a contract accountant.

accountable

[əˈkaʊntəbl]

adj. 负有责任的 (required to be responsible for something)

The owner was held accountable for his dog's biting of the child.

discount

[ˈdɪskaʊnt]

n. 折扣 (an amount of money that is taken off the usual cost of something)

The store offers a two percent discount when customers pay in cash.

recount

[rɪˈkaʊnt]

n. 重新计票 (an act of counting again to find the total number of something, especially votes at an election when the result is very close)

The election was very close and the loser demanded a recount.

v. 详细叙述 (to tell somebody about something, especially something that you have experienced)

He recounted how heavily armed soldiers forced him from the presidential palace.

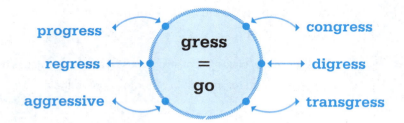

progress

[ˈprəʊgres]

n. 进步；前进 (movement forward or toward a place)

He's not a good reader, but he is making progress.

v. 进步；发展 (to move toward a higher, better, or more advanced stage)

The project has been progressing slowly.

progressive

[prəˈgresɪv]

adj. 逐渐的 (happening or developing gradually over a period of time)

One prominent symptom of the disease is progressive loss of memory.

congress

['kɒŋgres]

n. 国会；代表大会 (a formal assembly of representatives, as of various nations, to discuss problems)

She was recently elected to the country's congress.

aggressive

[ə'gresɪv]

adj. 好斗的 (showing a readiness to fight or argue)

He's a most aggressive boy—he is always fighting at school.

aggressor

[ə'gresə(r)]

n. 侵略者 (a person or country that attacks another)

Each country accused the other of being the aggressor.

digress

[daɪ'gres]

v. 离题 (to speak or write about something that is different from the main subject being discussed)

He digressed so often that it was hard to follow what he was saying.

regress

[rɪ'gres]

v. 倒退；退步 (to return to an earlier and usually worse or less developed condition or state)

① Many of the symptoms will regress or disappear.

② In extreme circumstances, people sometimes regress to the behavior they exhibited in childhood.

regressive

[rɪ'gresɪv]

adj. 后退的；退化的 (tending to return or revert to a previous state)

This regressive behaviour is more common in boy.

transgress

[trænz'gres]

v. 违反；违背 (to go beyond or over a limit or boundary)

No one is permitted to have privileges to transgress the law.

egress

['iːgres]

n. 出路；出口 (a way to get out of a place; the act of leaving a place)

The auditorium is designed to provide easy egress in an emergency.

Plate系列

plain

[pleɪn]

n. 平原；平地 (a large area of flat land without trees)

The first settlers in that area lived on the vast plains in lonely log cabins.

adj. 简朴的 (not having any added or extra things)

She was wearing plain black shoes.

adj. 清楚的；直白的 (easy to see or understand)

The lesson was explained in plain words.

explain [ɪk'spleɪn]	*v.*	讲解；解释 (to make something clear or easy to understand) Scientists could not explain the strange lights in the sky.
explanation [ˌeksplə'neɪʃn]	*n.*	解释；说明 (a statement that makes something clear or gives reasons for something) The professor's explanation was that the poem is really a parody.
platform ['plætfɔ:m]	*n.*	讲台；舞台 (a flat surface that is raised higher than the floor or ground and that people stand on when performing or speaking) He stepped up onto the platform and looked out into the audience.
plate [pleɪt]	*n.*	盘子 (a flat and usually round dish that is used for eating or serving food) Anita pushed her plate away; she had eaten virtually nothing.
plateau ['plætəʊ]	*n.* *n.*	高原 (a large flat area of land that is higher than other areas of land that surround it) A broad valley opened up leading to a high, flat plateau of cultivated land. 停滞时期 (a period when something does not increase or advance any further) The price of gas seems to have reached a plateau.
platitude ['plætɪtju:d]	*n.*	陈词滥调 (a statement that expresses an idea that is not new) His speech was filled with familiar platitudes about the value of hard work and dedication.

追根溯源

在希腊神话中，利希（Lethe）是冥界中的五条河流之一，被称为"忘却之河"。据说人死后都要喝下此河水，只有这样才能忘却前世的一切爱恨情仇，彻底斩断与前世的联系，有点像咱们中国传说中的孟婆汤。词根leth就来源于此，在英语中表示"致死的"，如lethal（致命的）。亡灵喝了利希（Lethe）的水，便会陷入昏睡，于是便有了lethargic（昏睡的；无精打采的）一词。

lethal ['li:θl]	*adj.*	致命的；致死的 (able to cause death) The barriers are lethal to fish trying to swim upstream.
lethargic [lə'θɑ:dʒɪk]	*adj.*	无精打采的 (feeling a lack of energy or a lack of interest in doing things) A big meal always makes me feel lethargic and sleepy.

eave [iːv]	*n.* 屋檐 (the lower edge of a roof that sticks out past the wall) These eave tiles are carved with many animal pictures.
eavesdrop [ˈiːvzdrɔp]	*v.* 窃听；偷听 (to listen secretly to what other people are saying) We caught him eavesdropping outside the window.
eavesdropper [ˈiːvzdrɒpə(r)]	*n.* 偷听者 (a secret listener to private conversations) The theory is simply that the eavesdropper will not know how to decrypt the message.

锦囊妙记

gangling [ˈgæŋglɪŋ]	*adj.* 又高又瘦且动作笨拙的 (tall, thin and awkward in their movements) The riders at the barn just loved the gangling newborn colt. 谐音法 gangling-杠铃，一个人长得像杠铃一样，身体又瘦又长 (gangling)。
gaunt [gɔːnt]	*adj.* 憔悴的；骨瘦如柴的 (very thin, usually because of illness, not having enough food, or worry) He left the hospital looking tired and gaunt. 联想法 g-干巴巴，aunt-姑姑，干巴巴的姑姑很憔悴（gaunt）。
idle [ˈaɪdl]	*adj.* 闲散的 (without work) I've never met such an idle bunch of workers. 谐音法 idle-爱斗！一般闲散的 (idle)人就爱斗殴！
siren [ˈsaɪrən]	*n.* 汽笛；警报器 (a device that makes a loud warning sound) He holed up inside the house and begged his wife to hide him whenever he heard a siren go by. 谐音法 si-死，ren-人，死人了，赶紧拉响警报 (siren)！

Unit 24

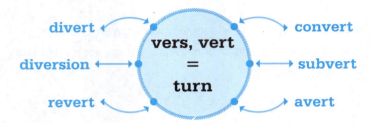

divert [daɪ'vɜːt]	**v.** 使转移；转向 (to make somebody/something change the direction)
	1 Police diverted traffic to a side street.
	2 The stream was diverted toward the farmland.
	v. 使……转移注意力 (to take somebody's attention away from someone or something)
	They want to divert the attention of the people from the real issues.
diversion [daɪ'vɜːʃn]	**n.** 转向；转移 (the act of changing the direction or use of something)
	We made a short diversion to go and look at the castle.
	n. 消遣；娱乐 (something that people do because it is enjoyable)
	Hiking is one of my favorite diversions.
subvert [səb'vɜːt]	**v.** 颠覆；推翻 (to secretly try to ruin or destroy a government, political system)
	The rebel army is attempting to subvert the government.
subversion [səb'vɜːʃn]	**n.** 颠覆 (活动) (a systematic attempt to overthrow or undermine a government or political system)
	He was arrested in parliament on a charge of subversion for organizing the demonstration.
convert [kən'vɜːt]	**v.** 使转变 (to change from one form to another)
	The signal will be converted into digital code.
	v. 使皈依 (to change from one belief, religion, view or party to another)
	He was converted to Christianity.
convertible [kən'vɜːtəbl]	**adj.** 可改变的；可变换的 (able to be changed into another form)
	The convertible sofa means that the apartment can sleep four.

revert [rɪ'vɜːt]	**v.** 恢复；回复 (to go back to a former condition or practice) Her boss became increasingly depressed and reverted to smoking heavily.
reverse [rɪ'vɜːs]	**v.** 使反转 (to change something to an opposite state or condition) **1** There is no way to reverse the aging process. **2** My mother and I reversed our roles. Now I'm taking care of her. **adj.** 相反的 (opposite to what is usual or stated) The drug is used to lower blood pressure but may have the reverse effect in some patients.
reversal [rɪ'vɜːsl]	**n.** 倒转；颠倒 (a change to an opposite or former state, condition, view or direction) In a sudden reversal, the mayor has decided not to run for reelection.
irreversible [ˌɪrɪ'vɜːsəbl]	**adj.** 不可逆的 (impossible to change back to a previous condition or state) Inaction on climate change could leave future generations with an irreversible catastrophe.
avert [ə'vɜːt]	**v.** 转移（目光等）(to turn your eyes, etc. away from something that you do not want to see) When asked if he had lied, he averted his eyes. **v.** 防止；避免 (to keep something bad or dangerous from happening) He sped up and averted an accident.
averse [ə'vɜːs]	**adj.** 厌恶的 (having a feeling of dislike) We are averse to such noisy surroundings.
aversion [ə'vɜːʃn]	**n.** 厌恶 (a strong feeling of not liking something) Many people have a natural and emotional aversion to insects.
adverse ['ædvɜːs]	**adj.** 不利的；有害的 (acting against or in an opposite direction) Despite the adverse conditions, the road was finished in just eight months.
adversary ['ædvəsəri]	**n.** 对手；敌手 (one that contends with or opposes another) His political adversaries tried to prevent him from winning the nomination.
invert [ɪn'vɜːt]	**v.** 使反向；使倒置 (to turn something upside down) The lens inverts the image.

Unit 25

inverse

[ˌɪn'vɜːs]

adj. 相反的 (opposite in order, nature or effect)

Addition and subtraction are inverse operations.

diverse

[daɪ'vɜːs]

adj. 不同的；多种多样的 (different from each other)

Members of the same family can have very diverse personalities.

diversity

[daɪ'vɜːsəti]

n. 多样化 (state of having many different forms, types or ideas)

The island has more diversity in plant life than other islands nearby.

diversify

[daɪ'vɜːsɪfaɪ]

v. 使多样化 (to change something so that it has more different kinds of people or things)

The country is diversifying its energy sources.

versatile

['vɜːsətaɪl]

adj. 多才多艺的 (able to do many different things)

She is a versatile athlete who participates in many different sports.

controvert

[ˌkɒntrə'vɜːt]

v. 驳斥；反驳 (to say or prove that something is not true)

The statement of the last witness controvert the evidence of the first two.

controversial

[ˌkɒntrə'vɜːʃl]

adj. 引起争论的；有争议的(causing a lot of angry public discussion and disagreement)

The issue of the death penalty is highly controversial.

controversy

['kɒntrəvɜːsi]

n. 争论；争议 (argument that involves many people who strongly disagree about something)

The decision aroused much controversy among the students.

vertigo

['vɜːtɪɡəʊ]

n. 眩晕；头晕 (a feeling of dizziness caused especially by being in a very high place)

If you have vertigo it seems as if the whole room is spinning round you.

vertebrate

['vɜːtɪbrət]

adj. 有脊椎的 (having vertebrae or a backbone)

Mammals are vertebrate animals.

invertebrate

[ɪn'vɜːtɪbrət]

adj. 无脊椎的 (having no backbone)

Half of all invertebrate species live in tropical rain forests.

converse

[kən'vɜːs]

adj. 相反的 (opposite or reverse)

One must also consider the converse case.

v. 谈话 (to have a conversation with somebody)

They conversed quietly in the corner of the room.

doctrine

['dɒktrɪn]

n. 教条；教义 (a set of ideas or beliefs that are taught or believed to be true)

The government was founded on a doctrine of equality for all people.

doctrinal

[dɒk'traɪnl]

adj. 学说的 (relating to doctrines)

Doctrinal differences were vigorously debated among religious leaders.

indoctrinate

[ɪn'dɒktrɪneɪt]

v. 向……灌输(信仰) (to teach especially the ideas, opinions or beliefs of a certain group)

The goal should be to teach politics, rather than to indoctrinate students in a narrow set of political beliefs.

document

['dɒkjumənt]

n. 文件；公文 (an official paper that gives information about something or that is used as proof of something)

An important classified document has been leaked to the media.

v. 记录 (to create a record of something through writing, film or photography)

Her study was the first to document this type of behavior in gorillas.

docile

['dəʊsaɪl]

adj. 温顺的；驯服的 (quiet and easy to control)

His students were docile and eager to learn.

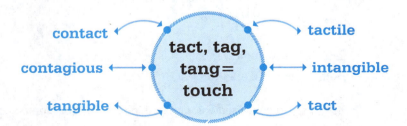

contact   tactile

contagious   tact, tag, tang＝touch   intangible

tangible   tact

contact

['kɒntækt]

n. 接触 (a meeting or touching of persons or things)

Physical contact between a mother and child is very important.

v. 接触；联系 (to communicate with someone or something)

For more information, contact the city's tourism office.

contagious

[kən'teɪdʒəs]

adj. 有传染性的 (able to be passed from one person or animal to another by touching)

The children are isolated because measles is the most contagious virus on Earth.

tangible

['tændʒəbl]

adj. 摸得着的；真实的 (possible to touch or handle)

① Sculpture is a tangible art form.

② The policy has not yet brought any tangible benefits.

intangible

[ɪn'tændʒəbl]

adj. 无形的 (not made of physical substance)

① Leadership is an intangible asset to a company.

② Electrical energy is completely intangible.

tactile

['tæktaɪl]

adj. 触觉的 (connected with the sense of touch; using your sense of touch)

Babies who sleep with their parents receive much more tactile stimulation than babies who sleep in a crib.

intact

[ɪn'tækt]

adj. 完整无缺的；未经触动的 (undamaged in any way)

Underneath the sediment, archaeologists imagine the vessel remains largely intact.

tact

[tækt]

n. (处事、言谈等的) 老练；圆通 (the ability to do or say things without offending or upsetting other people)

The peace talks required great tact on the part of both leaders.

tactful

['tæktfl]

adj. 圆通的；得体的；不得罪人的 (careful not to offend or upset other people)

It was tactful of her not to criticize me in front of my boss.

Integer系列

integer

['ɪntɪdʒə(r)]

n. 整数 (a whole number, such as 3 or 4 but not 3.5)

Both 10 and −10 are integers.

integrate

['ɪntɪɡreɪt]

v. 使一体化 (to combine two or more things to form or create something)

These programs will integrate with your existing software.

integration

[ˌɪntɪ'ɡreɪʃn]

n. 结合；整合 (process of uniting different things)

The aim is to promote closer economic integration.

integral

['ɪntɪɡrəl]

adj. 必需的；不可或缺的 (very important and necessary)

She had become an integral part of their lives.

integrity

[ɪn'teɡrəti]

n. 正直；诚实 (honest and firm in moral principles)

He was praised for his fairness and high integrity.

	n. 完整；完全 (state of being a united whole)
	Separatist movements are a threat to the integrity of the nation.
disintegrate	*v.* 碎裂；解体 (to break apart into many small parts or pieces)
[dɪsˈɪntɪɡreɪt]	① At that speed the plane began to disintegrate.
	② Rocks are disintegrated by rain and frost.

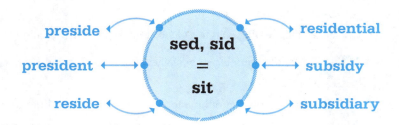

preside	*v.* 主持；指挥 (to be in charge of something)
[prɪˈzaɪd]	① The prime minister presided at the meeting.
	② She will preside over the company.
president	*n.* 总统 (the head of the government in some countries)
[ˈprezɪdənt]	The President will hold a news conference tomorrow.
reside	*v.* 住；居住 (to live in a particular place)
[rɪˈzaɪd]	He still resides at his parents' house.
	v. 存在于 (to exist or be present)
	The importance of this decision resides in the fact that it relates to people across the country.
resident	*n.* 居民 (someone who lives in a particular place)
[ˈrezɪdənt]	Ten percent of residents live below the poverty line.
residential	*adj.* 住宅的 (used as a place to live)
[ˌrezɪˈdenʃl]	This district is mainly residential.
subside	*v.* 减弱；平息 (to sink to a low or lower level)
[səbˈsaɪd]	① The earth subsided as the aquifer drained away.
	② Local officials say the flood waters have subsided.
subsidy	*n.* 补贴；津贴 (financial assistance given by one person or government to another)
[ˈsʌbsədi]	The government is planning to abolish subsidies to farmers.

subsidiary

[səb'sɪdiəri]

adj. 附属的；次要的 (not as important as something else)

The economics ministry has increasingly played a subsidiary role to the finance ministry.

n. 附属公司 (a business company that is owned or controlled by another company)

The company placed much money in its foreign subsidiary.

residual

[rɪ'zɪdjuəl]

adj. 残余的 (remaining after a process has been completed or something has been removed)

She's still dealing with the residual effects of the accident.

dissident

['dɪsɪdənt]

adj. 持异议的 (disagreeing especially with an established religious or political system)

She was suspected of having links with a dissident group.

n. 持异议者 (people who disagree with and criticize their government, especially because it is undemocratic)

The dissident was cast out from his country.

insidious

[ɪn'sɪdiəs]

adj. 隐伏的；潜在的 (causing harm in a way that is gradual or not easily noticed)

Most people with this insidious disease have no idea that they are infected.

assiduous

[ə'sɪdjuəs]

adj. 刻苦的；勤勉的 (showing great care, attention, and effort)

They were assiduous in gathering evidence.

sedate

[sɪ'deɪt]

v. 使镇静 (to give a person or animal drugs that cause relaxation or sleep)

The doctor sedated the patient heavily.

adj. 镇静的 (quiet and steady in manner or conduct)

He remained sedate under pressure.

sedentary

['sedntri]

adj. 久坐的 (involving a lot of sitting)

Their health problems were caused by their sedentary lifestyles.

sediment

['sedɪmənt]

n. 沉淀物 (material that sinks to the bottom of a liquid)

There was a layer of sediment in the bottom of the tank.

sedimentary

[ˌsedɪ'mentri]

adj. 沉积的 (made from material that sinks to the bottom of a liquid)

Sandstone is a sedimentary rock.

saddle	_v._ 给（马）备鞍 (to put a saddle on a horse)
['sædl]	He saddled his horse and mounted it.
	_v._ 使……负担 (to place somebody/something under a burden)
	The war saddled the country with huge foreign debt.

Guard系列

guard	_v._ 看守，监视（囚犯）(to prevent prisoners from escaping)
[gɑːd]	Two policemen were assigned to guard the prisoner.
	_n._ 卫兵 (a person whose job or duty is to watch and protect someone or something)
	We have a security guard around the whole area.
guardian	_n._ 监护人；保护者 (a person who guards or looks after something)
['gɑːdiən]	After the death of her parents, her uncle was appointed as her legal guardian.
safeguard	_v._ 保护；保卫 (to make someone or something safe or secure)
['seɪfgɑːd]	The laws safeguard the rights of citizens.
	_n._ 保护措施 (something that is designed to protect people from harm, risk or danger)
	There are many safeguards built into the system to prevent fraud.
guarantee	_v._ 保证；担保 (to make a promise about the condition or occurrence of something)
[ˌgærən'tiː]	① They guarantee that the diamonds they sell are top quality.
	② He guaranteed us that everything would go according to plan.

Tiny系列

tiny	_adj._ 极小的 (very small)
['taɪni]	He's from a tiny town that you've probably never heard of.
tenuous	_adj._ 脆弱的；微弱的；缥缈的 (flimsy, weak or uncertain)
['tenjuəs]	① The local theatre has had a tenuous existence in recent years.
	② The cultural and historical links between many provinces were seen to be very tenuous.

attenuate [ə'tenjueɪt]	**v.** 使减弱；使降低效率 (to make something weaker or less in amount, effect or force) You could never eliminate risk, but preparation and training could attenuate it.
extenuate [ɪks'tenjʊeɪt]	**v.** 减轻 (罪责或过错) 的程度；使看起来情有可原(to make guilt or an offence seem less serious or more forgivable) Nothing can extenuate such appalling behavior.

Text系列

text [tekst]	**n.** 文本 (the words that make up the main part of a book, magazine or newspaper, etc.) We examine the wording in detail before deciding on the final text. **v.** 发短信 (to send someone a text message) I texted a message to her.
textbook ['tekstbʊk]	**n.** 教科书 (a book used in the study of a subject) She wrote a textbook on international law. **adj.** 规范的；标准的 (very typical) The house is a textbook example of medieval domestic architecture.
context ['kɒntekst]	**n.** 上下文；背景 (the situation in which something happens) We need to look at the event within the larger context of world history.
textile ['tekstaɪl]	**n.** 织物；纺织品 (a fabric that is woven or knit) ① Various textile techniques will be explored to realise design possibilities. ② They import fine silk textiles from China.
texture ['tekstʃə(r)]	**n.** 质地；手感 (the way that something feels when you touch it) The plant's leaves are almost leathery in texture.

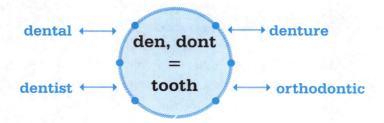

dentist ['dentɪst]	*n.* 牙科医生 (a person whose job is to care for people's teeth) He goes to the dentist's for a check-up every six months.
dental ['dentl]	*adj.* 牙齿的；牙科的 (relating to teeth or to the work dentists do) Regular dental care is essential for healthy teeth.
denture ['dentʃə(r)]	*n.* 假牙 (artificial teeth) He had a denture that he took out at night.
orthodontic [ˌɔːθəˈdɒntɪk]	*n.* 牙齿正畸 (a branch of dentistry that deals with helping teeth to grow straight) Adults make up a record high of nearly 1.5 million orthodontic patients in the U.S. and Canada.

追根溯源

　　单词narcissus 源于希腊神话。相传，那喀索斯(Narcissus)是河神刻斐索斯与水泽女神利里俄珀之子。他是一位长相十分清秀的美少年，却对任何姑娘都不动心，只对自己的水中倒影爱慕不已，最终在顾影自怜中抑郁死去，化作水仙花，仍留在水边守望着自己的影子。后来，人们便以那喀索斯的名字命名水仙花(narcissus)。

narcissus [nɑːˈsɪsəs]	*n.* 水仙花 (plants which have yellow or white flowers with cone-shaped centres that appear in the spring) Now I still do not know what a blooming narcissus looks like.
narcissism ['nɑːsɪsɪzəm]	*n.* 自我陶醉；自恋 (habit of always thinking about yourself and admiring yourself) Tens of thousands of people are calling for Donald Trump to be examined by doctors for narcissism, and a Harvard medical professor thinks they are right.

Flint与Skinflint

flint [flɪnt]	*n.* 燧石；火石 (a hard type of rock that produces a small piece of burning material, called a spark when it is hit by steel) Houses in this part of the country are built of flint.
skinflint ['skɪnflɪnt]	*n.* 吝啬鬼；一毛不拔的人 (a person who would save, gain or extort money by any means) She is a penny-pinching skinflint.

锦囊妙记

anchor ['æŋkə(r)]	*n.* 锚 (a heavy device that is attached to a boat or ship by a rope or chain and that is thrown into the water to hold the boat or ship in place) The ship dropped anchor in a secluded harbor. 谐音法 anchor-岸口，船到岸口要抛锚 (anchor)。
cactus ['kæktəs]	*n.* 仙人掌 (a plant that lives in the desert and that has many sharp points) It was the first year that the cactus had produced flowers. 谐音法 cactus-看看它刺，看看仙人掌(cactus)的刺。
cacophony [kə'kɒfəni]	*n.* 刺耳的声音 (unpleasant loud sounds) The sounds of barking dogs and sirens added to the cacophony on the streets. 谐音法 caco-咔咔声，phon-电话，电话中出现咔咔的声音，就是刺耳的声音 (cacophony)。
serene [sə'riːn]	*adj.* 沉静的；宁静的 (calm and peaceful) She looked as calm and serene as she always did. 谐音法 serene-死人了，人死之后归于宁静 (serene)。
labyrinth ['læbərɪnθ]	*n.* 迷宫 (a place that has many confusing paths or passages) We lost our way in the labyrinth of streets. 谐音法 labyrinth-来必晕死！当然是迷宫 (labyrinth)。

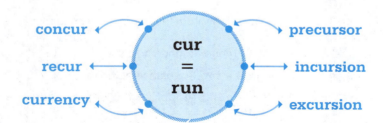

concur   ←→   **cur
=
run**   →   precursor

recur   ←→   ←→   incursion

currency   ←→   ←→   excursion

occur [əˈkɜː(r)]	*v.* 发生；出现 (to happen)
	① The deaths occurred when troops tried to disperse the demonstrators.
	② The disease tends to occur in children under the age of five.
occurrence [əˈkʌrəns]	*n.* 发生；事件 (something that happens)
	① Getting headaches has become a common occurrence for her.
	② Lightning is a natural occurrence.
recur [rɪˈkɜː(r)]	*v.* 再发生；复发 (to happen or appear again)
	① There is only a slight chance that the disease will recur.
	② The same problem keeps recurring.
recurrent [rɪˈkʌrənt]	*adj.* 复发的；复现的 (returning or happening time after time)
	The loss of innocence is a recurrent theme in his stories.
concur [kənˈkɜː(r)]	*v.* 同意 (to agree)
	We concur that more money should be spent on education.
current [ˈkʌrənt]	*adj.* 现在的 (happening or existing now)
	Current thinking holds that obesity is more a medical than a psychological problem.
	n. 气流；水流 (the part of a fluid body, as air or water, moving continuously in a certain direction)
	① Strong currents pulled the swimmer out to sea.
	② Air currents carried the balloon for miles.
currency [ˈkʌrənsi]	*n.* 货币 (the money that a country uses)
	A new currency has been introduced in the foreign exchange market.

Unit 26

incur [ɪn'kɜː(r)]	*v.* 招致；遭受 (to cause yourself to have or experience something unpleasant) The government had also incurred huge debts.
incursion [ɪn'kɜːʃn]	*n.* 侵犯；侵入 (a sudden invasion or attack) There were incursions from the border every summer.
cursory ['kɜːsəri]	*adj.* 粗略的；草率的 (done or made quickly) ① The mayor gave a cursory glance at the report. ② Even the most cursory look at the organization's records shows problems.
excursion [ɪk'skɜːʃn]	*n.* 短途旅行 (a short trip especially for pleasure) They went on a brief excursion to the coast.
excursive [eks'kɜːsɪv]	*adj.* 离题的 (characterized by digression) His speech was filled with excursive statements.
precursor [priː'kɜːsə(r)]	*n.* 先驱；先锋 (one that indicates or announces someone or something to come) Colonial opposition to unfair taxation by the British was a precursor of the Revolution.
course [kɔːs]	*n.* 航线；路线 (the path or direction that something or someone moves along) The ship was blown off course by a storm. *n.* 课程 (a series of classes about a particular subject in a school) She's taking a chemistry course this semester.
curriculum [kə'rɪkjələm]	*n.* 全部课程 (the courses that are taught by a school or college) Russian is the one compulsory foreign language on the school curriculum.

Later系列

lateral ['lætərəl]	*adj.* 侧面的；横向的；向侧面移动的 (toward, on, or coming from the side) Jets of compressed air gave the aircraft lateral and directional stability.

| **unilateral** | *adj.* 单边的；一方的 (involving only one group or country) |
| [juːnɪ'lætrəl] | Our country is prepared to take unilateral action. |

| **bilateral** | *adj.* 双边的；双方的 (involving two groups or countries) |
| [ˌbaɪ'lætərəl] | They have been negotiating a bilateral trade deal. |

| **equilateral** | *adj.* 等边的 (having all sides or faces equal) |
| [ˌiːkwɪ'lætərəl] | Its outline roughly forms an equilateral triangle. |

collateral	*adj.* 附属的；附加的 (related but not in a direct or close way)
[kə'lætərəl]	To minimize collateral damage maximum precision in bombing was required.
	n. 担保物 (something that you promise to give someone if you cannot pay back a loan)
	Many people use personal assets as collateral for small business loans.

collate	*v.* 核对；校对 (to gather together information from different sources in order to study it carefully)
[kə'leɪt]	① They are still collating the data.
	② The photocopier will collate the pages of the report.

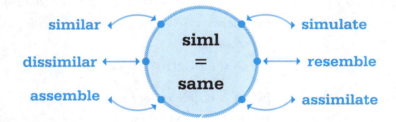

| **similar** | *adj.* 类似的；同类的 (almost the same as someone or something else) |
| ['sɪmələ(r)] | They had similar experiences growing up, even though they came from vastly different backgrounds. |

| **dissimilar** | *adj.* 不同的；不相似的 (not the same; different or unalike) |
| [dɪ'sɪmɪlə(r)] | The two movies are very dissimilar. |

| **simulate** | *v.* 假装；冒充 (to look, feel or behave like something) |
| ['sɪmjuleɪt] | The model will be used to simulate the effects of an earthquake. |

simulation

[ˌsɪmjuˈleɪʃn]

n. 模仿；模拟 (the process of simulating something)

They use computer simulation to predict weather conditions.

simulator

[ˈsɪmjuleɪtə(r)]

n. 模拟装置；模拟器 (a machine that is used to show what something looks or feel like and is usually used to study something or to train people)

People learning to fly often practices on a flight simulator.

assimilate

[əˈsɪməleɪt]

v. 吸收；消化 (to take in and make part of a larger thing)

The body assimilates nutrients in food.

v. 同化；使融入 (to absorb into the cultural tradition of a population or group)

She was completely assimilated into her new country.

assemble

[əˈsembl]

v. 集合；收集 (to collect things or gather people into one place or group)

1 She assembled all of her old photos into three albums.

2 A team of scientists was assembled to study the problem.

assembly

[əˈsembli]

n. 组装 (the act of connecting together the parts of something)

The parts are made in this factory and then shipped to another country for assembly.

n. 集会 (the meeting together of a group of people for a particular purpose)

The right of assembly is protected by the First Amendment to the United States constitution.

dissemble

[dɪˈsembl]

v. 假装；掩饰 (感情、意图等) (to hide under a false appearance)

1 He dissembled happiness at the news that his old girlfriend was getting married to someone else.

2 Children learn to dissemble at a surprisingly early age.

resemble

[rɪˈzembl]

v. 与……相像 (to look or be like someone or something)

He strongly resembles his father in appearance and in temperament.

resemblance

[rɪˈzembləns]

n. 相似；形似 (the state of looking or being like someone or something else)

He doesn't look exactly like his father, but there is some resemblance.

facsimile

[fækˈsɪməli]

n. 副本；传真 (an exact copy)

A facsimile of the world's first computer was exhibited in the museum.

simultaneous

[ˌsɪmlˈteɪniəs]

adj. 同时发生的 (existing or occurring at the same time)

There were several simultaneous attacks by the rebels.

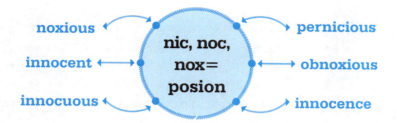

noxious ← → pernicious

innocent ← → obnoxious

nic, noc, nox= posion

innocuous ← → innocence

noxious [ˈnɒkʃəs]	*adj.* 有害的；有毒的 (harmful to living things) Heavy industry pollutes our rivers with noxious chemicals.
obnoxious [əbˈnɒkʃəs]	*adj.* 讨厌的；可憎的 (unpleasant in a way that makes people feel offended, annoyed or disgusted) He said some really obnoxious things about his ex-girlfriend at the party.
innocuous [ɪˈnɒkjuəs]	*adj.* 无害的 (not harmful) Both mushrooms look innocuous but are in fact deadly.
innocent [ˈɪnəsnt]	*adj.* 无辜的；无罪的 (free from guilt or blame) ① A person accused of a crime is considered innocent until proven guilty. ② Someone told your secret, but it wasn't me. I'm innocent.
innocence [ˈɪnəsns]	*n.* 清白 (the state of being not guilty of a crime or other wrong act) He vows that he will prove his innocence in court.
pernicious [pəˈnɪʃəs]	*adj.* 恶性的；有害的 (causing great harm or damage often in a way that is not easily seen or noticed) She thinks television has a pernicious influence on our children.

Emperor系列

empire [ˈempaɪə(r)]	*n.* 帝国 (a group of territories or peoples under one ruler) ① The Roman Empire was divided in the fourth century AD. ② She built a tiny business into a worldwide empire.
emperor [ˈempərə(r)]	*n.* 皇帝；君主 (a man who rules an empire) The Emperor must realize that he has us at his mercy.

Unit 26

empress	*n.* 女皇；皇后 (a woman who rules an empire or who is the wife of an emperor)
['emprəs]	They referred to the Empress as their venerable ancestor.
imperial	*adj.* 帝国的；皇帝的 (relating to an empire or its ruler)
[ɪm'pɪəriəl]	The company is the official provider of jewelry to Japan's imperial family.
imperious	*adj.* 专横的 (showing arrogant superiority)
[ɪm'pɪəriəs]	An imperious movie star thinks she's some sort of goddess.
imperialism	*n.* 帝国主义 (a policy of extending your rule over foreign countries)
[ɪm'pɪəriəlɪzəm]	Imperialism is monopolistic, parasitic and moribund capitalism.
imperative	*adj.* 重要紧急的；迫切的；急需处理的 (very important and needing immediate attention or action)
[ɪm'perətɪv]	The president said it was imperative that the release of all hostages be secured.
	adj. 表示权威的(expressing authority)
	People resented his imperative tone of voice.
	n. 必要的事 (a command, rule, duty that is very important or necessary)
	She considers it a moral imperative to help people in need.

Relation系列

relate	*v.* 叙述；讲述 (to tell something, such as a story)
[rɪ'leɪt]	We listened eagerly as she related the whole exciting story.
	v. 与……有关 (to show or make a connection between two or more things)
	Other recommendations relate to the details of how such data is stored.
relative	*adj.* 相关的；相对的 (compared to someone or something else or to each other)
['relətɪv]	We discussed the relative merits of each school.
	n. 亲戚 (a member of your family)
	He inherited a small piece of land from a distant relative.
relation	*n.* 关系；联系 (the way in which two or more people or things are connected)
[rɪ'leɪʃn]	The incident led to tense international relations.
relationship	*n.* 关系；联系 (the state of being related or connected)
[rɪ'leɪʃnʃɪp]	The relationship between the two countries has improved.

correlate ['kɒrələt]	*v.* 使互相关联 (to have a close connection with something) There is no evidence correlating height and intelligence.
correlation [ˌkɒrə'leɪʃn]	*n.* 相互关系 (the relationship between things that happen or change together) Researchers have found a direct correlation between smoking and lung cancer.

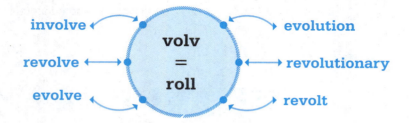

involve [ɪn'vɒlv]	*v.* 包含；使参与 (to have or include someone or something as a part of something) The teacher involved her students in the project.
involvement [ɪn'vɒlvmənt]	*n.* 加入；参与 (the act of sharing in the activities of a group) The statement by the military denied any involvement in last night's attack.
evolve [i'vɒlv]	*v.* 使发展；使进化 (to change or develop gradually) The bright plumage of many male birds has evolved to attract females.
evolution [ˌi:və'lu:ʃn]	*n.* 演变；进化 (the process of development of an animal or a plant) It has passed through an interesting procedure of evolution.
revolve [rɪ'vɒlv]	*v.* 使旋转 (to turn around a centre point or line) The planets revolve around the sun.
revolution [ˌrevə'lu:ʃn]	*n.* 巨变；彻底改变 (a sudden, extreme, or complete change in the way people live or work) This new theory could cause a revolution in elementary education. *n.* 旋转 (the action of moving around something in a path that is similar to a circle) The earth makes one revolution on its axis in 24 hours.

| revolutionary | *adj.* 革命的；革命性的 (connected with political revolution) |
| [ˌrevəˈluːʃənəri] | Revolutionary forces were easily defeated before reaching the capital. |

revolt	*v.* 反叛；背叛 (to fight in a violent way against the rule of a leader or government)
[rɪˈvəʊlt]	The army revolted against the dictator.
	n. 叛乱 (violent action against a ruler or government)
	Soon the entire armed forces were in open revolt.

| voluble | *adj.* 健谈的 (talking a lot in an energetic and rapid way) |
| [ˈvɒljʊbl] | She is an extremely voluble young woman who engages in soliloquies not conversations. |

Cross系列

| crucial | *adj.* 关键性的 (extremely important) |
| [ˈkruːʃl] | Vitamins are crucial for maintaining good health. |

| crucify | *v.* 严厉批评 (to criticize someone or something very harshly) |
| [ˈkruːsɪfaɪ] | Dishonest judges were crucified in the newspapers. |

| crusade | *n.* 斗争；运动 (a major effort to change something) |
| [kruːˈseɪd] | Football players launched an unprecedented crusade against racism on the terraces. |

| excruciating | *adj.* 极痛苦的 (causing great mental or physical pain) |
| [ɪkˈskruːʃieɪtɪŋ] | I was in excruciating pain and one leg wouldn't move. |

| cruise | *v.* 巡游；漫游 (to travel on a boat or ship to a number of places as a vacation) |
| [kruːz] | They cruised along the coast. |

Advance系列

| advance | *v.* 使前进 (to bring or move forward) |
| [ədˈvɑːns] | The car advanced slowly down the street. |

Unit 26

n. （知识、技术等）发展，进步 (if knowledge, technology, etc. advances, it develops and improves)

Our understanding of this disease has advanced rapidly in recent years.

n. 进展 (progress in development)

There has been little advance made in the treatment of this disease.

advantage

[əd'vɑːntɪdʒ]

n. 有利条件；益处 (something that benefits the one it belongs to)

① His plan has the advantage of being less expensive than other options.

② The company's only advantage over the competition is its location.

disadvantage

[ˌdɪsəd'vɑːntɪdʒ]

n. 不利；劣势 (a bad or undesirable quality or feature)

They argued that the new regulations would place their company at a competitive disadvantage in the marketplace.

Ornament系列

ornament

['ɔːnəmənt]

n. 装饰；装饰物 (a small, fancy object that is put on something else to make it more attractive)

The flowers were put on the table for ornament.

ornamental

[ˌɔːnə'mentl]

adj. 装饰的 (covered with a lot of decoration, especially when this involves very small or complicated designs)

The garden has many ornamental shrubs.

ornate

[ɔː'neɪt]

adj. 装饰华丽的 (covered with fancy patterns and shapes)

She doesn't like ornate jewelry.

adorn

[ə'dɔːn]

v. 装饰；修饰 (to make more attractive by adding something)

Her paintings adorn the walls.

Alt系列

alter

['ɔːltə(r)]

v. 改变；更改 (to make a change so that it will fit better)

I'll need to have the dress altered before the wedding.

alteration

[ˌɔːltə'reɪʃn]

n. 变化；改变 (the act or process of changing something)

She began alteration of the design.

Unit 26

altruistic [ˌæltrʊˈɪstɪk]	**adj.** 利他的；无私的 (caring about the needs and happiness of other people more than your own) Altruistic spirit should be cultivated by us vigorously.
altruism [ˈæltruɪzəm]	**n.** 利他主义；无私 (unselfish regard for or devotion to the welfare of others) Charitable acts should be motivated purely by altruism.
alternate [ɔːlˈtɜːnət]	**adj.** 轮流的；交替的 (occurring or following by turns) Stretch up 30 times with alternate arms as a warm-up exercise. **v.** 使交替 (to do different things so that one follows the other in a repeated series) For the best results, you should alternate between yoga and weightlifting every other day.
alternative [ɔːlˈtɜːnətɪv]	**adj.** 替代的；备选的 (offering or expressing a choice) Scientists are developing an alternative approach to treating the disease. **n.** 可供选择的事物 (a choice or option) The menu offered several vegetarian alternatives.

Urb系列

urban [ˈɜːbən]	**adj.** 都市的 (relating to cities and the people who live in them) The government is spending billions of dollars on new urban rail projects.
urbane [ɜːˈbeɪn]	**adj.** 温文尔雅的 (polite and confident) She describes him as urbane and charming.
urbanize [ˈɜːbənaɪz]	**v.** 使都市化 (to cause to take on urban characteristics) For China to modernize its economy, it must further industrialize, and urbanize.
suburb [ˈsʌbɜːb]	**n.** 郊区；城郊 (a town or other area where people live in houses near a larger city) His family lived in the suburb.

在罗马神话中，爱神被称为"维纳斯"（Venus），在希腊神话中被称为"阿芙洛狄忒"（Aphrodite）。金星就是以她的名字命名的。**Venus**在拉丁语中有"美；渴望"之意，并延伸出"**venerate**"（崇拜）之意。

venerate ['venəreɪt]	*v.* 崇敬；尊敬 (to show deep respect for somebody) They came to venerate him as a symbolic figure.
venerable ['venərəbl]	*adj.* 令人尊重的 (valued and respected because of old age, long use) The venerable old man was a cherished source of advice and wisdom for the villagers.

锦囊妙记

miser ['maɪzə(r)]	*n.* 守财奴；吝啬鬼 (a person who hates to spend money) The miser liked to sit and play with his money. 联想法 mis-miss（思念），一个总是思念(miss) money 的人是吝啬鬼(miser)。
misery ['mɪzəri]	*n.* 不幸；痛苦 (extreme suffering or unhappiness) The miser died in misery. 联想法 misery与miser有关系，吝啬鬼(miser)的结局一般都充满了不幸(misery)。
miserable ['mɪzrəbl]	*adj.* 不幸的 (very unhappy or distressed) He felt lonely and miserable after his divorce.
commiserate [kə'mɪzəreɪt]	*v.* 怜悯；同情 (to express sadness or sympathy for someone who has experienced something unpleasant) We commiserated with him on the loss of his mother. 拆分法 com-together, 和他人共同感受悲伤，就是同情、怜悯 (commiserate)他人。
stingy ['stɪndʒi]	*adj.* 小气的；吝啬的 (not liking or wanting to give or spend money) The company was too stingy to raise salaries. 谐音法 stingy-死盯着，死盯着money不放的人真小气(stingy)！

Unit 26

Unit 27

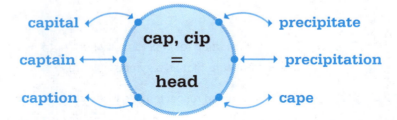

capital ['kæpɪtl]	*n.* 首都 (the most important town or city of a country, usually where the central government operates from) China hosted the Asia-Pacific Economic Cooperation meeting in the capital city of Beijing. *adj.* 死刑的 (punishable by or resulting in death) Espionage is a capital offence in this country. *n.* 资本 (a large amount of money that is invested) A large amount of capital is invested in all these branches.
captain ['kæptɪn]	*n.* 船长；机长 (a person who is in charge of a ship or an airplane) The captain is responsible for everything that happens to his ship in the course of a voyage.
caption ['kæpʃn]	*n.* 标题；说明文字 (title that goes with a picture) The caption on the picture says "This year's contest winners".
capitulate [kə'pɪtʃuleɪt]	*v.* 认输；屈服 (to surrender often after negotiation of terms) ① The enemy was forced to capitulate unconditionally. ② The company capitulated to the labor union to avoid a strike.
capitulation [kə,pɪtʃʊ'leɪʃn]	*n.* (有条件的) 投降 (the act of surrendering or yielding) Her sudden capitulation surprised everyone; she usually debated for hours.
decapitate [dɪ'kæpɪteɪt]	*v.* 将……斩首 (to cut off the head of somebody) The commander ordered his men to decapitate the prisoner.
recapitulate [,riːkə'pɪtʃuleɪt]	*v.* 重述要点；简要回顾 (to give a brief summary of something) We understood your point, there's no need to recapitulate.

precipitate [prɪˈsɪpɪteɪt]	*v.* 使······突然降临；加速 (坏事的发生) (to make something, especially something bad, happen suddenly or sooner than it should)
	Her death precipitated a family crisis.
	adj. 突然的；仓促的 (happening very quickly or too quickly without enough thought or planning)
	Many of our current problems have been caused by precipitate policy making in the past.
precipitation [prɪˌsɪpɪˈteɪʃn]	*n.* 降水 (water that falls to the ground as rain, snow)
	The weather forecast calls for some sort of frozen precipitation tomorrow—either snow or sleet.
	n. 沉淀 (the process of separating a solid substance from a liquid)
	Minerals are separated from the seawater by precipitation.
precipice [ˈpresəpɪs]	*n.* 悬崖；险境 (a very steep side of a mountain or cliff)
	① He stood on the edge of the precipice.
	② The King now stands on the brink of a political precipice.
precipitous [prɪˈsɪpɪtəs]	*adj.* 险峻的 (very steep)
	The town is perched on the edge of a steep, precipitous cliff.
	adj. 急剧的；剧烈的 (happening in a very quick and sudden way)
	① There has been a precipitous decline in home sales recently.
	② People were shocked by his precipitous fall from political power.
cape [keɪp]	*n.* 海角 (a point of land that juts out into the sea or into a lake)
	The fishing-boat rounded the cape.

Tailor系列

tailor [ˈteɪlə(r)]	*n.* 裁缝 (a person whose business is making or making adjustments in clothes)
	The tailor took him as his successor.
	v. 定制 (to change to fit a special need)
	They tailored the show for younger audiences.
retail [ˈriːteɪl]	*n.* 零售 (relating to the business of selling things directly to customers for their own use)
	Retail sales grew just 3.8 percent last year.

retailer ['riːteɪlə(r)]	*n.* 零售商 (a person or business that sells goods to the public) Furniture and carpet retailers are among those reporting the sharpest annual decline in sales.
detail ['diːteɪl]	*n.* 细节 (a small part of something) Every detail of the wedding was perfect. *v.* 详述 (to report with attention to each item) The book details the series of events that led to the tragedy.

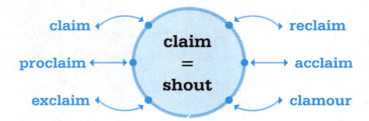

claim [kleɪm]	*v.* 声称 (to say that something belongs to you or that you deserve something) The terrorist group claimed responsibility for the attack. *v.* 要求 (to ask for as something that is a right or is deserved) You should claim compensation for the hours you worked. *n.* 要求 (a statement saying that something happened a certain way or will happen a certain way) He made false claims about his past job experience.
proclaim [prəˈkleɪm]	*v.* 宣告；公布 (to announce officially and publicly) ❶ The President proclaimed a national day of mourning. ❷ She proclaimed that she will run for president.
proclamation [ˌprɒkləˈmeɪʃn]	*n.* 宣布；公布 (an official statement or announcement made by a person in power or by a government) The President issued a proclamation which freed the slaves.
acclaim [əˈkleɪm]	*v.* 称赞；赞扬 (to praise enthusiastically and often publicly) He was acclaimed as the country's greatest modern painter.
acclamation [ˌækləˈmeɪʃn]	*n.* 欢呼；喝彩 (a loud eager expression of approval or praise) She has earned worldwide acclamation for her charitable works.

Unit 27

exclaim [ɪkˈskleɪm]	*v.* 突然呼喊；惊叫 (to cry out or speak in strong or sudden emotion) **1** The children exclaimed with wonder when they saw the elephant. **2** "Here he comes!" someone exclaimed.
exclamation [ˌekskləˈmeɪʃn]	*n.* 呼喊；惊叫 (a sharp or sudden cry or expression of strong feeling) The good news was greeted with a chorus of joyous exclamations.
reclaim [rɪˈkleɪm]	*v.* 要求归还 (to get back something that was lost or taken away) You might be able to reclaim some of the money you contributed. *v.* 开垦荒地 (to make land available for use by changing its condition) The Netherlands has been reclaiming farmland from water.
declaim [dɪˈkleɪm]	*v.* 高声朗诵 (to say something in usually a loud and formal way) **1** The actress declaimed her lines with passion. **2** He raised his right fist and declaimed, "Liar and cheat!"
clamour [ˈklæmə(r)]	*n.* 喧哗声；喧闹 (a loud persistent outcry, as from a large number of people) She could hear a clamour in the road outside.

Phone系列

prophet [ˈprɒfɪt]	*n.* 预言家；先知 (a person who predicts the future) A prophet made a prophecy that the kingdom would fall.
prophecy [ˈprɒfəsi]	*n.* 预言 (a statement that something will happen in the future) The prophecies of the author have all come true.
prophetic [prəˈfetɪk]	*adj.* 预言的 (correctly stating what will happen in the future) A young girl in the village experienced a prophetic vision.
symphony [ˈsɪmfəni]	*n.* 交响乐 (a usually long musical composition for a full orchestra) Each musician is an active member of the symphony.
euphony [ˈjuːfəni]	*n.* 悦耳的声音 (pleasing or sweet sound) Such euphony is hard to resist.
infant [ˈɪnfənt]	*n.* 婴儿；幼儿 (a child in the first period of life) He showed us a picture of his infant daughter.

| **phonetic** | *adj.* 语音的；语音学的 (relating to spoken language or speech sounds) |
| [fə'netɪk] | This dictionary uses the International Phonetic Alphabet. |

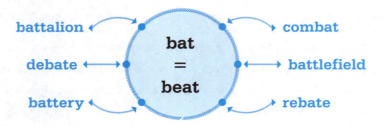

debate	*n.* 讨论；辩论 (a discussion, especially of a public question in an assembly)
[dɪ'beɪt]	After a long debate, Congress approved the proposal.
	v. 讨论 (to discuss something with people whose opinions are different from your own)
	Whether or not the tax cuts benefit the lower classes is still hotly debated among economists.

| **abate** | *v.* 减少；减轻 (to reduce in amount, degree or intensity) |
| [ə'beɪt] | The doctor gave him some medicine to abate the powerful pain. |

| **rebate** | *n.* 折扣；回扣 (an amount of money that is paid back to you because you have paid too much) |
| ['riːbeɪt] | Customers are to benefit from a rebate on their electricity bills. |

combat	*n.* 格斗；搏斗 (active fighting especially in a war)
['kɒmbæt]	Over 16 million men died in combat during the war.
	v. 防止；减轻 (to stop something unpleasant or harmful from happening or from getting worse)
	❶ Exercise can help combat the effects of stress.
	❷ The mayor pledged to combat crime.

| **combative** | *adj.* 好斗的 (having or showing a willingness to fight or argue) |
| ['kɒmbətɪv] | He conducted the meeting in his usual combative style, refusing to admit any mistakes. |

| **battlefield** | *n.* 战场；战地 (an area where a battle is fought) |
| ['bætlfiːld] | Hundreds of dead soldiers lay on the battlefield. |

battery ['bætri]	*n.*	蓄电池 (a combination of two or more cells connected to produce electric energy) He is using your mains electricity to recharge his car battery.
	n.	一组；一群 (a usually large group of similar people, things, or ideas that work together) The operation was performed by a battery of doctors.
battalion [bə'tæliən]	*n.*	大军；部队 (a large group of soldiers that consists of three or more companies) He was ordered to return to his battalion.
batter ['bætə(r)]	*v.*	连续猛击 (to beat with repeated violent blows) ❶ Waves battered the shore. ❷ He was battered to death with a large stick.
baton ['bætɒn]	*n.*	警棍 (a short heavy stick which is sometimes used as a weapon by the police) The policeman used his baton to battle the rascal.

Circle系列

circle ['sɜːkl]	*n.*	圆 (something in the form of a circle or part of a circle) We gathered in a circle around the fireplace.
	v.	圈出；包围 (to form or draw a circle around) The pilot circled the airport before landing.
encircle [ɪn'sɜːkl]	*v.*	包围；围绕 (to form a circle around someone or something) A crowd of reporters encircled the mayor.
circulate ['sɜːkjəleɪt]	*v.*	循环；流转 (to move around in a course) ❶ Blood circulates through the body. ❷ Rumors are circulating around town.
circulation [ˌsɜːkjə'leɪʃn]	*n.*	流通 (movement of air, water through the different parts of something) A fan will improve the circulation of air in the room.
	n.	循环；流通 (passage from place to place or person to person) The coins have recently entered circulation.

circuit [ˈsɜːkɪt]	*n.* 电路；线路 (the complete path that an electric current travels along) Any attempts to cut through the cabling will break the electrical circuit. *n.* 环形 (movement around something) It takes a year for the Earth to make one circuit around the sun.
circuitous [səˈkjuːɪtəs]	*adj.* 迂回的；绕行的 (not straight, short and direct) **1** We took a circuitous route to the airport so as to avoid the massive traffic jam on the highway. **2** Their logic seems a bit circuitous.
circular [ˈsɜːkjələ(r)]	*adj.* 圆形的；环行的 (shaped like a circle; round) That planet has a more circular orbit than our planet does.
circus [ˈsɜːkəs]	*n.* 马戏；马戏团 (a group that consists of clowns, acrobats and animals which travels around to different places and performs shows) My real ambition was to work in a circus.

Curve系列

curve [kɜːv]	*n.* 弧线；曲线 (a smooth, rounded line, shape or path) Both he and the crew are on a steep learning curve. *v.* 弯曲；弯成曲线 (to form a curve) **1** The ball curved strangely in the air. **2** The road curved to the left.
curl [kɜːl]	*n.* 卷发 (a lock of hair that coils) Her daughter has cute blonde curls. *v.* 弯曲；卷曲 (to become curved or rounded) **1** Smoke was curling from the chimney. **2** The cat curled into a ball and went to sleep.
coil [kɔɪl]	*n.* 卷；圈 (a circle, a series of circles, or a spiral made by coiling) The steel arrives at the factory in coils. *v.* 卷；盘绕 (to move in a circular or spiral course) She coiled the loose thread around her finger.
recoil [rɪˈkɔɪl]	*v.* 退缩 (to quickly move away from something that is shocking, frightenin or disgusting) She recoiled hastily at seeing a snake in the path.

Unit 27

	v. (枪炮) 反冲；产生后坐力 (to move suddenly backwards when you fire it)
	The rifle recoils when it is fired.

Scrub系列

scrub [skrʌb]	*v.* 用力擦洗；刷洗 (to clean something with hard rubbing) We scrubbed and scrubbed until the floor was clean.
scrape [skreɪp]	*v.* 擦；刮 (to remove by repeated strokes with something sharp or rough) ① She scraped her fingernails across the blackboard. ② Someone had scraped the car with a key.
scratch [skrætʃ]	*v.* 挠痒 (to scrape or rub lightly) You shouldn't scratch. It'll just make your itch worse. *v.* 划伤；划出痕迹 (to rub a surface or object with something sharp or rough) The branches tore at my jacket and scratched my hands and face.
scramble ['skræmbl]	*v.* 迅速地爬 (to climb over something quickly especially while also using your hands) We scrambled over the boulders and kept climbing up the mountain. *v.* 争夺；抢夺 (to move to do, find or get something often before someone else does) More than three million fans are expected to scramble for tickets.
scrawl [skrɔːl]	*v.* 潦草地写 (to write something in a careless and untidy way) He scrawled a hasty note to his wife.

Ough系列

rough [rʌf]	*adj.* 粗糙的 (having a surface that is not even) We traveled over rough dirt roads. *adj.* 粗野的；粗鲁的 (not gentle or careful) They have complained of discrimination and occasional rough treatment.

tough [tʌf]	*adj.* 粗暴的；粗野的 (physically strong and likely to be violent) He's been hanging around with a bunch of tough guys. *adj.* 坚强的 (physically or emotionally strong enough to put up with hardship) He built up a reputation as a tough businessman.
cough [kɒf]	*v.* 咳嗽 (to force air through your throat with a short, loud noise often because you are sick) She was coughing and sneezing all day.

Nish系列

varnish ['vɑːnɪʃ]	*n.* 清漆 (a liquid that is spread on a surface and that dries to form a hard, shiny coating) Give the cardboard two or three coats of varnish to harden it. *v.* 给……涂上清漆 (to put varnish on the surface of something) The floors have been varnished.
tarnish ['tɑːnɪʃ]	*v.* 使失去光泽 (to become or cause metal to become dull and not shiny) Wear cotton gloves when cleaning silver, because the acid in your skin can tarnish the metal. *v.* 玷污；破坏 (to damage or ruin the good quality of something, such as a person's reputation) The scandal tarnished his reputation.
burnish ['bɜːnɪʃ]	*v.* 擦亮金属等 (to make something, such as metal or leather, smooth and shiny by rubbing it) We burnished the floor of the ballroom to a soft luster.
garnish ['gɑːnɪʃ]	*v.* (用菜) 为 (食物) 加装饰；加饰菜于 (to put something on food as a decoration) Chocolate curls garnished the cake.

Audi系列

audience ['ɔːdɪəns]	*n.* 观众 (the people who watch, read or listen to something) The concert attracted a large audience.

Unit 27

audible [ˈɔːdəbl]	*adj.* 听得见的 (loud enough to be heard) She'd lowered her voice until it was barely audible.
audio [ˈɔːdiəʊ]	*adj.* 音频的 (connected with sound that is recorded) ① They listened to an audio recording of the speech. ② The picture was clear but the audio was very poor.
inaudible [ɪnˈɔːdəbl]	*adj.* 听不见的 (impossible to hear) The sound is inaudible to humans but can be heard by dogs.
auditorium [ˌɔːdɪˈtɔːriəm]	*n.* 礼堂；会堂 (a hall where people gather as an audience) The town meeting will be held in the high school auditorium.

追根溯源

　　从医学观点来看，"心"的功能主要是输送血液，而血液也是人体中必不可少的部分，词根称之为"sangui"。中古和文艺复兴时代的人，相信人体是由四种液体组成，包括血液、黏液、黄胆汁和黑胆汁。我们的脾性便是由这四种体液消长的多寡来决定。当人体中血液占优势时，人会变得开朗，充满愉快的感觉（sanguine）。如果黏液（phlegm）过重的话，一个人便会冷漠，沉着（phlegmatic）。当一个人的黄胆汁（choler）过重时，表示一个人容易愤怒，暴躁（choleric）。黑胆汁（melan）是忧郁的象征，当一个人的黑胆汁过重时，会变得抑郁不快（melancholy）。

sanguine [ˈsæŋgwɪn]	*adj.* 充满自信的；乐观的 (confident and hopeful) He is sanguine about the company's future.
phlegmatic [flegˈmætɪk]	*adj.* 冷漠的；镇定的 (not easily upset, excited or angered) A phlegmatic man is unmoved by tears.
choleric [ˈkɒlərɪk]	*adj.* 易怒的；性情暴躁的 (easily made angry) He was affable at one moment, choleric the next.
melancholy [ˈmelənkəli]	*adj.* 忧郁的；悲伤的 (feeling or showing sadness) He became quiet and melancholy as the hours slowly passed. *n.* 忧郁 (a sad mood or feeling) The bleakness of winter sometimes gives me cause for melancholy.

morose [məˈrəʊs]	*adj.* 闷闷不乐的；阴郁的 (very sad or unhappy; gloomy) He became morose and withdrawn and would not talk to anyone. **拆分法** mo-没，rose-玫瑰，过情人节没有玫瑰，当然是闷闷不乐的 (morose)。
intuition [ˌɪntjuˈɪʃn]	*n.* 直觉 (the ability to know something without having proof) Intuition was telling her that something was very wrong. **拆分法** in-内心，tui-推理，内心推理靠直觉 (intuition)。
split [splɪt]	*v.* 分裂；分开 (to break apart or into pieces especially along a straight line) ① The river splits the town in two. ② Two of the band members split off to form their own band. **谐音法** plit-劈了它，当然是分裂，分开 (split)。
distasteful [dɪsˈteɪstfl]	*adj.* 讨厌的 (not pleasant or enjoyable) The work was distasteful, but it was the best I could find at the time. **拆分法** dis-no，taste-品味，没有品味，品味太差，是令人讨厌的 (distasteful)。
familiar [fəˈmɪliə(r)]	*adj.* 熟悉的；通晓的 (frequently seen, heard, or experienced) Parents should be familiar with their children's schools. **联想法** family-家庭，跟家人当然是熟悉的(familiar)。

Unit 28

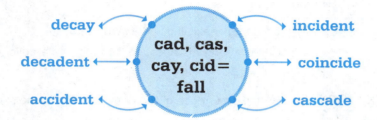

decay — decadent — accident — **cad, cas, cay, cid= fall** — incident — coincide — cascade

decay [dɪˈkeɪ]	*v.* 腐烂；腐朽 (to break down or cause to break down slowly by natural processes) Dead plants and leaves decayed by bacteria. *n.* (社会、机构，制度等的) 衰败 (the gradual destruction of a society, an institution, a system, etc.) She writes about the moral decay of our society.
decadence [ˈdekədəns]	*n.* 衰落；堕落 (behavior, attitudes, etc. which show low morals and a great love of pleasure, money, fame) The book condemns the decadence of modern society.
decadent [ˈdekədənt]	*adj.* 堕落的；颓废的 (having or showing low morals and a great love of pleasure, money or fame) The book condemns some of society's wealthiest members as decadent fools.
accident [ˈæksɪdənt]	*n.* 意外事件；事故 (an event that is not planned or intended) Investigators are still trying to determine the cause of the accident.
accidental [ˌæksɪˈdentl]	*adj.* 偶然的 (happening in a way that is not planned or intended) The timing of the announcement was purely accidental.
incident [ˈɪnsɪdənt]	*n.* 事件；事变 (an unexpected and usually unpleasant thing that happens) 1 Two people were shot yesterday in two separate incidents. 2 The bombing caused an international incident.
incidental [ˌɪnsɪˈdentl]	*adj.* 附属的 (happening as a minor part or result of something else) The discovery was incidental to their main research.

coincide [ˌkəʊɪnˈsaɪd]	*v.* 与……一致 (to happen at the same time as something else) The band's performance is scheduled to coincide with the fireworks. *v.* 同意 (to agree with something exactly) The kids' views on life don't always coincide, but they're not afraid of voicing their opinions.
coincidental [kəʊˌɪnsɪˈdentl]	*adj.* 巧合的 (occurring or existing at the same time) The fact that he and his boss went to the same college was purely coincidental.
coincidence [kəʊˈɪnsɪdəns]	*n.* 巧合；一致 (the occurrence of two or more things at the same time) Scientists have no explanation for the coincidence of these phenomenon.
casual [ˈkæʒuəl]	*adj.* 不经意的；漫不经心的；不在乎的 (done without much thought, effort or concern) ① The atmosphere at the meeting was quite casual. ② He made a casual remark about her shoes.
casualty [ˈkæʒuəlti]	*n.* 伤员；遇难者 (a person who is hurt or killed during an accident or a war) Troops fired on the demonstrators, causing many casualties.
occasion [əˈkeɪʒn]	*n.* 场合 (a particular time when something happens) Roses are the perfect flower for any occasion. *n.* 时机 (a situation that allows something to happen) We had occasion to watch her perform last summer.
occasional [əˈkeɪʒənl]	*adj.* 偶尔的；不经常的 (happening or done sometimes but not often) ① She receives occasional phone calls from her mother. ② He tells an occasional joke to keep his students interested.
cascade [kæˈskeɪd]	*v.* 倾泻；流注 (to flow or hang down in large amounts) ① Tears cascaded from the baby's eyes. ② The water cascades over the rocks.

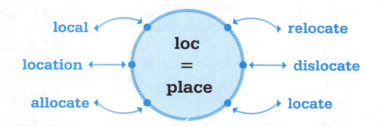

local ['ləʊkl]	*adj.* 地方的；当地的 (occurring in a particular area, city or town) 　　The police have arrested a local man for the crime.
location [ləʊ'keɪʃn]	*n.* 位置；场所 (a place or position) 　　Radar established the precise location of the aircraft.
locate [ləʊ'keɪt]	*v.* 确定……的位置 (to find the place or position of something or someone) 　　The missing boy was located by police in the woods. *v.* 放置；设立 (to put something in a particular place) 　　The company chose to locate its factory near the airport.
allocate ['æləkeɪt]	*v.* 分配；分派 (to set apart for a specific purpose or to particular persons or things) 　　Local authorities have to learn to allocate resources efficiently.
allocation [ˌælə'keɪʃn]	*n.* 配给；分配 (the act of giving something to somebody for a particular purpose) 　　His sons quarrelled bitterly over the allocation of family resources.
dislocate ['dɪsləkeɪt]	*v.* 使脱离位置 (to force someone or something to move from a place or position) 　　Thousands of workers have been dislocated by the latest economic crisis. *v.* 使混乱 (to stop a system, plan, etc. from working or continuing in the normal way) 　　It would help to end illiteracy and disease, but it would also dislocate a traditional way of life.
relocate [ˌriːləʊ'keɪt]	*v.* 使迁移 (to move to a new place) 　　The company decided to relocate its headquarters.

Unit 28

Sage系列

sage [seɪdʒ]	*n.* 圣人；智者 (a very wise person) The sage is the instructor of a hundred ages. *adj.* 明智的 (very wise) He was famous for his sage advice to younger painters.
sagacious [sə'geɪʃəs]	*adj.* 精明的 (quick and wise in understanding and judging something) He is a sagacious businessman.
presage ['presɪdʒ]	*v.* 预示；预兆 (to give or be a sign of something that will happen or develop in the future) Those black clouds presage a storm.

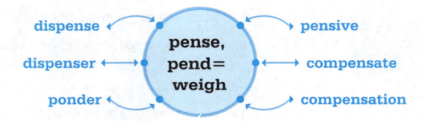

dispense → ← pense, pend = weigh → pensive

dispenser ← → compensate

ponder ← → compensation

dispense [dɪ'spens]	*v.* 分配；分给 (to give out something in portions or shares) The machine dispenses candy. *v.* 配 (药)；发 (药) (to prepare medicine and give it to people, as a job) Pharmacists are certified to dispense medication.
dispenser [dɪ'spensə]	*n.* 配药师 (a person who gives or provides medition to people) The dispenser quickly filled the prescription for me. *n.* 自动售卖机 (a machine or container that lets you take small amounts of something) I bought a cup of coffee from the dispenser.
dispensable [dɪ'spensəbl]	*adj.* 非必需的；可省去的 (not necessary or required) Computers have made typewriters dispensable.
indispensable [ˌɪndɪ'spensəbl]	*adj.* 不可缺少的；绝对必要的 (extremely important or necessary) An intelligent computer will be an indispensable diagnostic tool for doctors.

ponder ['pɒndə(r)]	*v.* 思索；衡量 (to weigh something carefully in the mind; to consider something thoughtfully) He didn't waste time pondering the questions.
pensive ['pensɪv]	*adj.* 沉思的；深思的 (lost in serious or sad thought) The child sat by himself, looking pensive.
compensate ['kɒmpenseɪt]	*v.* 补偿；赔偿 (to make up for some defect or weakness) To ease financial difficulties, farmers could be compensated for their loss of subsidies.
compensation [ˌkɒmpen'seɪʃn]	*n.* 补偿；赔偿 (something good that acts as a balance against something bad or undesirable) He received a large sum of money as compensation when he was injured at work.

Temperature系列

temperature ['temprətʃə(r)]	*n.* 温度；体温 (degree of hotness or coldness as measured on a scale) ① His temperature continued to rise alarmingly. ② The weatherman predicted unusually low temperatures for the area.
temper ['tempə(r)]	*n.* 性情；脾气 (characteristic state of feeling) It's often difficult for parents not to lose their tempers.
temperament ['temprəmənt]	*n.* 性格；性情 (the usual attitude, mood, or behavior of a person or animal) The two women were opposite in temperament.
tepid ['tepɪd]	*adj.* 微温的 (not hot and not cold) Your child's temperature rises, sponge her down gently with tepid water. *adj.* 冷淡的 (not energetic or excited) My suggestion was given a tepid response.
temperate ['tempərət]	*adj.* 温和的；温带的 (having temperatures that are not too hot or too cold) The Nile Valley keeps a temperate climate throughout the year. *adj.* 节制的 (emotionally calm and controlled) Though angry, he used temperate language.

tempest ['tempɪst]	*n.* 暴风雨 (a violent storm) The sudden summertime tempest drove us off the golf course and into the clubhouse.
tempestuous [tem'pestʃuəs]	*adj.* 激烈的；狂暴的；骚动的 (very strong and intense emotions, especially anger, are involved) In terms of social change, the 1960s are generally considered the most tempestuous decade in recent American history.

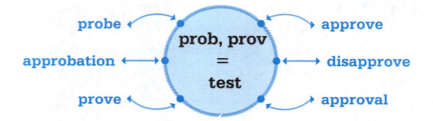

prove [pruːv]	*v.* 证明；证实 (to test by experiment or by a standard) ① Tests proved that the vaccine is effective. ② The climb proved more difficult than they had expected.
disprove [ˌdɪs'pruːv]	*v.* 反驳 (to show that something is false or wrong) The statistics to prove or disprove his hypothesis will take years to collect.
proof [pruːf]	*n.* 证据；证物 (something which shows that something else is true or correct; evidence) ① The document was proof that her story was true. ② He claims that he was home when the murder was committed, but he has no proof.
approve [ə'pruːv]	*v.* 批准；通过 (计划、要求等) (to officially agree to a plan, request, etc.) The state has approved the building plans, so work on the new school can begin immediately.
approval [ə'pruːvl]	*n.* 同意；批准 (permission to do something) ① The chairman has also given his approval for an investigation into the case. ② The testing and approval of new drugs will be speeded up.

disapprove [ˌdɪsəˈpruːv]	_v._	反对；否决 (to believe that someone or something is bad or wrong)
	①	She married him even though her parents disapproved.
	②	The treaty was disapproved by the congress.
improve [ɪmˈpruːv]	_v._	改进；改善 (to make something/somebody better than before)
	①	This operation will greatly improve her chances of survival.
	②	The company has been steadily improving sales.
improvement [ɪmˈpruːvmənt]	_n._	改进；改善 (the act or process of making something better)
		Doctors were amazed by the sudden improvement in her medical condition.
probe [prəʊb]	_v._	调查；探究 (to search into and explore very thoroughly)
		She probed the files for evidence that would help the investigation.
approbation [ˌæprəˈbeɪʃn]	_n._	认可；许可 (praise or approval)
		That plan has the approbation of the school board.
reprove [rɪˈpruːv]	_v._	责骂；指摘 (to criticize or correct someone usually in a gentle way)
		The teacher reproved the student for being late.

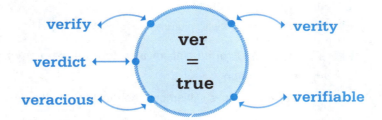

verify [ˈverɪfaɪ]	_v._	核实；证明 (to prove, show, find out, or state that something is true or correct)
		The government has not verified any of those reports.
verifiable [ˈverɪfaɪəbl]	_adj._	能证实的 (be proved to be true or genuine)
		We're not sure whether that's a verifiable hypothesis.
verdict [ˈvɜːdɪkt]	_n._	裁决；裁定 (the decision made by a jury in a trial)
		The jury reached a guilty verdict.
veracious [vəˈreɪʃəs]	_adj._	(指人) 诚实的 (marked by truth)
		She has a reputation for being veracious, so people generally take his word for things.

verity	*n.* 真实；事实 (something that is regarded as true)
['verəti]	The local tourist bureau is less concerned with the verity of the legend than the fact that it attracts visitors to the area.

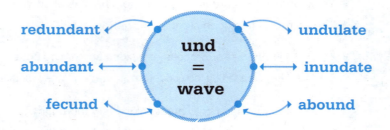

abundant	*adj.* 大量的；充足的 (more than enough)
[ə'bʌndənt]	① Rainfall is more abundant in summer.
	② Mosquitoes are extremely abundant in this dark wet place.
abundance	*n.* 丰富；充裕 (a large quantity)
[ə'bʌndəns]	The area has an abundance of wildlife.
abound	*v.* 丰富；盛产 (to be present in large numbers or in great quantity)
[ə'baʊnd]	① Salmon abound in the river.
	② The book abounds with pictures.
fecund	*adj.* 多产的；富饶的 (producing or able to produce many babies, young animals, or plants)
['fi:kənd]	The Amazon basin is still among the most fecund lands in the world.
redundant	*adj.* 多余的；累赘的 (repeating something else and therefore unnecessary)
[rɪ'dʌndənt]	He edited the paper and removed any redundant information or statements.
inundate	*v.* 淹没；泛滥 (to cover something with a flood of water)
['ɪnʌndeɪt]	Rising rivers could inundate low-lying areas.
	v. 使应接不暇 (to take in a large amount of things at the same time)
	Her office was inundated with requests for tickets.
undulate	*v.* 起伏；波动 (to form or move in waves)
['ʌndjuleɪt]	① Gleaming seaweed curls and undulates with the tide.
	② His body slowly undulated in time to the music.

Number系列

enumerate [ɪˈnjuːməreɪt]	*v.* 列举；枚举 (to name things one after another in a list) Let me enumerate my reasons for doing this.
numerous [ˈnjuːmərəs]	*adj.* 很多的；许多的 (existing in large numbers) The birds are becoming more numerous in this area.

Mun系列

communal [kəˈmjuːnl]	*adj.* 共享的；共有的；共用的 (shared or used by members of a group or community) The toilets and other communal facilities were in a shocking state.
community [kəˈmjuːnəti]	*n.* 社区；共同团体 (a group of people who live in the same area such as a city, town or neighborhood) The festival was a great way for the local community to get together.
communicate [kəˈmjuːnɪkeɪt]	*v.* 沟通；交流 (to exchange information, news ideas, etc. with somebody) We communicate a lot of information through body language. *v.* 传达；传递 (to get someone to understand your thoughts or feelings) He was asked to communicate the news to the rest of the people.
communication [kə,mjuːnɪˈkeɪʃn]	*n.* 交流；传播 (exchange of information between individuals through a common system of signs symbols or behavior) Honeybees use one of the most sophisticated communication systems of any insect.
immune [ɪˈmjuːn]	*adj.* 有免疫力的 (not capable of being affected by a disease) This blood test will show whether or not you're immune to the disease. *adj.* 不受影响的 (not influenced or affected by something) ① Football is not immune to economic recession. ② She is immune to criticism.
immunize [ˈɪmjunaɪz]	*v.* 使免疫 (to give someone a vaccine to prevent infection by a disease) Many people had to be immunized after being exposed to the disease.

Unit 28

immunity [ɪ'mjuːnəti]	*n.* 免疫力 (the power to keep yourself from being affected by a disease) They have developed immunity to the virus. *n.* 豁免 (special protection from what is required for most people by law) The embassy official claimed diplomatic immunity and was later released.
municipal [mjuː'nɪsɪpl]	*adj.* 市的；市政的 (relating to the government of a town or city) The city is planning to build a municipal library.
communism ['kɒmjunɪzəm]	*n.* 共产主义 (a social system or theory in which property and goods are held in common) Our ultimate aim is to realize communism.
communist ['kɒmjənɪst]	*n.* 共产主义者 (a person who supports communism) He was a convinced communist.

追根溯源

　　古罗马时期，国家的司法权力掌握在"裁判官"手中。这个职位最早设立于公元前376年，是从执政官的职权中分离出来的，地位仅次于执政官，享有在其职责范围内的法律方面的最高权威。但裁判官并不参与具体案件的审判，而是交给审判员去审理。审判员不是国家官吏，他是由裁判官从预定名单中选定并授权处理特定案件的公断人。因此在拉丁语中这个职位担任者被称为"arbiter"，由ad（to）和baetere（来、去）构成，字面意思就是"去某地（审案）的人"。arbiter和arbitrator同源，都能表示"仲裁人"，区别在于：arbiter一词更为古老，是书面用语，通常应用于文学领域，"审判"的意味胜过"仲裁"；而arbitrator比较通俗，通常表示受争议双方所托，居中仲裁，拥有较大的自由裁量权，甚至可以是arbitrary（独断的）。

arbitrate ['ɑːbɪtreɪt]	*v.* 仲裁；公断 (to settle a disagreement after hearing the arguments of both sides) She agreed to arbitrate their dispute.
arbitrator ['ɑːbɪtreɪtə(r)]	*n.* 仲裁人；公断人 (a person chosen to settle differences in a disagreement) Both sides agreed to accept a decision by an impartial arbitrator.
arbitrary ['ɑːbɪtrəri]	*adj.* 随意的；任性的 (done without concern for what is fair or right) Although arbitrary arrests are illegal, they continue to occur in many parts of the country.

Unit 28

jubilee原指犹太教每50周年，即每7年为一周期，7个周期之后的大周期之年，在这一年里人们会吹起羊角，奴隶被释放，土地得到休耕或进行重新分配，以表达与上帝的和好的诚意。

jubilee ['dʒu:bɪli:]	*n.* 周年纪念 (a special anniversary) The town is planning a year-long jubilee in celebration of its founding 200 years ago.
jubilant ['dʒu:bɪlənt]	*adj.* 喜气洋洋的 (feeling or expressing great joy) The hero was greeted by a jubilant crowd.

锦囊妙记

derive [dɪ'raɪv]	*v.* 起源于 (to come from a certain source) Some modern holidays derive from ancient traditions. 联想法 rive-river（河流），世界上的很多文明都是起源于(derive)河流.
thrive [θraɪv]	*v.* 兴盛；兴隆 (to grow or develop successfully) These plants thrive with relatively little sunlight. 联想法 rive-river，世界上的很多文明都在河流旁发展兴盛 (thrive)。
scream [skri:m]	*v.* 尖叫 (to make a very loud, high sound) The crowd screamed with excitement. 联想法 ice cream（冰淇淋），孩子们见到好吃的冰淇淋(ice cream)会尖叫(scream)。
coerce [kəʊ'ɜːs]	*v.* 强迫；强制 (to make someone do something by using force or threats) Confession was coerced from the suspect by police. 谐音法 coerce-渴饿死，一个人受到了强迫 (coerce)，如果不服从就会被渴死、饿死。
dilapidated [dɪ'læpɪdeɪtɪd]	*adj.* 残破的；失修的 (in very bad condition because of age or lack of care) The house is very dilapidated but it has value. 谐音法 di-地，lapi-烂破，地又烂又破，当然是残败的，失修的 (dilapidated)。

Unit 28

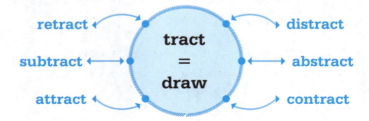

retract ← → tract = draw → distract

subtract ← → abstract

attract ← → contract

tractor ['træktə(r)]	*n.* 拖拉机 (a short, heavy truck that is designed to pull a large farm equipment) Paul hooked his tractor to the car and pulled it to safety.
attract [ə'trækt]	*v.* 吸引；诱惑 (to cause someone to like or be interested in something) ❶ The museum attracts visitors from all over the world. ❷ The bird's colorful feathers are used to attract a mate.
attractive [ə'træktɪv]	*adj.* 迷人的；有魅力的；英俊的 (pleasant to look at) I thought he was very attractive and obviously very intelligent. *adj.* 吸引人的 (having the power or quality of drawing interest) Smoking is still attractive to many young people who see it as glamorous.
attraction [ə'trækʃn]	*n.* 吸引力；诱惑力 (something interesting or enjoyable that people want to visit, see or do) ❶ The town's big attraction for movie lovers is the annual film festival. ❷ The waterfall continues to be the main attraction at the park.
retract [rɪ'trækt]	*v.* 收回；撤回 (to say that something you have said earlier is not true or correct or that you did not mean it) He hurriedly sought to retract the statement. *v.* 缩回；拉回 (to move back into the main part of something; to pull something back into the main part of something) A cat can retract its claws, but a dog can't.
retreat [rɪ'triːt]	*v.* 撤退；后退 (to move back to get away from danger or attack) When the enemy attacked, our troops were forced to retreat.

n. 撤退；隐退 (an act of going back or away especially from something dangerous, difficult, or disagreeable)

Some of her friends were surprised by her retreat from public life following her defeat in the election.

distract
[dɪ'strækt]

v. 使分心；使混乱 (to draw a person's thoughts or attention to something else)

1 The video games distract me when I'm studying.

2 The local story distracted attention from news of the war overseas.

distraction
[dɪ'strækʃn]

n. 分散注意力的事 (something that makes it difficult to think or pay attention)

It was hard to work with so many distractions.

n. 娱乐；消遣 (something that amuses or entertains you)

A weekend at the beach was a good distraction from her troubles.

distraught
[dɪ'strɔːt]

adj. 心神错乱的 (so upset that you are not able to think clearly or behave normally)

She was distraught over the death of her partner.

extract
['ekstrækt]

v. 提取 (to remove something by pulling it out or cutting it out)

Citric acid can be extracted from the juice of oranges.

v. 索取；设法得到（对方不愿提供的信息、钱财等）(to obtain information, money, etc., often by taking it from somebody who is unwilling to give it)

He tried to extract further information from the witness.

protract
[prə'trækt]

v. 延长；拖延 (to make something last longer)

1 Disagreements protracted the negotiation.

2 The highway project was protracted by years of litigation.

abstract
['æbstrækt]

adj.&n.

[æb'strækt] *vt.*

adj. 抽象的 (involving general ideas or qualities rather than specific people, objects or actions)

Truth, poverty and bravery are abstract nouns.

n. 摘要 (a brief written statement of the main points or facts in a longer report or speech)

If you want to submit a paper, you must supply an abstract.

v. 提取；摘取 (to obtain or remove something from a source)

Data for the study was abstracted from hospital records.

contract

['kɒntrækt] *n.*

[kən'trækt] *v.*

n. 合同；契约 (a legal agreement between people or companies)

The contract requires him to finish work by the end of the year.

v. 签订合同 (to make a contract)

You can contract with us to deliver your cargo.

v. 使收缩；缩小 (to become less or smaller; to make something become less or smaller)

The muscle expands and then contracts.

---

contraction

[kən'trækʃn]

n. 收缩；缩减 (process of making something smaller or of becoming smaller)

① The contraction of muscles uses energy and releases heat.

② The hot metal undergoes contraction as it cools.

---

subtract

[səb'trækt]

v. 减去；扣除 (to take a number or amount from another number or amount)

① If you subtract 10 from 23, you get 13.

② You can subtract the time you spent daydreaming from your total homework time.

---

tractable

['træktəbl]

adj. 易处理的；驯服的 (easily managed or controlled)

① This new approach should make the problem more tractable.

② Children are no longer as tractable as they used to be.

---

trace

[treɪs]

n. 痕迹；踪迹 (a mark or line left by something that has passed)

① Wash them in cold water to remove all traces of sand.

② He disappeared mysteriously without a trace.

v. 跟踪；追溯 (to follow the path or line of something)

This book traces the history of art through the ages.

---

traceable

['treɪsəbl]

adj. 可归因于……的 (be attributed to something specified)

The probable cause of his death is traceable to an incident in 1724.

---

retrace

[rɪ'treɪs]

v. 沿原路返回 (to go back along exactly the same path or route that you have come along)

She lost her keys somewhere on the way to the station, and had to retrace her steps until she found them.

---

track

[træk]

n. 赛道；轨道 (a line or route along which something travels or moves)

The two men turned to watch the horses going round the track.

Unit 29

v. 跟踪；追踪 (to find somebody/something by following the marks, signs, information, etc. that they have left behind them)

①The ship can track incoming missiles with radar.

②The study tracked the patients over the course of five years.

trail
[treɪl]

n. 林间小道 (a path through a forest, field, etc.)

He was following a broad trail through the trees.

n. (一串) 痕迹，足迹 (a trace or mark left by something that has passed or been drawn along)

The car left a trail of smoke as it sped off.

v. 跟踪；追踪 (to follow somebody/something by looking for signs that show you where they have been)

Police trailed the robbers.

trek
[trek]

v. 长途跋涉 (to make a long and difficult journey, especially by walking)

①On their vacation last year they went trekking in the Himalayas.

②We trekked across the country in her old car.

n. 艰难旅程 (a slow or difficult journey)

Our car broke down and we had a long trek back to town.

trudge
[trʌdʒ]

v. 跋涉；吃力地走 (to walk slowly and heavily because you are tired or working very hard)

I was trudging through the snow.

Snake系列

snake
[sneɪk]

n. 奸险的人 (a person who pretends to be your friend but who cannot be trusted)

I thought she was my friend, but she turned out to be a snake in the grass.

snap
[snæp]

v. 咬 (to try to bite somebody/something)

The dogs snarled and snapped at our heels.

v. 突然折断 (to break something suddenly with a sharp noise; to be broken in this way)

The branch snapped and fell to the ground.

sneak
[sniːk]

v. 潜行；偷偷溜走 (to go somewhere secretly, trying to avoid being seen)

They tried to sneak into the movie without paying.

sneaky ['sniːki]	*adj.* 鬼鬼祟祟的 (behaving in a secret and usually dishonest manner) It is a sneaky and underhand way of doing business.
sneaker ['sniːkə(r)]	*n.* 运动鞋 (a sports shoe with a rubber sole) The motto is written on their sneakers.

Dense系列

dense [dens]	*adj.* 密集的；稠密的 (having its parts crowded together) ① They cut a path through the dense jungle. ② That part of the city has a dense population of immigrants.
density ['densəti]	*n.* 密度；稠密 (the condition of having parts that are close together) These instruments are used for measuring the density of the atmosphere.
condense [kən'dens]	*v.* 压缩；精简 (to make something shorter or smaller by removing parts that are less important) The information is collected and then passed on to the CEO in condensed form. *v.* (使) 冷凝 (to change from a gas into a liquid) The cooler temperatures cause the gas to condense into a liquid.

Dole系列

doleful ['dəʊlfl]	*adj.* (表情、声音等) 悲伤的，忧郁的 (very sad) ① The girl had a doleful look on her face. ② You sounded so doleful about your future that night.
condole [kən'dəʊl]	*v.* 表示同情 (to express sympathetic sorrow) We condole with him on his father's death.
condolence [kən'dəʊləns]	*n.* 同情；吊唁 (a feeling or expression of sympathy and sadness especially when someone is suffering) ① The governor issued a statement of condolence to the victims' families. ② We wish to express our sincere condolences to your family.

Unit 29

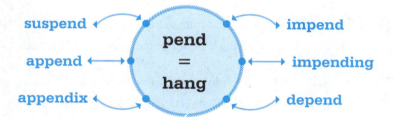

depend [dɪˈpend]	*v.* 依靠；依赖 (to rely for support) ① Children depend on their parents. ② I know I can always depend on you for help when I really need it. *v.* 取决于 (to be determined by or based on a person, action or condition) He either resigned or was sacked, depending on who you talk to.
dependent [dɪˈpendənt]	*adj.* 依靠的；依赖的 (decided or controlled by something else) ① The local economy is overwhelmingly dependent on oil and gas extraction. ② Our plans are dependent on the weather.
interdependent [ˌɪntədɪˈpendənt]	*adj.* 互相依赖的 (depending on one another) We live in an increasingly interdependent world.
suspend [səˈspend]	*v.* 暂停；延缓 (to stop something for a usually short period of time) The company was forced to suspend operations.
suspension [səˈspenʃn]	*n.* 暂停；延缓；停职 (the act of stopping, removing, or making someone or something ineffective for a time) ① He's under suspension for breaking the rules. ② She was punished by suspension of her driver's license.
impend [ɪmˈpend]	*v.* 即将发生 (to be about to occur) ① Crucial events impend in Europe. ② He felt that danger impended.
impending [ɪmˈpendɪŋ]	*adj.* 即将发生的；迫在眉睫的 (about to occur at any moment) On the morning of the expedition I awoke with a feeling of impending disaster.
append [əˈpend]	*v.* 附加；添加 (to add as something extra) It was a relief that his real name hadn't been appended to the manuscript.

Unit 29

appendix [ə'pendɪks]	*n.* 附录 (extra information that is placed after the end of the main text) Details of the investigation are set out in the appendix.
pendant ['pendənt]	*n.* 垂饰；坠儿 (an ornament on a chain that you wear round your neck) The pendant was hanging by a thin gold chain.

Pair系列

parallel ['pærəlel]	*adj.* 平行的 (extending in the same direction) Parallel lines will never meet no matter how far extended. *v.* 与……平行 (to place so as to be parallel in direction with something) Rising prices parallel increasing fuel costs.
unparalleled [ʌn'pærəleld]	*adj.* 绝无仅有的 (better or greater than anyone or anything else) The new telescope offers an unparalleled opportunity to conduct research.
parasite ['pærəsaɪt]	*n.* 寄生物；寄生虫 (an animal or plant that lives in or on another animal or plant and gets food or protection from it) Many diseases are caused by parasites. *n.* 不劳而获者 (a person who lives at the expense of another) The lazy man was a parasite on his family.
disparage [dɪ'spærɪdʒ]	*v.* 轻视；贬低 (to describe someone or something as unimportant, weak or bad) Voters don't like political advertisements in which opponents disparage one another.
compare [kəm'peə(r)]	*v.* 比较；对比 (to examine people or things to see how they are similar and how they are different) ❶ She compared the activity of ants to the behavior of humans. ❷ We compared the two products for quality and cost.
comparable ['kɒmpərəbl]	*adj.* 可比较的；相当的 (being similar or about the same) In other comparable countries real wages increased much more rapidly.
incomparable [ɪn'kɒmprəbl]	*adj.* 无双的；无敌的 (better than any other) ❶ The quality of their products is incomparable. ❷ The views from the house are incomparable.

comparison [kəm'pærɪsn]	*n.* 比较；对照 (the act of looking at things to see how they are similar or different) I don't think comparisons of her situation and mine are appropriate.
separate ['seprət]	*v.* 分开；分离 (to move apart; to make people or things move apart) Oil and water separate when combined together. *adj.* 单独的；分开的 (not joined, connected, or combined; different) ① They walked together to the corner, but then they separated and went their separate ways. ② There are separate restrooms for men and women.
disparate ['dɪspərət]	*adj.* 完全不同的 (different from each other) ① Scientists are trying to pull together disparate ideas. ② The nine republics are immensely disparate in size, culture and wealth.

Aware系列

aware [ə'weə(r)]	*adj.* 知道的；明白的 (knowing that something, such as a situation, condition, or problem, exists) ① They are well aware of the dangers. ② Smokers are well aware of the dangers to their own health.
unaware [ˌʌnə'weə(r)]	*adj.* 不知道的；未察觉到的 (not having knowledge about something) She was unaware of the change in travel plans.
wary ['weəri]	*adj.* 谨慎的；警惕的 (very cautious) ① People did not teach their children to be wary of strangers. ② Investors are increasingly wary about putting money into stocks.

Point系列

appoint [ə'pɔɪnt]	*v.* 任命；指定 (to give someone a position or duty) ① The school board appointed three new teachers. ② After his parents died, the boy's uncle was appointed as his guardian.

appointment
[əˈpɔɪntmənt]

n. 任命；职务 (a job or duty that is given to a person)
The court ordered the appointment of an attorney to represent the child.

n. 约会 (an agreement to meet with someone at a particular time)
I have a doctor's appointment tomorrow morning at nine o'clock.

disappoint
[ˌdɪsəˈpɔɪnt]

v. 使失望；使破灭 (to fail to satisfy the hope or expectation of somebody)
❶ Her decision to cancel the concert is bound to disappoint her fans.
❷ I was disappointed to see that my suggestions had been ignored.

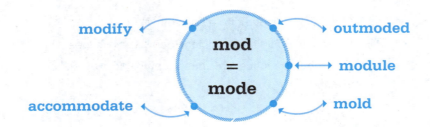

outmoded
[ˌaʊtˈməʊdɪd]

adj. 过时的；不流行的 (no longer in style or in use)
❶ People in positions of power continue to promote outmoded ideas.
❷ The political system has become thoroughly outmoded.

mold
[məʊld]

n. 模子；铸模 (a hollow form in which something is shaped)
Make a candle by pouring wax in a mold.

v. 塑造 (to influence or affect the character of somebody)
Parents try to mold their children into responsible adults.

module
[ˈmɒdjuːl]

n. 模块；组件 (one of a set of parts that can be connected or combined to build or complete something)
The factories build engines, transmissions, brakes, and other modules for cars.

modify
[ˈmɒdɪfaɪ]

v. 修改；改进 (to change something slightly, especially in order to make it more suitable for a particular purpose)
❶ He modified the recipe by using oil instead of butter.
❷ We can help you modify an existing home or build a new one.

accommodate
[əˈkɒmədeɪt]

v. (调整以) 适应 (to provide what is needed or wanted for someone or something)
❶ My teacher will change her schedule to accommodate her students.
❷ Smart investors quickly accommodated to the new market conditions.

accommodation [əˌkɒmə'deɪʃn]	*v.* 容纳；接纳 (to provide a place to stay and sleep for someone) The bus accommodates 40 people.
	n. 住处 (a place where travelers can sleep and find other services) They weren't sure if they could provide food and accommodations for the whole group.
	n. 和解；调和 (an agreement that allows people, groups, to work together) Negotiators were convinced that accommodation with the union was possible.

追根溯源

在希腊神话中，海吉亚（Hygieia）是医药神埃斯库拉庇乌斯的女儿，她掌管清洁卫生和健康，其形象通常是一个拿着碗喂蛇的少女。海吉亚的碗跟其父亲埃斯库拉庇乌斯的蛇杖一样，有一条蛇盘旋在上，两者同样具备医学、健康的象征意义，是现今世界常用的符号之一。单词hygiene（健康）便是来自海吉亚（Hygieia）的名字。

hygiene ['haɪdʒiːn]	*n.* 卫生(conditions or practices, as of cleanliness, conducive to health) Poor sanitation and hygiene caused many of the soldiers to get sick.
hygienic [haɪ'dʒiːnɪk]	*adj.* 卫生的；保健的 (conducive to health) For hygienic reasons, restaurants should wash silverware and drinking glasses more than once.

twi是"two"的意思，light指"光线"。黄昏时阴阳交替的时候，即白日光线与黑夜光线相互交替，所以twilight是指"黄昏"。

twilight ['twaɪlaɪt]	*n.* 黄昏；薄暮 (the light from the sky at the end of the day when night is just beginning) They returned at twilight and set off for the bar.
	n. 衰落时期 (the final stage of something when it becomes weaker or less important than it was) Now they are both in the twilight of their careers.

Unit 29

dismal
['dɪzməl]

adj. 忧郁的；令人沮丧的 (showing or causing unhappiness or sad feelings)

My prospects of returning to a suitable job are dismal.

拆分法 dis-no (没有)，mal-mall (购物中心)，对于爱购物的女人来说，没有购物中心可逛太令人沮丧了(dismal)！

boisterous
['bɔɪstərəs]

adj. 狂暴的；喧闹的 (very noisy and active in a lively way)

1 Most of the children were noisy and boisterous.

2 A large and boisterous crowd attended the concert.

联想法 boi-boil (沸腾)，ous-形容词后缀，像沸腾的 (boiling)水一样喧闹 (boisterous)。

spoil
[spɔɪl]

v. 宠坏 (to give someone, such as a child, everything that he or she wants)

Grandparents are often tempted to spoil their grandchildren whenever they come to visit.

v. 损坏；糟蹋 (to damage something badly)

Peaceful summer evenings can be spoilt by mosquitoes.

联想法 p-泡，oil-油，泡在油里宠爱，肯定要被宠坏 (spoil)。

irate
[aɪ'reɪt]

adj. 盛怒的 (very angry)

He was so irate he almost threw me out of the place.

联想法 i-我，rat-老鼠，我看到偷大米的老鼠，非常愤怒 (irate)，追着老鼠打。

shrewd
[ʃruːd]

adj. 精明的；敏锐的 (having or showing an ability to understand things and to make good judgments)

She's shrewd about her investments.

谐音法 音近"鼠"，老鼠是很精明敏锐的 (shrewd)。

Unit 29

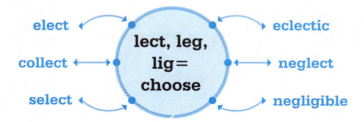

elect → ← lect, leg, lig= choose → eclectic
collect ↔ ← → neglect
select ← → negligible

elect [ɪ'lekt]	*v.* 选举；推选 (to choose somebody to do a particular job by voting for them)
	❶ He hopes to be elected to the committee.
	❷ The people of the Philippines have voted to elect a new president.
election [ɪ'lekʃn]	*n.* 选举；当选 (the act or process of choosing someone for a public office by voting)
	❶ The scandal may affect his chances for election.
	❷ During his election campaign he promised to put the economy back on its feet.
electorate [ɪ'lektərət]	*n.* 选民 (全体) (the body of persons entitled to vote in an election)
	The government largely misread the mood of the electorate.
collect [kə'lekt]	*v.* 收集 (to bring things together from different people or places)
	❶ We collected soil samples from several areas on the site.
	❷ She collected stories from all over the world.
recollect [ˌrekə'lekt]	*v.* 记起；想起 (to remember something, especially by making an effort to remember it)
	❶ I don't recollect telling him anything, but maybe I did.
	❷ She could no longer recollect the details of the letter.
recollection [ˌrekə'lekʃn]	*n.* 回忆；追忆 (the act or power of remembering something)
	His novel is largely based on his own recollections of his childhood in the inner city.
select [sɪ'lekt]	*v.* 选择；挑选 (to choose someone or something from a group)
	❶ We selected the ripest pears at the orchard.
	❷ You have been selected to represent us on the committee.

selective [sɪˈlektɪv]	*adj.* 精心选择的；严格筛选的 (careful to choose only the best people or things)
	① The club is selective in choosing members.
	② The college has a highly selective admissions process.
neglect [nɪˈɡlekt]	*v.* 疏忽；忽略 (to fail to take care of or to give attention to someone or something)
	① He'd given too much to his career, worked long hours, neglected his children.
	② They never neglect their duties.
neglectful [nɪˈɡlektfl]	*adj.* 疏忽的；不注意的 (not giving enough care or attention to someone or something)
	Children who are neglected tend to become neglectful parents.
negligible [ˈneɡlɪdʒəbl]	*adj* 可以忽略的；微不足道的 (very small or unimportant)
	① Crops received a negligible amount of rainfall.
	② A negligible amount of damage was done to the vehicle.
eclectic [ɪˈklektɪk]	*adj.* 兼收并蓄的 (composed of elements drawn from various sources)
	The museum's eclectic collection has everything from a giraffe skeleton to medieval musical instruments.
elegant [ˈelɪɡənt]	*adj.* 优美的；漂亮的 (showing good taste; graceful and attractive)
	Michelle Obama is the most elegant First Lady in the nation's history.
eligible [ˈelɪdʒəbl]	*adj.* 有资格的；符合条件的 (qualified to be chosen, to participate or to receive)
	① You could be eligible for a university scholarship.
	② Almost half the population are eligible to vote in today's election.
elite [eɪˈliːt]	*n.* 精锐；精英 (the most powerful, rich or talented people within a particular group, place or society)
	① The winners of this science award represent the elite of our high schools.
	② The country's elite owned or controlled most of the wealth.
legion [ˈliːdʒən]	*n.* 大批部队 (a large group of soldiers)
	The last of the Roman legions left Britain in AD 410.
	n. 众多；大量 (a very large number of people)
	His delightful sense of humour won him a legion of friends.

delegate

['delɪgət]

n. 代表 (a person who is chosen or elected to vote or act for others)

He's been chosen as a delegate to the convention.

v. 授权；委派 (to give control, responsibility, authority, etc. to someone)

1 A manager should delegate authority to the best employees.

2 The voters delegate power to their elected officials.

colleague

['kɒliːg]

n. 同事 (a person who works with you)

On her first day at work her colleagues went out of their way to make her feel welcome.

intellect

['ɪntəlekt]

n. 智力；理解力 (the ability to think in a logical way)

1 She is a woman of superior intellect.

2 We were required to read a book every week in order to develop our intellects.

intellectual

[ˌɪntə'lektʃuəl]

adj. 智力的；有才智的 (connected with or using a person's ability to think in a logical way and understand things)

As the daughter of college professors, she's used to being around intellectual people.

n. 知识分子 (a person who takes pleasure in serious study and thought)

She's a hard worker but she's no great intellectual.

intelligent

[ɪn'telɪdʒənt]

adj. 聪明的；理解力强的 (having or showing serious thought and good judgment)

1 He's a hard worker but he's not very intelligent.

2 An intelligent computer will be an indispensable diagnostic tool for doctors.

intelligence

[ɪn'telɪdʒəns]

n. 智力；智慧 (the ability to learn and understand)

1 She impressed us with her superior intelligence.

2 The test measures intelligence.

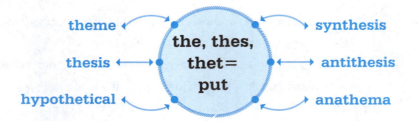

theme ← → the, thes, thet = put → synthesis

thesis ← → the, thes, thet = put ← → antithesis

hypothetical ← → the, thes, thet = put ← → anathema

theme [θiːm]	*n.* 主题 (a particular subject or issue that is discussed often or repeatedly) ① Adventures are popular themes in children's books. ② The quest for power is the underlying theme of the film.
thesis ['θiːsɪs]	*n.* 命题；论点 (a statement that a person wants to discuss or prove) The book's central thesis is that propaganda influences the masses in important ways.
hypothesis [haɪ'pɒθəsɪs]	*n.* 假设；假说 (an idea or theory that is not proven but that leads to further study or discussion) ① The results of the experiment did not support his hypothesis. ② Their hypothesis is that watching excessive amounts of television reduces a person's ability to concentrate.
hypothetical [ˌhaɪpə'θetɪkl]	*adj.* 假设的；假定的 (involving or based on a suggested idea or theory) ① We talked about what we would do in various hypothetical emergencies. ② She described a hypothetical case to clarify her point.
synthesis ['sɪnθəsɪs]	*n.* 综合；合成 (something that is made by combining different things, such as ideas or styles) ① His novels are a rich synthesis of Balkan history and mythology. ② This kind of lightening encourages vitamin D synthesis in the skin.
synthesize ['sɪnθəsaɪz]	*v.* 综合；人工合成 (to make something by combining different things) ① He synthesized old and new ideas to form his theory. ② A vitamin is a chemical compound that cannot be synthesized by the human body.
antithesis [æn'tɪθəsɪs]	*n.* 对立 (the state of two things that are directly opposite to each other) ① Hope is the antithesis of despair. ② There is an antithesis between the needs of the state and the needs of the people.

antithetical	*adj.* 正相反的；对立的 (directly opposite or opposed)
[ˌæntɪ'θetɪkl]	Spiritual concerns and ideals are antithetical to the materialism embraced by modern society.
anathema	*n.* 可憎的事物 (someone or something that is very strongly disliked)
[ə'næθəmə]	Violence was anathema to them.

Cast系列

cast	*v.* 投射 (to make light, a shadow, etc. appear in a particular place)
[kɑːst]	① The moon cast a bright light over the yard.
	② The tree cast a long shadow on the lawn.
	n. 全体演员 (the characters or the people acting in a play or story)
	The show is very amusing and the cast are very good.
broadcast	*v.* 广播；播出 (to send out signals, programs, etc. by radio or television)
['brɔːdkɑːst]	The concert will be broadcast live on television and radio.
	n. 广播节目；电视节目 (a radio or television program)
	In a broadcast on state radio the government also announced that it was willing to resume peace negotiations.
forecast	*v.* 预报；预测 (to predict often after thought and study of available evidence)
['fɔːkɑːst]	① They're forecasting rain for this weekend.
	② Experts forecast that the economy will slow in the coming months.
	n. 预报；预测 (a statement about what will happen in the future)
	He delivered his election forecast.

Police系列

policy	*n.* 政策；策略 (a plan of action adopted by an individual or social group)
['pɒləsi]	There were significant changes in Britain's policy on global warming.
politician	*n.* 政治家 (someone who is active in government usually as an elected official)
[ˌpɒlə'tɪʃn]	They have arrested a number of leading opposition politicians.

Unit 30

political [pəˈlɪtɪkl]	*adj.* 政治的 (relating to politics or government) **1** We need a political solution rather than a military solution. **2** All other political parties there have been completely banned.
metropolitan [ˌmetrəˈpɒlɪtən]	*adj.* 大都会的；大城市的 (relating to a large city and the surrounding cities and towns) This is one of the best seafood restaurants in metropolitan Los Angeles.
cosmopolitan [ˌkɒzməˈpɒlɪtən]	*adj.* 世界性的；国际化的 (containing people of different types or from different countries, and influenced by their culture) London has always been a cosmopolitan city.
monopoly [məˈnɒpəli]	*n.* 垄断；专卖 (complete control of the entire supply of goods or of a service in a certain area or market) **1** The government passed laws intended to break up monopolies. **2** In the past central government had a monopoly on television broadcasting.
monopolize [məˈnɒpəlaɪz]	*v.* 独占；垄断 (to get or have complete control over something) The company has monopolized the market for computer operating systems.

Sane系列

sanitation [ˌsænɪˈteɪʃn]	*n.* 公共卫生 (the state of being clean and conducive to health) Diseases can spread from poor sanitation.
sane [seɪn]	*adj.* 心智健全的；明智的 (having a healthy mind; able to think normally) No sane person could do something so horrible.
insane [ɪnˈseɪn]	*adj.* 疯狂的；精神病的 (not normal or healthy in mind) **1** Some people simply can't take it and they just go insane. **2** He had this insane idea that he could get rich by selling old computers.

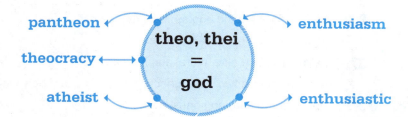

theo, thei = god

pantheon ← → enthusiasm
theocracy ← →
atheist ← → enthusiastic

pantheon ['pænθiən]	*n.* 万神庙 (a temple dedicated to all the gods) The emperor Marcus Agrippa had a pantheon built in Rome. *n.* 名流 (a group of people who are famous or important) He occupies a place in the pantheon of great American writers.
theocracy [θi'ɒkrəsi]	*n.* 神权政治 (a form of government in which a country is ruled by religious leaders) Humanistic artists opposed asceticism with humanism, opposed theocracy with human rights.
atheist ['eɪθiɪst]	*n.* 无神论者 (a person who believes that there is no god) Abolishing this to appease a few atheists hardly makes sense.
enthusiastic [ɪnˌθjuːziˈæstɪk]	*adj.* 热烈的；狂热的 (feeling or showing strong excitement about something) ① They were enthusiastic supporters of the president. ② She received an enthusiastic welcome.
enthusiasm [ɪnˈθjuːziæzəm]	*n.* 热情；热忱 (strong excitement about something) ① The party supported its candidate with enthusiasm. ② He seems to lack enthusiasm for the work he's doing.

Dign系列

dignity ['dɪgnəti]	*n.* 尊严；高尚 (the quality or state of being worthy of honor and respect) ① She showed dignity in defeat. ② Our country cherishes freedom and human dignity.
indignity [ɪn'dɪgnəti]	*n.* 侮辱；轻蔑 (an act that offends against a person's dignity or self-respect) ① He remembers all the indignities he had to suffer in the early years of his career. ② He suffered the indignity of being forced to leave the courtroom.

decent ['diːsnt]	*adj.* 合宜的；得体的 (good enough but not the best) I've got to get some decent clothes. *adj.* 正派的；正直的 (polite, moral and honest) The corruption allows the unscrupulous to grow rich while decent people labor to earn an honest wage.
indecent [ɪn'diːsnt]	*adj.* 粗鄙的；下流的 (using language that offends people) She accused him of making indecent suggestions.
disdain [dɪs'deɪn]	*n.* 轻视；鄙视 (a feeling of dislike for someone or something considered not good enough) He regarded their proposal with disdain. *v.* 轻视；鄙视 (to feel dislike for something or someone usually for not being good enough) They disdained him for being weak.

Sol系列

solace ['sɒləs]	*n.* 安慰；慰藉 (comfort in times of sorrow or worry) ❶ The kind words brought a little solace to the grieving parents. ❷ Books were his only solace.
console [kən'səʊl]	*v.* 安慰；慰问 (to try to make someone feel less sadness or disappointment) ❶ She could not console the weeping child. ❷ I can console myself with the thought that I'm not alone.
consolation [ˌkɒnsə'leɪʃn]	*n.* 安慰；慰问 (something that lessens disappointment, misery, or grief) His great wealth was no consolation for the loss of his reputation.
inconsolable [ˌɪnkən'səʊləbl]	*adj.* 伤心欲绝的 (extremely sad and not able to be comforted) He was inconsolable after the death of his wife.

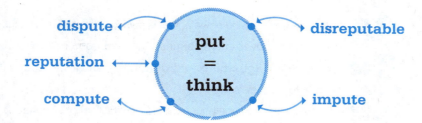

compute [kəm'pjuːt]	**v.** 计算；估算 (to calculate something) For the test we were required to compute the answers without using a calculator.
dispute [dɪ'spjuːt]	**v.** 对……表示异议 (to say or show that something may not be true, correct or legal) You can dispute your bill if you believe it is inaccurate. **v.** 争论 (to argue about something) The source of the text has been disputed for centuries. **n.** 争议 (an argument or disagreement between people or groups) Negotiators failed to resolve the bitter dispute between the European Community and the United States over cutting subsides to farmers.
reputation [,repju'teɪʃn]	**n.** 名气；名声 (overall quality or character as judged by people in general) **1** Poor customer service has ruined the company's reputation. **2** He has earned a reputation as a first-class playwright.
disreputable [dɪs'repjətəbl]	**adj.** 名誉不好的 (not respected or trusted by most people) The disreputable Internet retailer had a record of hundreds of complaints for shoddy merchandise and slow refunds.
impute [ɪm'pjuːt]	**v.** 把 (错误等) 归咎于 (to suggest that someone or something has or is guilty of something) People often impute his silence to unfriendliness and not to shyness.

Terra系列

territory ['terətri]	**n.** 领地 (an area of land that belongs to or is controlled by a government) The goal of the expedition is to map unexplored territory. **n.** 领地；地盘 (an area that is occupied and defended by an animal or group of animals) The birds are busy establishing territories and building nests.

territorial [ˌterəˈtɔːriəl]	*adj.* 领土的 (relating to land or water that is owned or controlled by a government) A number of governments banned the ship from their territorial waters. *adj.* 地盘意识强的 (guarding and defending an area of land that they believe to be their own) Two cats or more in one house will also exhibit territorial behavior.
terrestrial [təˈrestriəl]	*adj.* 陆地的；地球的 (relating to or occurring on the earth) ① The toad has terrestrial habits, spending most of its time on shore. ② Scientists haven't even found all the terrestrial life on our planet.
subterranean [ˌsʌbtəˈreɪniən]	*adj.* 地表下面的；地下的 (located or living under the surface of the ground) London has 9 miles of such subterranean passages.
Mediterranean [ˌmedɪtəˈreɪniən]	*adj.* 地中海的 (relating to the Mediterranean Sea or to the lands or peoples surrounding it) An American naval force is showing the flag in various Mediterranean ports.
terrain [təˈreɪn]	*n.* 地形；地势 (the features of the surface of a piece of land) ① The terrain changed quickly from arable land to desert. ② We had to drive over some rough terrain.

追根溯源

古时，人们认为蟾蜍(toad)有毒，而实际上蟾蜍对人的身体是无害的，江湖游医往往会利用这一点行骗，他们让自己的下人做出将死之状，然后为其解毒，拯救其生命。游医通过耍这种小手段忽悠人们来买他的药。吃蟾蜍的人被称为"toad-eater"，因此就有江湖游医的下人吞食蟾蜍来展示主人解毒有方的隐喻。有些地位低下的人为了迎合主人而做恶心的事（比如吃蟾蜍），这类人就是我们所说的马屁精、谄媚者(toady)。

toad [təʊd]	*n.* 蟾蜍 (a small animal that looks like a frog but has dry skin and lives on land) His eyes seemed to bulge like those of a toad.
toady [ˈtəʊdi]	*n.* 谄媚者；马屁精 (a person who praises and helps powerful people in order to get their approval) No one liked the office toady, who spent most of her time complimenting the boss on what a great job he was doing.

Unit 30

atone（赎罪）是at和one的合成词，指的是与上帝保持和谐一致（to be one with God）。在基督教中，一个人若做了对上帝不敬的事情，要想重新与上帝保持和谐一致，就要进行祈祷、苦修和行善，来弥补自己的罪行，这种做法就有了赎罪（atone）之意。

atone [ə'təʊn]	*v.* 补偿；赎罪 (to do something good as a way to show that you are sorry about doing something bad) He gave large sum of money to charities in an effort to atone for his sins.
atonement [ə'təʊnmənt]	*n.* 弥补；赎罪 (a making up for an offense or injury) They are still trying to make some sort of atonement and reparation.

锦囊妙记

retire [rɪ'taɪə(r)]	*v.* 退休 (to stop a job or career because you have reached the age when you are not allowed to work anymore) My grandfather retired at 65 years old. 联想法 tire—tired (劳累的)，到了年龄，累了，当然要退休 (retire)。
itch [ɪtʃ]	*v.* 痒，发痒 (to have or produce an unpleasant feeling that causes a desire to scratch) His eyes began to burn and itch because of his allergies. 拆分法 it—它，ch—吃，蚊子它吃我，让我感觉很痒(itch)。
hostile ['hɒstaɪl]	*adj.* 敌人的，敌对的 (not friendly; having or showing unfriendly feelings) It was a small town that was hostile to outsiders. 谐音法 hostile—耗死他！因为跟他是敌对的(hostile)关系，所以要耗死他!
courteous ['kɜːtiəs]	*adj.* 有礼貌的；谦恭的 (showing respect and consideration for others) Their customer service department always gives courteous responses, even to rude people. 联想法 court—宫廷，到了宫廷上当然要谦恭，有礼貌的 (courteous)。

Unit 30

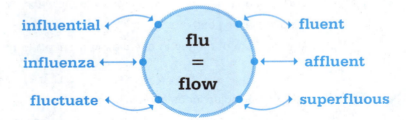

influence	*n.* 影响；势力 (the power to change or affect someone or something)
['ɪnfluəns]	Recent years have seen a decline in the company's influence within the industry.
	v. 影响 (to affect or change someone or something in an indirect but usually important way)
	No one knows how this decision will influence the outcome of the election.

| **influential** | *adj.* 有影响的；有权势的 (having the power to cause changes) |
| [ˌɪnflu'enʃl] | My parents have been the most influential people in my life. |

| **influenza** | *n.* 流行性感冒 (a very contagious virus disease like a severe cold with fever) |
| [ˌɪnflu'enzə] | They took steps to prevent the spread of influenza. |

fluid	*n.* 液体；流体 (a substance that is able to flow freely)
['fluːɪd]	She needs to drink plenty of fluids.
	adj. 不稳定的 (unstable and is likely to change often)
	The situation is extremely fluid and it can be changing from day to day.

influx	*n.* 流入；注入 (the arrival of a large number of people or something)
['ɪnflʌks]	① The city is preparing for a large influx of tourists this summer.
	② The company has had a sudden influx of capital.

fluctuate	*v.* 变动；波动 (to change continually and especially up and down)
['flʌktʃueɪt]	① In the desert, the temperature fluctuates dramatically.
	② The actual cost may fluctuate above and below that standard.

fluent ['fluːənt]	*adj.* 流利的 (able to speak a language easily and very well) ① She studied eight foreign languages but is fluent in only six of them. ② A very fluent speaker can always communicate his points well.
affluent ['æfluənt]	*adj.* 富裕的；富足的 (having plenty of money and expensive things) ① Cigarette smoking used to be commoner among affluent people. ② He is affluent and can afford to send his children to the best school.
affluence ['æfluəns]	*n.* 富裕；富足 (the state of having much money and expensive things) The postwar era was one of new affluence for the working class.
superfluous [suː'pɜːfluəs]	*adj.* 过多的；多余的 (going beyond what is enough or necessary) ① Her story was filled with superfluous details. ② I rid myself of many superfluous belongings and habits that bothered me.
inflate [ɪn'fleɪt]	*v.* (使)充气；(使)膨胀 (to add air or gas to something, such as a tire or a balloon and make it larger) Airbags inflate instantaneously on impact. *v.* (使) 通货膨胀 (to cause to increase beyond proper limits) Economists warn that rapid economic growth could inflate prices.
deflate [dɪ'fleɪt]	*v.* 放 (轮胎、气球等)的气 (to let air or gas out of a tyre, balloon, etc.) The birthday balloons deflated after a few days. *v.* 使泄气 (to make somebody feel less confident or less important) The criticism deflated her confidence.

Clog系列

clog [klɒg]	*n.* 阻塞；堵塞 (something that hinders or holds back) There's a clog in the kitchen sink. *v.* 阻碍；堵塞 (to make passage through difficult or impossible) ① The drain clogs easily because the opening is so small. ② Snow clogged the roads.
clot [klɒt]	*n.* 凝块 (a lump made by some substance getting thicker and sticking together) He needed emergency surgery to remove a blood clot from his brain. *v.* 凝结成块 (to become thick and partly solid) Aspirin apparently thins the blood and inhibits clotting.

cluster	*n.* 丛；簇；群 (a group of things or people that are close together)
['klʌstə(r)]	A small cluster of people had gathered at the scene of the accident.
	v. （人)聚集 (to come together to form a group)
	The children clustered around the storyteller.

Band系列

band	*n.* 乐队；乐团 (a group of musicians performing together)
[bænd]	① He was a drummer in a rock band.
	② Local bands provide music for dancing.
disband	*v.* (使) 解散；散伙 (to end an organization or group such as a club)
[dɪs'bænd]	① All the armed groups will be disbanded.
	② The members of the organization have decided to disband.
bind	*v.* 束；系；捆绑 (to tie or wrap something with rope, string, etc.)
[baɪnd]	She bound her hair in a ponytail.
	v. 约束；限制 (to constrain with legal authority)
	The treaty binds them to respect their neighbour's independence.
bond	*n.* 纽带；联系 (the condition of being held together)
[bɒnd]	Recent events have helped to strengthen the bonds between our two countries.
	v. 与……黏合（或连接） (to join things together)
	① The poster was bonded to the wall with glue.
	② Heat is used to bond the plastic sheets together.
bondage	*n.* 奴役；束缚 (the state of being a slave)
['bɒndɪdʒ]	The Civil War ended over 200 years of bondage for black Africans in America.
bandage	*n.* 绷带 (a strip of material used to cover and wrap up wounds)
['bændɪdʒ]	He wrapped a bandage around his knee.
	v. 用绷带包扎 (to cover or wrap something with a bandage)
	Her mother always bandages her scraped knees very carefully.
bundle	*n.* 捆；束 (a group of things that are fastened, tied or wrapped together)
['bʌndl]	He gathered the bundles of clothing into his arms.
	v. 收集；打包 (to fasten, tie, or wrap a group of things together)

Unit 31

	① Someone had bundled the wet towels into a big pile.
	② They've increased sales by bundling their most popular programs.
bunch [bʌntʃ]	*n.* 束；串；捆 (a number of things of the same type which are growing or fastened together)
	① He had left a huge bunch of flowers in her hotel room.
	② He always had a bunch of keys on his belt.

Population系列

populate ['pɒpjuleɪt]	*v.* 居住于；生活于 (to live in a country, city or area)
	Immigrants began to populate the area in the late 19th century.
population [ˌpɒpju'leɪʃn]	*n.* 人口 (the number of people who live in a place)
	① There has been a sharp reduction in the bat population in this region.
	② Food production has already fallen behind the population growth.
popular ['pɒpjələ(r)]	*adj.* 流行的；大众化的 (liked or enjoyed by many people)
	① Spicy foods have become increasingly popular.
	② Her theories are popular among social scientists.
unpopular [ʌn'pɒpjələ(r)]	*adj.* 不受欢迎的；不流行的 (not liked by many people)
	① Recent conflicts have made him unpopular among the staff.
	② The military regime in power was unpopular and repressive.

Fence系列

fence [fens]	*n.* 栅栏；篱笆 (a structure made of wood or wire supported with posts that is put between two areas of land as a boundary, or around a garden/yard, field, etc. to keep animals in, or to keep people and animals out)
	The garden was surrounded by a wooden fence.
	v. 击剑 (to fight with swords)
	I used to be very good at fencing.
offend [ə'fend]	*v.* 冒犯；得罪 (to cause a person or group to feel hurt, angry or upset by something said or done)

① She uses language that offends people.

② He apologizes for his comments and says he had no intention of offending the community.

offensive

['ə'fensɪv]

adj. 无礼的；冒犯的 (causing someone to feel hurt, angry, or upset)

Some friends of his found the play horribly offensive.

n. 进攻 (a large military attack)

The armed forces have launched an offensive to recapture lost ground.

defend

[dɪ'fend]

v. 防御；保卫 (to protect somebody/something from danger or attack)

① She defended her teacher against the class's complaints.

② The company must defend its own interests.

defensive

[dɪ'fensɪv]

adj. 防御用的；防守的；保护的 (defending or protecting someone or something from attack)

① The city began building a defensive wall around its borders.

② The government decided to join a defensive alliance with several other nations.

defendant

[dɪ'fendənt]

n. 被告 (a person who is being sued or accused of a crime in a court of law)

The jury believed that the defendant was guilty.

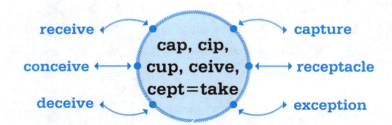

capture

['kæptʃə(r)]

v. 俘获；夺取 (to get control of a place or person especially by using force)

① The army has captured a strategic city in the north.

② The company plans on capturing a larger segment of the market.

captive

['kæptɪv]

n. 战俘；俘虏 (someone who is held prisoner)

He described the difficulties of surviving for four months as a captive.

adj. 被俘的 (kept within bounds or under control)

The captive soldiers were treated cruelly by the guards.

capable

['keɪpəbl]

adj. 能干的；有才能的 (having the qualities or abilities that are needed to do something)

	1 I believe I am capable of calculating the political consequences accurately.
	2 The kitchen is capable of catering for several hundred people.
capacity [kə'pæsəti]	*n.* 能力；才能 (the ability to do something)
	In your capacity as team captain, you can set a good example.
	n. 容量 (the ability to contain or deal with something)
	This tank has a capacity of 300 gallons.
capacious [kə'peɪʃəs]	*adj.* 宽敞的；容量大的 (able to hold a great deal)
	The car has a capacious trunk that makes it a good choice for families.
incapacitate [ˌɪnkə'pæsɪteɪt]	*v.* 使无能力 (to make someone or something unable to work, move, or function in the usual way)
	1 His poor health incapacitate him for work.
	2 The class teaches you how to incapacitate an attacker.
capsule ['kæpsjuːl]	*n.* 胶囊 (a very small container that is filled with medicine and swallowed whole)
	You are asked to swallow a capsule containing vitamin B.
	n. 航天舱 (a closed compartment for travel in space)
	A Russian space capsule is currently orbiting the Earth.
anticipate [æn'tɪsɪpeɪt]	*v.* 预感；预见 (to think of something that will or might happen in the future)
	1 We could not have anticipated the result of our campaigning.
	2 The cost turned out to be higher than anticipated.
anticipation [æn,tɪsɪ'peɪʃn]	*n.* 预计 (the act of preparing for something)
	Investors were storing up a lot of cash in anticipation of disaster.
	n. 期待 (excitement about something that's going to happen)
	She had a feeling of great anticipation before her graduation ceremony.
receive [rɪ'siːv]	*v.* 收到；接到 (to get or be given something)
	1 I received a letter from her yesterday.
	2 You will receive a discount if you spend over $100.
receipt [rɪ'siːt]	*n.* 收到 (the act of receiving)
	I acknowledged receipt of the letter.
	n. 收据；发票 (a written statement saying that money or goods have been received)
	I wrote her a receipt for the money.

Unit 31

receptacle

[rɪ'septəkl]

n. 容器 (a container that is used to hold something)

① She used the box as a receptacle for her jewelry.

② Place all wrappers in the trash receptacles at the entrances of the theatre.

deceive

[dɪ'siːv]

v. 欺诈；误导 (to make someone believe something that is not true)

① He was accused of deceiving the customer about the condition of the car.

② Her parents punished her for trying to deceive them.

deception

[dɪ'sepʃn]

n. 瞒骗；欺诈 (the act of making someone believe something that is not true)

① She accuses the company of willful deception in its advertising.

② His clever deception fooled me.

deceptive

[dɪ'septɪv]

adj. 欺诈的；骗人的 (intended to make someone believe something that is not true)

In his deceptive answer about the vehicle's history, the salesman said that the used car had never been hit by another car.

conceive

[kən'siːv]

v. 构思；设想 (to think of or create something in the mind)

She had conceived the idea of a series of novels.

v. 怀孕 (to become pregnant)

Women, he says, should give up alcohol before they plan to conceive.

conceivable

[kən'siːvəbl]

adj. 可想到的 (able to be imagined)

① They discussed the question from every conceivable angle.

② Without their support the project would not have been conceivable.

concept

['kɒnsept]

n. 观念；概念 (an idea of what something is or how it works)

She is familiar with basic concepts of psychology.

perceive

[pə'siːv]

v. 意识到；察觉 (to notice or become aware of something)

① He was beginning to perceive the true nature of their relationship.

② I perceived a change in her attitude.

perception

[pə'sepʃn]

n. 知觉；察觉力 (the ability to understand or notice something easily)

He is interested in how our perceptions of death affect the way we live.

perceptive

[pə'septɪv]

adj. 观察敏锐的；有洞察力的 (showing an ability to understand or notice something easily or quickly)

① He was one of the most perceptive US political commentators.

② This is a very perceptive assessment of the situation.

Unit 31

exception [ɪkˈsepʃn]	*n.* 例外；除外 (someone or something that is not included) ① There will be no exceptions to this rule. ② There were no floral offerings at the ceremony, with the exception of a single red rose.
exceptional [ɪkˈsepʃənl]	*adj.* 例外的 (unusual or uncommon) Capital punishment is allowable only under exceptional circumstances. *adj.* 优越的；杰出的 (unusually good; much better than average) The seafood dishes at this restaurant are exceptional.
inception [ɪnˈsepʃn]	*n.* 开始；开端 (the time at which something begins) ① Since its inception, the business has expanded to become a national retail chain. ② Since its inception the company has produced 53 different aircraft designs.
intercept [ˌɪntəˈsept]	*v.* 拦截；拦住 (to stop before reaching an intended destination) ① Gunmen intercepted him on his way to the airport. ② Detectives have been intercepting her mail.
occupy [ˈɒkjupaɪ]	*v.* 居住 (to live in a house or apartment) They have occupied the apartment for three years. *v.* 占据 (to fill or be in a place or space) ① Reading occupied me most of the summer. ② U.S. forces now occupy a part of the country.
occupation [ˌɒkjuˈpeɪʃn]	*n.* 占领 (the act of using or taking possession and control of a place) Human occupation of this area began thousands of years ago. *n.* 职业；工作 (the work that a person does) He is thinking about changing occupations and becoming a police officer.
emancipate [ɪˈmænsɪpeɪt]	*v.* 解放；解脱 (to free someone from someone else's control or power) ① He felt the only way to emancipate himself from his parents was to move away. ② That war preserved the Union and emancipated the slaves.
emancipation [ɪˌmænsɪˈpeɪʃn]	*n.* 解放 (an act of setting someone free from control or slavery) The book discussed the role that the emancipation of slaves played in the nation's history.

Canoe系列

canoe [kə'nu:]	*n.* 独木舟 (a long light narrow boat with pointed ends and curved sides that is usually moved by a paddle) We attempted to manoeuvre the canoe closer to him. *v.* 划独木舟 (to go or travel in a canoe) We canoed across the lake.
cane [keɪn]	*n.* 藤条 (a short stick that often has a curved handle and is used to help someone to walk) ① The chair seat is made of cane. ② This sugar cane is quite a sweet and juicy.
canal [kə'næl]	*n.* 运河；沟渠 (an artificial waterway for boats or for irrigation of land) The Panama Canal opened a much easier and shorter passageway from the Atlantic to the Pacific.
cannon ['kænən]	*n.* 大炮；机关炮 (a large gun that shoots heavy metal or stone balls and that was once a common military weapon) The stillness of night was broken by the boom of a cannon.

追根溯源

在16世纪的法语中，etiquette原指"标签"，英文单词ticket（票；标签）也来源于此。法国的宫廷礼节非常的繁琐，每有宴会，宾客都会收到一张纸条或者卡片，上面列出了宾客应该遵循的礼节和着装要求。因此这种卡片后来引申为"礼节"(etiquette)的意思。

etiquette ['etɪket]	*n.* 礼仪；礼节 (the rules indicating the proper and polite way to behave) ① Her failure to respond to the invitation was a serious breach of etiquette. ② Etiquette is still important on occasions such as weddings and funerals.

undermine是一个合成词，本意是"暗中挖地道破坏敌人堡垒"。mine有"矿井"和"挖矿"的意思，under是下面，合意就是"从下面挖地道"。古代两军交战，为了摧毁敌人的堡垒，士兵们往往会暗中挖地道来接近敌人的堡垒，然后发起攻击，达到歼灭敌人的目的。后来，undermine就有了暗中破坏之意。

mine [maɪn]	*v.* 开采；采掘 (to dig a mine in order to find and take away coal, gold or diamonds) The area was soon filled with prospectors who were mining for gold. *n.* 矿井 (a pit or excavation in the earth from which mineral substances are taken) A gold mine is not a bottomless pit, the gold runs out.
undermine [ˌʌndəˈmaɪn]	*v.* 削弱；损害 (to make something, especially somebody's confidence or authority, gradually weaker or less effective) Their criticisms undermine my confidence.

锦囊妙记

ellipse [ɪˈlɪps]	*n.* 椭圆 (a shape that looks like a flattened circle) The Earth orbits in an ellipse. **联想法** lip-嘴唇，嘴唇的形状是椭圆的 (ellipse)。
scorch [skɔːtʃ]	*v.* 烧焦；烤焦 (to burn on the surface) The fire scorched the bottom of the pan. **谐音法** scorch-死烤着！当然会烧焦，烤焦 (scorch)。
nostalgia [nɒˈstældʒə]	*n.* 怀旧；乡愁 (the state of being homesick) A wave of nostalgia swept over me when I saw my childhood home. **拆分法** no-不，sta-stay (逗留)，充满了对故乡的思念 (nostalgia)，不想在异乡逗留！
allot [əˈlɒt]	*v.* 分配；分派 (to give someone an amount of something to use or have) The seats are allotted to the candidates who have won the most votes. **联想法** lot-lot of (很多的)，把东西分配 (allot) 给很多人。

Unit 31